CONTENTS

Essays on European History 1453-1648   Vol. II
ISBN 1 85944 184 X

Contents

27. Why did civil war break out in France so soon after the death of Henry II in 1559?
28. To what extent were French civil wars about religion?
29. Why was Spain unable to crush the Dutch revolt?
30. Assess the importance of the House of Orange to the revolt of the Netherlands between 1563 and 1609.
31. Why was Henry IV more successful than Catherine de Médici in controlling the forces which threatened disorder in France?
32. How far can Philip II's foreign policy be explained as an attempt to defend the Catholic faith against protestant and Muslim forces?
33. Why, despite imports of bullion from the New World, did Philip II often find himself in financial difficulty
34. Why did the economy of the northern provinces of the Netherlands remain strong in the years to 1609, in spite of the war of independence?
35. Was Spain in steep decline in the early seventeenth century?
36. 'Gustavus Adolphus gave Sweden a greatness which it could not sustain'. Discuss this assessment.
37. To what extent were the policies of Richelieu and Mazarin dominated by their wish to break the Habsburg encirclement of France?
38. 'The most important turning point in the 30 Years War'. Do you agree with this assessment of the Edict of Restitution (1629)?
39. Discuss the claim that the basis of the scientific revolution in the seventeenth century was observation.
40. What issues were settled by the Treaties of Westphalia (1648)?

1. Europe in 1453

Europe in the middle of the fifteenth century was thinly populated, overwhelmingly agrarian in its economy and rural in its settlement patterns. It corresponded, more or less, with Christendom, and was divided into two broad areas of religious allegiance, the Roman and the Greek. Christian communities survived under Islamic rule in the Levant, and autonomously in Ethiopia and North India, but Christianity was the religion of Europe, and one of its very few identifying characteristics. Its social structure followed one of two main patterns; the rural, embracing between 80% and 90% of the total, and the urban, which contained the remainder. Rural society was aristocratic and hierarchical, based upon the holding of land in return for military service, and the actual working of land by peasant communities which had been unfree or semi-free in origin. Aristocrats by custom lived on the rents and dues derived from their lands, exercised the profession of arms, and did not pursue any craft or manual labour. They also exercised *dominium,* or rule, over their tenants and other workers living on their lands, being answerable in turn to their own overlords. The nature and extent of this aristocratic jurisdiction varied from one part of Europe to another. In Poland it amounted to almost complete autonomy, in England it was largely confined to office under the Crown. Society was thus divided into two broad categories, the noble and the non-noble, and status was hereditary. In most places noble status carried legal and fiscal privileges, and was sharply defined, although not all nobles were rich. There were many degrees of noble rank, from the royal kindred down to gentlemen, hidalgos and seigneurs, but all were armigerous - that is to say entitled to heraldic identification - and shared many of the same values and attitudes. The rural non-nobles were also divided into many different degrees, and the blanket term 'peasant' is extremely misleading. In some parts of Europe there were substantial non-noble freeholders, men of considerable wealth, and most village communities had their 'aristocracies' of substantial tenant farmers and craftsmen such as millers and blacksmiths. Such men might hold only minor public offices, but they were leaders in their own context. At the bottom of the social pyramid were the landless labourers, and the nomads and vagabonds who existed on sufferance, an 'underclass' of considerable dimensions. Urban society was more complex, but towns existed principally as trading centres, and the social structure reflected that priority. The wealthiest section of the population was the merchants, who neatly always constituted the ruling elite, and who were frequently organised into companies according to the nature of their businesses. Craftsmen similarly organised themselves into guilds, and there was frequently political conflict between the companies and the guilds. Both merchants and craftsmen were citizens, but the bulk of the urban population was not enfranchised, consisting of hired workers, day labourers, and the rootless who drifted into the towns in search of support.

Towns varied greatly in their status, and in their degree of independence. Some were little more than local markets, controlled by a territorial lord and trading only within a narrow hinterland. Others were chartered corporations, controlling their own affairs and owing allegiance only to a distant king or emperor. Such towns usually practised long distance trade, and might control important routes along or across rivers. London, Paris and Augsburg all came into this category. Others again might be independent states, with distant commercial outposts or colonies, operating a seaborne trade of immense value. Venice was the most conspicuous example, a city where the rural nobility had become urbanised and subjected to commercial priorities; the most powerful and outstanding example of a republican system of government.

The most valuable long distance trade, and that which provided the foundation for the wealth of such cities as Florence and Antwerp, was that in woollen cloth. Cloth was bulky, but valuable enough to be worth transporting. The other main commodities tended to be light in proportion to value, particularly spices of oriental origin, and luxury goods such as silks and jewelry. The main internal trade routes were along the great rivers, the Danube, the Rhine, the Elbe, the Seine, and many others; and the spinal route, connecting the systems of northern and southern Europe, ran from the Netherlands up the Rhine and over the Alpine passes into northern Italy. Lombardy and Brabant were the two most highly urbanised regions in Europe, and the commercial wealth which they generated had also, by 1450, led to the development of a sophisticated banking and credit transfer system, epitomised by the success of the Médici bank in Florence. Most bulky trade was carried by sea, partly because the roads connecting the river systems were deficient, partly because vehicles were primitive, and partly because all internal routes were forced to pay numerous dues to the jurisdictions through which they passed. This was true even in supposedly unified kingdoms, such as France, and much worse in the Holy Roman Empire or Burgundy. The most important sea routes passed from the Baltic and Eastern England to the Netherlands and thence to Northern Spain, Portugal and the Mediterranean. Other routes linked Venice with the Levant; Genoa with Aragon, and Naples and Sicily with southern France. A network of lesser systems connected all the ports of the western seaboard, and Scotland with Scandinavia. The population of Europe had peaked in the late thirteenth century, declined steeply during the fourteenth (largely, but not entirely, because of the Black Death) and was still low in 1450. The population of England, for example, had fallen from about six million to about two and a half million, and had stayed at that level. At the same time France contained some twelve to thirteen million people, and the Empire about fifteen million. Great cities were few. Paris, Rome and Naples probably held over 100,000 each; Florence and Venice about 80,000; London 50,000; Cologne 35,000; Strasbourg 25,000; Arras and Bruges about 20,000. After London, the next largest English city was York with 12,000. Sizeable areas of France were still desolate from the ravages of the Hundred Years War, and marginal settlements had been abandoned all over Europe in the wake of the plague. On the other hand the chronic labour shortage had served to weaken the system of labour services everywhere, and enabled workers to negotiate freer and more remunerative terms for themselves. The fifteenth century has been described as 'the golden age of the peasant'. Legal restraints on movement and employment relaxed, personal freedom increased, and the age of marriage began to fall, creating a situation in which a recovery of population levels could begin. The political map was exceedingly complex, because a network of feudal relationships had long outlived their original purposes, and had left behind an Empire, several Kingdoms, Duchies and Counties, and a handful of republics, whose jurisdictions conflicted and over-lapped in a bewildering variety of ways. The Holy Roman Empire was theoretically the most extensive and prestigious power in Europe, but it was not a state in the modern sense, and since the Golden Bull of 1356 the Emperor had been little more than an elected president over a federation of principalities, lay and ecclesiastical, free cities, and even free villages. These units owed allegiance to the Emperor, and in theory paid Imperial taxes and obeyed Imperial law, but in practice they conducted themselves as independent entities unless it was in their interests to do otherwise. Unless the Electoral College selected a prince who already had extensive lands and resources of his own, the Empire was doomed to weakness. In 1453 the Emperor was Frederick III, the second ruler of the house of Habsburg. He was battered and undermined by the Hussite wars in Bohemia; a man of some ability, but crippled by poverty and by a frustrating lack of constitutional authority. During his long reign, which lasted from 1440 until 1493, the Empire, which embraced the whole of modern Germany, plus the Netherlands and Northern Italy apart from Venice, was incapable of unified and purposeful action. Although the empire possessed a set of central institutions, without the co-operation of the princes, they were as powerless as the Emperor himself. By contrast the kingdom of France was emerging from the chronic weakness which had afflicted it during the early years of the century. 1453 saw the expulsion of the English from Gascony and Guienne, and the victorious conclusion of the Hundred Years War. Although in a sense France was also a federation of provinces, the position of the monarch was incomparably stronger than in the Empire. Indeed, too much depended upon the king himself. The guile and determination of Charles VII and Louis XI could restore the kingdom, but it had been the feebleness of Charles VI which had undermined it. The French nobility were not quasi-independent princes, but they did have great estates and extensive jurisdictions, so that the stability of the kingdom depended very largely upon their relations with the king. Fortunately the French Crown had great prestige, and if it was worn by a competent soldier, such as Charles VII, he could usually control his vassals and collect the taxes and dues to which he was entitled. In terms of political evolution, France represented the future, and Burgundy represented the past. The Dukes of Burgundy were a cadet branch of the Valois dynasty, and had originally been vassals of the French Crown. However, by a series of skilful marriages in the early fifteenth century they also acquired a number of Imperial fiefs, and by taking the English side against their French cousins became effectively independent sovereigns. In 1453, in spite of being a vassal of both the Emperor and the King of France, the Duke of Burgundy was actually more powerful than either. However, his territories were held together by little more than personal union. Attempts were made to create a federal structure, but the time was too short and the lands too diverse for them to succeed. In spite of its wealth and sophistication, Burgundy was not a state in any modern sense. It was the private honour of its Dukes, and when Charles the Bold was killed in battle in 1477 its constituent parts were dispersed by marriage and resumption. Burgundy is a very good example of the feudal honour at its most developed without territorial unity or a constitutional structure, and it was the last of its kind. The other monarchies of western Europe may be summarily described at this stage. England was descending into civil strife under a weak king, Henry VI, and following its defeat by France. The English Crown was institutionally the strongest in Europe, and the English state the most centralised, but its limited resources confined it to a secondary role. Scotland was far poorer, and was similarly a prey to domestic strife. It also lacked England's constitutional strength, and tended to rely for protection and survival on France. Denmark, Norway and Sweden, at one time separate kingdoms had been drawn together in 1393 into the Union of Kalmar, and until the Swedish war of independence in the 1520s remained under the Crown of Denmark. Iberia, which had once comprised as many as a dozen different units, had by this time been reduced to five; Castile, Aragon, Portugal, Navarre and Granada. The last was a Moorish Emirate, a remnant of the Islamic conquest which had once subdued the whole peninsula; the remainder were Christian kingdoms created by the *reconquista*. In the middle of the fifteenth century both Castile and Aragon were weakened by internal divisions, although Aragon also controlled the Balearic Islands and the Italian kingdoms of Naples and Sicily. Portugal, relatively stable and looking for expansion, had since the early years of the century been putting out probes into Muslim North Africa, and also exploratory voyages down the West African coast, which were eventually to have momentous consequences for the relationship between Europe and the outside world. By 1453 these voyages had barely reached the equator. South eastern Europe lay under the shadow of the advancing Ottoman Turks, who, since the late fourteenth century had been picking off the crumbling Byzantine Empire. The Ottomans were already established in the Balkans in the early fifteenth century, but it was the fall of Constantinople in 1453 which signalled the final end of the second Rome, and should have alerted the remainder of Christendom to its danger. Serbia collapsed in 1459, leaving Hungary and the Venetian colonies in the Levant exposed to the next wave of Turkish aggression. Further north the main power was Poland, which had united with Lithuania in the early fifteenth century under King Jagiello. He had died in 1434, but the combined kingdom retained its strength, beating off attacks from both the Teutonic Knights (1466) and the Russians. The Grand Duchy of Muscovy was at this time just beginning a century and a half of expansion, mostly at the expense of the decaying Tartar states to the east and South, which was to create a new Russian Empire, and to convert the Grand Dukes into Tsars.

Russia, Serbia and Bulgaria acknowledged the religious authority of one or other of the Orthodox patriarchs. The remainder of Europe in theory acknowledged the leadership of the Pope. The Roman Catholic church was an omnipresent institution, long since adjusted to the feudal hierarchy with which it had to co-exist. In the thirteenth century Popes had challenged the authority of emperors and kings on the grounds that this world was merely an antechamber to the next, but exile to Avignon, followed by a prolonged schism had weakened the Papacy severely. By 1450 it had survived the challenge of the conciliar movement, but was enmeshed in the intricacies of Italian politics, and its spiritual leadership was largely in abeyance. Nevertheless the pervasive quest for salvation preserved the authority of the clergy in general, and the accumulated endowments of the church gave it the power of wealth at every social and political level. Bishops and Abbots were the equals of noblemen, and some of them were virtually independent princes. Cathedral chapters often over-matched the corporations with which they shared urban space and were constantly enmeshed in litigation over both property and jurisdiction. The church had a virtual monopoly of higher education, except in some of the Italian universities; it had a sophisticated administrative system and a uniform code of law, which ran throughout its extensive jurisdiction. Quite apart from the content of its teaching or the meaning of its sacraments, it was an unavoidable fact of life, completely integrated into the social and political system. Secular governments strove to imitate its efficiency, but the secular equivalent of the Canon law, the Civil law, was only used in Italy and in certain parts of southern France. Elsewhere (except in England which had a common code) a jumble of local customary laws prevailed, varying from town to town, principality to principality, and even village to village. The chanceries and treasuries of kings, their courts, and even their households, were modelled on those of Rome. England France and the Italian republics were beginning to develop secular legal professions, and in the following century the future was to lie with them, but there was not much sign of that in 1450. The professionalism of secular government could not yet match that of the church. In an age when kings and nobles were still expected to be soldiers, the arts of peace were largely in the keeping of the clergy.

2. Economic and Social Geography

With the possible exception of cloth weaving, large-scale industry was unknown in medieval Europe. Glassware, ceramics, armour and weapons were traded over long distances, but in small quantities and were literally manufactures - what we would now call craft products. Most foodstuffs were highly perishable, and only a few were traded in any quantity. Grain, wine and salt fish were the most conspicuous. The overwhelming bulk of trade was local; eggs, cheese, fruit and vegetables to the nearest market; shoes and boots, hats and caps over a radius of forty or fifty miles. Commercial wealth was consequently very widely distributed, and is almost impossible to calculate. Local or regional self-sufficiency was the rule rather than the exception but partly for this reason, where free wealth was created it became disproportionately important. A few major cities controlled the important trade routes, and their strategic positions gave them power. Danzig controlled the Vistula, Hamburg, the Elbe, and Venice the Adriatic. Whether or not they were technically independent states, such cities controlled their hinterlands, and dealt with kings and princes on terms of equality. The Hanseatic League, a federation of Baltic and north German cities, not only established a monopolistic control over trade entering or leaving the Baltic, it also fought a successful war against the king of Denmark and its warfleet continued to be widely-feared in northern waters well into the sixteenth century. Political generalisations, however, are difficult to sustain. Free Imperial cities such as Strassburg or Magdeburg paid little attention to their nominal overlord, but equally wealthy places like Bruges and Ghent suffered severely for falling foul of the Count of Brabant, within whose territories they were situated. It would also be difficult to say whether the rise of Antwerp in the later fifteenth century owed more to its strategic position, or to the patronage and protection of the Habsburgs. Princes and cities needed each other, because political protection fostered trade, created wealth, and wealth created banking facilities. Money was the sinew of war, and the prince who had to gather his revenues before he could pay his army was at a crippling disadvantage against a prince who could borrow large sums in cash from the Medici, the Frescobaldi or the Fuggers. The citizens of Lombardy and Brabant consequently exercised an influence out of all proportion to their numbers, or even to the share of the total wealth of Europe which they deployed, simply because they were organised to concentrate that wealth and to make it available.

War required money, but it also required men, and the feudal structure of society had been designed for that purpose. The purely feudal host, consisting of men raised by knights and barons in fulfilment of the contracts whereby they held their lands, had long since disappeared. Such hosts had served without pay for very limited periods, and were of little use for prolonged campaigns. On the other hand straightforward mercenaries could meet only a small proportion of the need for manpower, and were notoriously untrustworthy. The Swiss Cantons made a regular trade of mercenary soldiers, and there were also English Free Companies and Italian *condottieri*, but most troops were raised by what might be called 'quasi-feudal' means. A ruler wishing to make war issued instructions to his nobles, and to the corporations of cities under his control, requiring them to raise a given number of men by a certain date, to equip them and to send them to a named rendezvous. For all this provision the king would, sooner or later, pay; and the commanders, captains and men so provided would be paid at a given rate for as long as the service lasted. This method may be called 'quasi-feudal' because it was the traditional military role of the feudal nobility which suited them to act as agents and recruiting officers, and because the core of their 'bands' usually consisted of their own servants and retainers. The armies raised by these means were usually small, and bore no relation to the huge professional hosts of the eighteenth century, which might number 100,000 or 200,000 men, let alone to the conscript citizen armies of the first or second World Wars. A typical fifteenth century army numbered about 10,000, and was mobilised and de-mobilised afresh for each campaigning season. Key

5

fortresses were garrisoned all the year round, but field armies seldom, if ever, went into winter quarters. Consequently although wars might last for many years, actual campaigning was sporadic, occupying no more than a few weeks in each year. It was also very limited in its effects. A town which was besieged and captured might be sacked and virtually destroyed, as happened to Limoges, but nearby places of less strategic importance would be almost unaffected. Villages which lay within the path of an advancing army might well be burned, and their crops destroyed, but wattle and thatch houses were easily rebuilt, and the effect of a single such experience would be short lived. Only in areas which were repeatedly fought over did the people give up and the fields become desolate. The biggest hazard of warfare was often not the battles themselves, nor even the random atrocities perpetrated upon civilians and their property, but disease. Even small armies bred influenza, typhus and venereal diseases which not only decimated their own numbers, but infected the whole area within which they were operating. In spite of its recognised evils, war in itself was not a moral issue. Princes regarded it as a normal aspect of dynastic rivalry, cities used it to expand their markets, or to intimidate commercial rivals, and the church hardly bothered to apply rules as to how it should be conducted. There were grey areas, but these related less to the conduct of armies than to the status of the participants. When was it legitimate for a vassal to attack his overlord, or vice versa? Could an ecclesiastical Prince be a lawful belligerent? When, if ever, could the traditional immunity of clerical property and personnel be ignored? In other words war was a normal and legitimate instrument of policy. There were those who felt passionately that Christians should not make war upon each other, but principled pacifism was virtually unknown.

Politics were highly personalised, and the distinction between a state and the inheritance of a ruler was frequently unclear. Principalities might be broken up or held together in accordance with the customs of inheritance followed by the family concerned. The Habsburg estates, for example, were divided and re-united afresh in each generation, while the territorial integrity of the Kingdoms of France and England was protected by the laws of succession. The law, moreover, was frequently unclear, and dynastic conflicts over inheritance were frequent. It was the fact that the French had applied the Salic law, debarring claims transmitted through the female line, on the death of Charles IV in 1328 that provoked the Hundred Years War with England. Within England the dispute between the heirs general and the heirs male of Edward III resulted in a civil war which lasted, on and off, for thirty years. Castile suffered a similar affliction after the death of Henry IV in 1474. Consequently the births, marriages and deaths of princes were of the highest political significance. Their fertility, state of health and mental stability could determine the fate of kingdoms. All power came of God, and was answerable to him. So just as the crops depended upon the sunshine and rain, which only God could deliver, so the peace and prosperity of civil societies depended upon accidents of heredity which were determined in the same way. It is not surprising that men had a powerful sense of their dependence upon the supernatural, nor a very modest estimate of their own capacity to control their lives. Such modesty was also greatly encouraged by the uncertainty of life itself. The life expectancy of a man of aristocratic rank was about forty years, for a woman somewhat less; for ordinary people the corresponding figures were twenty-five and twenty-three. Not only was infant mortality astronomical by modern standards, plague and sweating sickness remained endemic and were particularly lethal to the young. The average duration of a first marriage was about three years, not because of divorce (which was virtually unknown), but because of death, most frequently the death of the woman in childbirth. Medical care was primitive or non-existent; hygiene and sanitation alike unknown. The population of great cities expanded by immigration, but their mortality rates remained far higher than those of the surrounding countryside. There was little sense of the old being closer to death than the young. Every age group was, in a sense, equidistant from death, and equally in need of some means of coping with such proximity. The church, as the monopolistic purveyor of religious consolation, was consequently an essential and pervasive presence. Its teaching offered hope as well as moral discipline, and its sacraments were the gateway to salvation. However unhappy' some people may have been with certain aspects of the church's activities, its services could no more be dispensed with than those of the farmer or the fisherman. Unhappiness was always the result of conviction that the church was not providing the right remedies - never that such remedies were unnecessary.

Only occasionally did that unhappiness develop a political dimension By 1450 Christendom was less divided than it had been at the time of the Avignon captivity, or the Schism. Only in Bohemia had violent reaction to the execution of John Hus in 1417 produced a portent of what was to come in the following century. Thirty years of strife there had demonstrated the disruptive possibilities of ideological warfare, but the Hussite example had not been followed elsewhere. After the demise of the Council of Basle the authority of the papacy in the west was once again a seamless web - if somewhat discoloured in places. Nevertheless Europe was politically fragmented, because the uniting forces of religion and trade were more than balanced by the local priorities of a largely immobile population, devoted to its own customs and circumscribed by regional geography. The identities of Christendom, Empire and Kingdom were balanced by allegiance to a local lord - a Châtillon, a Wittlesbach or a Percy. Northern Europe was dominated by the great chivalric courts of France and Burgundy, and southern Europe by the renaissance republics of Venice, Genoa and Florence; each representing cultures which recognised no national boundaries, but which were in many ways profoundly different. It was a Europe without natural frontiers, except for the English channel, which had acquired a new significance with the recent loss of the English lands in France; but with many natural and economic divisions. These divisions were provided not only by mountains, such as the Alps, the Apennines and the Pyrenees, but also by great rivers and by large areas of swamp and forest. It was a Europe of slow communications, where it took a month to travel from Paris to Rome, or from Brussels to Lisbon, and where urgent correspondence could be delayed for weeks by the vagaries of wind and tide. Barely ten per cent of the population was literate, and news travelled largely by word of mouth, making rumour king. Authority was wielded by men, and not by institutions or instruments of government, making obedience and personal allegiance the determining political forces in a world where bureaucratic resources and coercive force were alike in short supply. Europe was also a veritable Tower of Babel, in which scores of languages and dialects lived side by side in mutual incomprehension. Latin was the language of learning, and French was the language of chivalry, but linguistic nationalism was still a thing of the future. This was a Europe upon which the outside world impinged but little. The Americas were still unknown; Asia more dimly perceived than it had been two centuries earlier. Only the marauding Ottomans posed an outside threat, and they had so far impinged mainly upon the East, driving Greek fugitives into Italy and Germany, and alarming only the more perceptive rulers of the western Mediterranean. Iberian seamen were colonising the islands of the Atlantic, but it would have needed a prophetic vision of no common order to see in the Europe of the fifteenth century the dynamic culture and economy which was about to transform the world.

3. The Legacy of the Hundred Years War

The Treaty of Troyes in 1420 had marked the nadir of French fortunes. England and Burgundy in alliance held the north east and south west of the country, and Henry V, the husband of Charles VI's daughter Katherine had been recognised as the heir to Charles for the remainder of the kingdom. Charles had a son, also called Charles, but his legitimacy was conveniently disputed and his claim was set aside. It had seemed as though the kingdom of France was about to disappear. However, Henry V and Charles VI died within months of each other in 1422, and the situation had begun to change. England had lost a strong ruler, and France a desperately weak one. The infant Henry VI was proclaimed on both sides of the Channel, but the English never succeeded in extending their effective power beyond the regions which they already held. The Dauphin maintained his claim, and his following, but had at first little credibility, and was known contemptuously as the 'roi de Bourges'. Although there was powerful dislike of English overlordship, there was little unity among those who wished to remove it, and noble factions fought a civil war in what was, in effect, a political vacuum. Rather surprisingly, the minority of the young king did not at first make much difference. His uncle the Duke of Bedford was a strong and capable regent in France, the Burgundian alliance held, and the French continued to squabble among themselves. Moreover the Regency Council in England, headed by the Duke of Gloucester, was also effective and maintained the English military presence in France at a suitable level. It was not until 1429 that the balance of power began to change significantly. At that point Joan of Arc appeared. Who or what she was is immaterial. She was certainly not a soldier of any competence, and her role was psychological rather than military. The Dauphin could be described as devout or superstitious, according to taste, and he became convinced of the authenticity of her vision. He put aside his own crippling self-doubt, and advanced his claim to the throne with conviction and determination. Given a leader who was prepared to take himself seriously, the inherent strength of French identity began to revive. Nor was Charles the only person Joan succeeded in convincing. The factional strife subsided, and the French won two rapid victories at Orleans and Patay. The Dauphin was crowned at Rheims as Charles VII on 17 July 1429, with full traditional and sacramental splendour. He was no more intelligent or politically skilful than he had been before, but he was a presentable figure as a legitimate king.

The capture of Joan in 1430, and her execution for heresy in the following year exposed some of the weaknesses of Charles VII's character, but did not undo her work. Nevertheless it might have taken Charles a very long time to end the English occupation entirely if events had not then conspired to favour him. In 1432 Anne, Duchess of Bedford, died. Not only had she been a popular figure, and the centre of a glittering court at Paris, she was also the sister of Duke Philip of Burgundy. Philip had become increasingly disenchanted with the English alliance after an unnecessary quarrel with the Duke of Gloucester in 1425, and the death of his sister removed another bond which had held the two parties together. The political and military situation was thus slowly deteriorating when the death of the Duke of Bedford in 1435 greatly accelerated the process. Bedford had been a good soldier and a strong governor, as well as being Philip's brother in law. Within weeks of his death, Philip changed sides, coming to terms with Charles at the Treaty of Arras. In 1436 the French recovered control of Paris and the Isle de France, a success which had both practical and symbolic significance, and year by year the English were pushed back in a series of grinding and unspectacular campaigns. By 1439 Charles was strong enough to carry out a number of military reforms, and to get rid of the troublesome mercenary 'free companies' by hiring them out to the Emperor and the Duke of Lorraine. Thereafter he had an increasingly secure control over his own army. By 1444 both sides were exhausted and a truce was agreed, which was sealed with a marriage alliance between Henry VI (now twenty three) and Margaret, the daughter of Renee, Duke of Anjou. Charles used the respite much more effectively than his rival, continuing his military reforms and strengthening his financial position. Henry, by contrast, became increasingly enmeshed in factional conflict between the Duke of Suffolk, his favourite, and the Duke of Gloucester, his former regent, which resulted in the fall and death of the latter in 1447. Partly discredited, and in serious financial difficulties because of his inability to refuse petitions, Henry found the regime of Suffolk an increasing liability, but was unable or unwilling to do anything about it.

Sooner or later the French would have been bound to resume the offensive, but in 1449 the English in Normandy very foolishly broke the truce with a small-scale incursion into Brittany. Brittany was an independent Duchy, not a part of France, but Charles seized the opportunity to come to the aid of the Bretons in great force, and swept into Normandy. Rouen fell in October 1449, and by the following spring the English had been entirely expelled. In England the Duke of Suffolk was blamed for both weakness and ineptitude. An attempt was made to impeach him, which was frustrated by the king, and he was sent into exile. On the way he was intercepted and murdered by the servants of one of his political rivals, and the country tottered on the brink of civil war. In these circumstances the defence of the last English provinces in France, Guienne and Gascony, faltered, and both were lost by 1453, leaving only the Calais Pale in English hands out of the extensive empire which Henry V had created. Over the next few years, as the English government collapsed and the Duke of York advanced his rival claim to the throne, Charles concentrated his attention upon asserting his control over his nobility, a task which became harder as the likelihood of an effective English riposte receded. Nevertheless, victory had given him great prestige, and he succeeded in establishing a standing army of 12,000 men under his exclusive control, which was the key to subduing disaffected feudatories, and obtained the right to levy taxation without consulting the Estates General. This not only enabled him to pay his army without having to obtain any consent, it also undermined the effectiveness of the Estates General to the point where it was virtually to disappear in the following century. These successes were not unqualified. During the latter part of his reign he was on extremely bad terms with his son and heir Louis, who at one point sought refuge at the court of Burgundy. His main support came from the towns and the lesser nobility, but by the time that he died in 1461 the strength of the, French crown had entirely recovered from the debility of half a century before.

Louis XI continued this development in his own way. His style of government was well expressed in his nickname, 'the universal spider'. He was a great admirer of the Italians, and enjoyed their subtle and unscrupulous style of diplomacy. He inherited his father's successes but not his father's military prestige, and it soon became apparent that the threat from the great nobles was reduced rather than eliminated. Charles had relied to some extent on the creation of a number of family *appanàges,* conferring titles, revenues and jurisdiction upon his own kinsmen in the hope that the relationship would keep them loyal. This worked up to a point, but it meant that Louis was confronted by Dukes of Anjou, Orleans, Burgundy and Alençon who were all Princes of the Blood, with huge fiefs and patronage systems. In addition the Duke of Anjou had allied himself by marriage to the Lancastrian royal house of England, which might make him an unreliable subject should the ancient war be resurrected. It may have been for this reason that Louis tended at first to sympathise with the Yorkist cause in England, and accepted the fall of Henry VI with equanimity. Within three years of his accession, in 1464, Louis was confronted with a major conspiracy of discontented nobles, who called themselves the 'Public Weal' movement *(Le Bien Publique).* Nothing could have been less accurate as a description of an essentially reactionary attempt to recover the virtual autonomy of the 1420s, and in the event their lack of a coherent cause enabled the king to defeat the rebels in detail in the course of 1464, but they had briefly threatened the whole achievement of Charles VII, and served as a warning that aristocratic separatism was not dead. Quite typically, Louis overreached himself in the wake of this success with his own plot, the elaborate cunning of which left him temporarily at the mercy of Charles the Bold of Burgundy but Charles was preoccupied with other business, and the king was lucky to be able to make a humiliating escape (1467).

By this time Edward IV of England was angling for a Burgundian alliance, in spite of the sympathetic reception which his accession had received from Louis. There were good reasons for this, both economic and political. Edward could not afford to give up the English claim to France. One of the reasons for his success had been the supine manner in which Henry VI had appeared to acquiesce in the loss of his French possessions, so Edward had to make at least a show of determination in that direction. He was also genuinely alarmed by Louis' success in escaping from and overcoming his enemies. At the same time 70% of the increasingly important cloth trade of London was going to Flanders and Brabant, so that the goodwill of the Duke of Burgundy was important to the citizens who were Edward's main financial backers. In 1468 a marriage was contracted between Margaret, Edward's sister and Charles the Bold, who had succeeded his father in the previous year. This did not bring about a close relationship between the brothers-in-law, but it did serve to anger both the French king and Edward's powerful subject the Earl of Warwick, who had been trying to steer the king in the direction of a French alliance. Warwick was already annoyed because the king had chosen a domestic marriage for himself, ignoring the Earl's advice, and this second rebuff drove him into treasonable conspiracy. Louis promoted a reconciliation between Warwick and Henry VI's exiled queen, Margaret of Anjou, and when a rebellion in England caught Edward unawares in 1470, he backed their successful bid to restore Henry to the throne. Charles was by no means pleased to see a fugitive Edward, but his own self-interest prompted him to assist the exile's cause, and within a year Edward had regained his throne, and both Henry and the Earl of Warwick were dead. Louis' role in the crisis of 1470/71 naturally caused both Edward and Charles to capitalise upon the situation for their own benefit. A joint Anglo-Burgundian invasion of France was planned for 1474, ostensibly as the first step in Edward's recovery of his inheritance. How serious either party was must be open to question. Edward raised an army and duly marched into Picardy, but Charles was preoccupied with another campaign further south, and his support never materialised, whereupon Edward commenced negotiations with suspicious facility, and allowed himself to be bought off with an advantageous peace at Pecquigny in 1475. This has been called 'the end of the Hundred Years War', and when Charles was killed at Nancy in 1477 leaving only a female heir, Burgundy collapsed and the political map of northern Europe was re-drawn. Louis did well out of Charles's death, but not as well as he should have done. He secured Picardy, and the Duchy of Burgundy itself, but lost the marriage of the heiress, Mary, to Maximilian of Habsburg, the son of the Emperor Frederick III. In due course this was to have momentous consequences, but at the time it seemed a minor set back, because in other respects fortune continued to favour him. Rene of Anjou died in 1480, leaving no male heir and the whole of his vast estate escheated to the Crown. Louis had also contrived to marry two of his own daughters to the Dukes of Orleans and Bourbon. By the time of his death in 1483 only Britanny remained as an independent entity.

Louis' heir, Charles VIII, was only thirteen on his accession, and the Regency was held by his sister Anne and her husband, Pierre de Beaujeu. This was not undisputed, and France suffered from minority weakness for about five years, but it was a measure of Louis' achievement (and that of Charles before him) that the monarchy came nowhere near to collapse during this vulnerable period. Indeed, when Francis II of Britanny died in 1488, Charles was already able to move decisively. In spite of intervention from both Maximilian and Henry VII of England, who had signed the Treaty of Redon to guarantee Breton independence, Charles was able to secure the marriage of the heiress, Anne, and thus to bring Britanny into a personal union with the Crown of France. In that relationship it was to remain until 1532 when it was constitutionally absorbed into the kingdom. Henry, who was not at all anxious to renew the hundred years war, and who had received French support during his successful bid for the English throne in 1485, allowed himself to be bought off after the most perfunctory of campaigns at Étaples in 1492. By that time Charles's thoughts were, in any case, elsewhere. France had claims on both the Duchy of Milan, through the Orleans line, and the Kingdom of Naples (Anjou). Northern Italy was rich, and its politics were unstable. There was also the distant possibility of a crusade against the still advancing Ottomans, and a mirage of the Imperial hegemony of Europe. The temptation to intervene in Italy became overwhelming. Having secured peace on his northern border in 1492, he entered into a similar treaty with Ferdinand and Isabella of Spain in 1493 at Barcelona, and with the Emperor at Senlis in the same year. In 1494, having been conveniently invited to participate in Italian affairs by Ludovico Sforza of Milan, he launched his armies southward. Humanism was basically the rediscovery of pagan antiquity, and particularly of Greek antiquity.

4. Humanism and Intellectual Curiosity.

Humanism was basically the rediscovery of pagan antiquity, and particularly of Greek antiquity. It was not, as is sometimes alleged, a nineteenth century invention, although the word 'humanist' in the sense of 'atheist' or 'non-Christian' is a purely modern usage. What late fourteenth century Italian scholars like Petrarch discovered in antiquity was a quality of moral autonomy. Virtue was not formulated in imitation of a revealed model, but in a philosophical understanding of the nature of good and evil. The biblical understanding rested not on philosophy but upon mythology, and was expressed through such media as the Fall narrative in the Book of Genesis. To the humanist virtue lay not in obedience but in knowledge; but not just any knowledge. What was required was an understanding of the moral consequences of human action. Put very simply, the formula could be expressed; 'If 1 do x, it will cause y; do 1 want to cause y?' The determinant of moral action was not the furtherance of an ideological goal, such as the rule of the saints or the classless society, but the formulation of a stable and peaceful society, based upon principles of justice and self-development. A human society should be orderly and rational, living in obedience to agreed laws. This was not unlike the eighteenth century Utilitarian principle of the greatest happiness of the greatest number, except that the humanists realised that numbers alone carried no moral weight. Such philosophy had developed before the Christian faith, but it was not necessarily or exclusively pagan. It could be linked to orthodox Christian teaching by the concept of free will, and very few of the renaissance humanists were even suspected of infidelity. Free will is the Christian equivalent of the moral autonomy of the ancients, because although the Christian is bound to see moral action in terms of the Divine will, he exercises his judgement over the application of that will to his own circumstances. Many humanists also maintained Christian and pagan principles of moral action side by side without any sense of conflict or incongruity.

These ideas were expressed in the literature of pagan antiquity, and primarily in the writings of the Roman republican orator, Cicero. Cicero was the Latin link to the great moralists of Greek antiquity, and particularly via Plato to Socrates. The numerous works of that other giant of the ancient world, Aristotle, had been known in the west since the twelfth century. But they had come largely in Latin translations from Arabic texts, and had already been assimilated into orthodox Christian doctrine by the intellectual labours of St. Thomas Aquinas and others. The passionate enthusiasm of the renaissance was thus less for ancient literature as such than for fresh ancient literature, in which the wisdom and moral understanding of antiquity could be obtained unaltered through Christian intermediaries. It is superficial to denigrate the earnestness of this scholarship, and to claim that renaissance humanists were mainly interested in the rhetorical skills of Cicero in order to further their immediate careers as civil servants or teachers of grammar.

They were also interested in history, seeing it particularly as a storehouse of moral *exempla*. The historians of the ancient world, such as Thucydides, had been nothing if not didactic, and their narratives bristled with carefully pointed illustrations of how good rulers should behave, and of the fate awaiting tyrants or blasphemers. But the humanists also wanted their history to be accurate, because the moral force of the example was destroyed if the events could be shown to have been fictitious. Ancient history also provided illustrations of culture heroes struggling with various kinds of adversity, and linked the fortunes of states to the fortunes of their rulers, thereby increasing the moral significance of individual action. The ancients had had no sense of eschatological purpose. The Gods might determine particular events in accordance with their own whims and purposes, but there was no sense of an overall design, let alone of history moving towards a predetermined conclusion. Consequently history had tended to be seen as cyclical. Societies were developed by virtue, became corrupted by human failings, broke down, and then were renewed by fresh moral effort. As renaissance scholars saw themselves as the recoverers of ancient virtue, and hoped to revive what they saw as their decaying civilisation by that means, this was a pattern which appealed to them greatly.

Because knowledge was conducive to virtue, historical knowledge was necessary to those exercising political power. The more that man was seen to have control over his own future, the more important therefore a proper education for kings and princes became. Hence the very large numbers of manuals of guidance and instruction which were produced all over western Europe in the late fifteenth and early sixteenth centuries. This campaign was also remarkably successful. Starting in Italy the purveyors of this educational theory converted the courts of kings and princes into centres of patronage and learning, to their own immense advantage. The traditional education of the western aristocracy had been military and courtly, with much emphasis upon skill in arms and hunting, and literary tastes confined largely to the romances of chivalry. Beyond bare literacy 'book learning' tended to be treated with contempt as fit only for clerks. But by the middle of the sixteenth century kings were priding themselves upon their elegant Latin, and making it clear that they expected their servants to be conversant with the latest scholarly fashions. Nobles wishing to sustain their places at court hired the best humanist tutors for their sons - and even daughters.

As respect for the ancients which had originated in respect for their moral wisdom and human values, could, however, have other consequences. One of these was a slavish regard for the *ipse verbes* of ancient texts, which produced a rather stifling kind of grammatical pedantry. Another was a tendency to respect, quite uncritically, any knowledge which appeared to be ancient. A good example of this was the *Corpus Hermeticum,* a Greek text discovered and translated into Latin in the early fifteenth century. Ostensibly this was a text of secret wisdom, in the form of numbers based magic, written down by a Greek speaking Egyptian priest called Hermes Trismegisthus at about the time of Moses. It thus had all the ingredients of prestige, and bedevilled the growth of true mathematics for at least two generations. Eventually it was discovered to have been the concoction of an anonymous bunch of Alexandrian Jews in about the second century A.D., but that analysis eluded scholars until the early years of the seventeenth century.

More beneficial was the awareness that the ancients had disagreed among themselves, and consequently the wisdom of antiquity was not a monolithic orthodoxy. Aristotle's views on the nature of matter (for example) had been vigorously challenged by his own contemporaries. This awareness helped to stimulate some of the more energetic and original minds of the period, such as Leonardo da Vinci, to seek for their own solutions rather than depending upon authority, whether ancient or ecclesiastical. but that remained a minority position, and it took the discovery of the New World, and the dramatic developments which took place in firearms in the century after 1450 to convince many students that the ancients (collectively) had not known everything that there was to know. In fact the stimulation of intellectual curiosity was much more apparent in moral and political thinking than it was in thinking about the material world, which continued to be regarded as of secondary importance. Only the artists, such as Leonardo and Albrecht Dürer, who wrote theoretically about the material world which they painted, managed to some extent to bridge the gap between the physical and the intellectual. There was little scientific progress, as we now understand it, during the period of the renaissance, largely because there was no conception of verification by repeatable experiment, which is the basis of scientific methodology. However, as moral values required a political setting, there was a good deal of speculation about the nature of the state, and about proper forms of political action. Most of this focussed upon the state as an artifact, and considered the methods whereby a just constitution could be constructed, and what constituted justice in any particular set of circumstances. This led to a mechanical rather than an organic image of the state, which was fine in Italy, where it corresponded with the reality of many small states with ingeniously contrived republican constitutions, but did not make much sense in the feudal monarchies of the north. Northern humanists who wrote upon political themes tended either to concentrate upon the education of princes, like Erasmus or Sir Thomas Elyot, or upon the creation of moral fantasies, such as Thomas More's *Utopia*. *Utopia* was less a work of political philosophy than a satire upon the hopelessness of the human situation. If we draw any practical conclusions from it at all, they should probably be that for most social and political evils the remedy is at least as bad as the disease.

Italians, on the other hand, either sought to draw lessons from the idealised history of their own societies like Guicciardini, or strove to divorce politics from morality altogether. Niccolo Machiavelli, who was the most skilful practitioner of the latter approach, earned for himself in consequence a sinister reputation which has survived to the present day. This was not entirely undeserved, because to Machiavelli the stability of the state was the greatest good, subsuming the well-being of all its citizens. It was therefore better to preserve a bad order than to risk the turmoil involved in seeking to improve it. He did not, therefore, devote much time to the legitimacy of constitutions, and his most notorious book, *The Prince*, has been described as a handbook for usurpers. It is not true to say that Machiavelli was indifferent to either morality or religion, but for him the state was morally neutral, and he was prepared to distinguish between public and private morality. In order to preserve his authority, and hence the peace and order of the community, it may be necessary for a ruler to do things which would be immoral if done by a private citizen. Looking at the turmoil of Florentine politics which constituted Machiavelli's practical experience, to say nothing of the revolutions and civil wars of more recent times, it is not difficult to understand his point of view. However, his critics were not only correct in seeing him as completely out of step with the majority of humanist thinkers, they were also right to suspect the lack of moral content in his excellent pragmatic constructions. The most constructive contribution of the humanists to modern political thought was the idea of politics as a practical craft or skill with a moral purpose determined internally by the needs of human society, rather than externally by the revelation of transcendental purpose.

Eventually, although it took a long time to come, the humanists greatest contribution to western civilisation was the idea that man is master of his own fate, and consequently responsible for the consequences of his actions. During the renaissance most humanists continued to believe in God, and some resurrected the essentially pagan determinant of fate, but the greater the moral autonomy of man, and the greater his consequent domination of his environment, the less possible it becomes to blame either for the mistakes and follies of the human race.

5. From Burgundy to the Netherlands

In the fifteenth century the Duchy of Burgundy controlled the crossroads of Europe. Originally the Dukes had been simply vassals of the kings of France, but in addition Eudes IV (1315-1349) had set an example to his successors by securing it to the Imperial fief of Franche Compte. In 1361 the Duchy had escheated to the Crown, but it had been regranted by King John the Good to his youngest son, Philip the Bold, in 1364. Partly to further his own dynastic ambitions, and partly to check English moves in that direction, in 1369 Philip had married Margaret, the daughter and heir of Count Louis of Flanders. When Louis died in 1384 this paid off spectacularly, and Philip not only became Count of Flanders, but also secured control of Louis's other fiefs, Artois, Nevers and Franche Compte. This was probably the most important single move in the rise of Burgundy to power status. In spite of this, relations with France remained amicable, possibly because of the strength of that Valois family compact. However, this came to an abrupt end in 1392, when Philip's nephew, Charles VI, became insane. A power struggle then ensued between Philip and Louis of Orleans, the king's younger brother. Philip died in 1404, and was succeeded by his son, John the Fearless. John not merely continued the struggle, but raised (or lowered) it to a different plane by having the Duke of Orleans murdered in 1407. This provoked the blood feud between the Burgundians and the Armangnacs which tore France apart, and prompted the English intervention of 1415. In 1417 John reached an understanding with Henry V of England, and recognised him as heir to the French throne, a position which was confirmed three years later at the treaty of Troyes. John married his son Philip to Michele, a daughter of Charles VI, perhaps in the hope of ending the feud. If so, it was of little avail, because in 1419 he was murdered in his turn by the agents of Michele's brother, the Dauphin Charles. If Charles had hoped to weaken the Burgundian position by this move, then he also miscalculated. His revenge not merely prolonged the blood feud, it drove the English and the Burgundians closer together. Philip the Good succeeded his father, and married his own sister, Anne, to the Duke of Bedford, the English Regent in France, in 1423. For twelve years thereafter Philip remained allied to the English, although with diminishing enthusiasm, and helped to maintain English rule over that part of the kingdom which they controlled. One of the reasons why this came to an end was a private dispute over the Duchy of Brabant. Jacqueline of Holland was the daughter and heir of William VI of Holland, and was married to John IV, Count of Brabant. The marriage was childless, and in 1422 Jaqcueline abandoned her husband, who secured a divorce. Four years later she married Humphrey, Duke of Gloucester, the uncle of King Henry VI of England, and brother of the Duke of Bedford. In 1426 Humphrey very ill-advisedly began a campaign to secure control of his wife's inheritance of Holland Hainault, Zeeland and Frisia; and when John of Brabant died without heirs in the following year, even more ill-advisedly, extended his claim to Brabant. This was patently absurd. John was succeeded first by his brother Philip, and when Philip died, also childless, in 1430, Philip of Burgundy secured control by a legitimate, if distant, kinship. In 1433 Humphrey recognised the impossibility of the situation, and Jacqueline surrendered all her lands to the Duke of Burgundy. This was a second major step forward for the Duchy, but Philip felt that he had no particular reason to feel grateful to the Duke of Gloucester, regarding him instead as a rival and a nuisance, and Anglo-Burgundian relations were seriously impaired. When Philip finally broke the English alliance in 1435, he was in a very much stronger position than his father had been in 1417, when the connection had been established. Burgundy had been anxious to abandon the sinking English ship, but that did not imply any great cordiality in relations with France. The steady advance of royal power under Charles VII was a cause of constant suspicion, and the events of 1419 had not been forgotten. Consequently when Charles's disaffected son Louis took refuge at Philip's court from 1456 to 1461 he was made welcome, and relations between the two courts became distant and frosty. Burgundy also continued to show expansionist tendencies. In 1443 Philip secured the Duchy of Luxembourg by inheritance, and began to intrude his influence into those ecclesiastical states, such as Liege and Utrecht, which lay intermingled with his existing lands. It was also a constant aim of Burgundian policy to secure a bridge between The Netherlands and the Burgundian lands proper, and the Duchy of Bar was a continuous object of attention.

Philip's son, Charles the Bold, who succeeded him in 1467, married Margaret, the sister of Edward IV of England, and although that did not produce much cordiality, he pursued a generally anti-French policy. Charles, however, was too ambitious. He over-extended himself both physically and financially, and was killed in battle with the Swiss at Nancy in 1477. Although his revenues, at 773,000 livres per annum, were more than twice those of his great grandfather, in a period innocent of inflation, at his death he was virtually bankrupt. After 1477 Charles's daughter, Mary, was unable to hold her inheritance together. Louis XI secured Burgundy proper, Picardy and Artois, fiefs of the French Crown: but the richest part, Flanders, Brabant, Holland, Zeeland, Hainault and Frisia, went with Mary's marriage to Maximilian of Habsburg. This was not quite as splendid as it at first appeared, partly because Mary died in 1482, leaving her lands theoretically in the hands of her infant son, Philip, and partly because the old cloth towns, Bruges, Ypres and Ghent, were all in difficulties during the late fifteenth century. The economic future lay rather with towns such as Brussels and Antwerp. The latter doubled in size between 1436 and 1460, but it had barely reached the front rank when Mary's death ushered in a period of political trouble. The Estates of Flanders refused to accept Maximilian as Regent, and set up their own Regency Council, while Louis XI used the opportunity to insinuate a measure of French control. The driving force behind the Regency government at this time was the town of Ghent, but in 1483 Maximilian managed to regain some control over the Bishopric of Liege, and consequently to drive a wedge between Ghent and Antwerp, which at that point was supporting it. At the same time, Louis IX died, and Maximilian was able to dismiss the Regency Council of Flanders, and take power himself. Civil war ensued, but the other provinces had little enthusiasm for the conflict, and quickly came to terms. By 1485 only Flanders was resisting the Archduke, and within Flanders, only Ghent. Before the end of the year the city came to terms, and it appeared that Maximilian's Regency was finally established. However he then tried to use his newly established authority to support a military campaign against France, and quickly over-reached himself. In 1488 his Regency collapsed, and the government of all Philip's provinces was in chaos. Civil strife continued, with intermittent intervention from France, until 1493, and a number of the cities, most notably Bruges, suffered severe economic and physical damage.

In 1493 the Emperor Frederick III died, and his son Maximilian was elected in his place. This ended his attempts to impose a Regency in the Netherlands and Philip, by then aged fifteen, was able to make a show of taking over the government in person. In this fragile situation, the diversion of French energies into Italy in 1494 was a great blessing, and the stability and prosperity of The Netherlands began to recover. In 1496 Philip married Juana, the eldest daughter of Ferdinand and Isabella of Spain. After her brother's death in 1499, Juana became the heir to her mother's kingdom of Castile, and when Isabella died in 1504, Philip claimed the Crown in the right of his wife. Although Juana was supported by a strong party in Castile, the couple never succeeded in making their rule effective, and in 1506 Philip himself died. This left his eldest son, Charles, as Archduke of Burgundy at the age of six. There was, however, no return to the confusion of his father's minority. In theory the Regency was again exercised by Maximilian, but in practice by Philip's competent and level-headed sister, Margaret of Austria.

Juana played no part in the government of either the Netherlands or Castile. She suffered a nervous collapse after her husband's death, and since it was politically convenient to eliminate her, was regarded thereafter as hopelessly insane. She lived in seclusion and virtual imprisonment until 1556. Almost as soon as Charles was old enough to assume responsibility for the government, in 1516, he succeeded his grandfather Ferdinand as king of both Aragon and Castile. In 1519 he was elected to succeed his other grandfather, Maximilian, as Holy Roman Emperor, and for the remainder of his long reign, down to 1555, The Netherlands were governed by a succession of Regents.

This did not mean, however, that the provinces were neglected. The Imperial court was frequently at Brussels, and Charles assiduously expanded his inheritance in that corner of Europe. When the French enclave of Tournai was recovered from the English in 1518, it was almost immediately taken by the Emperor, in 1521 at the outset of his protracted struggle against Francis The Lordship of Friesland was annexed after a prolonged period of civil strife in 1524, and the temporal sovereignty of the bishopric of Utrecht in 1527/8, after a conflict with the Duke of Gelderland. Overijessel was acquired in 1528, the Lordship of Gröningen and the County of Drenthe in 1536, and finally the Duchy of Gelderland and the County of Zutphen in 1543. Although the bishopric of Liege remained theoretically an independent ecclesiastical principality, Charles treated its independence very cavalierly, even building the fortress of Marienburg on its territory in 1546. These years saw the spectacular rise of Antwerp to prominence as the centre of European banking and international finance, not least because of the constant demands which Charles made upon the money market to finance his endless wars. The connection with Spain was a mixed blessing. Spanish trade with the New World was conducted through Seville, but it was Antwerp which reaped the main commercial benefit. On the other hand, taxation was heavy to support both Spanish and Imperial commitments, and garrisons of Spanish troops were no more welcome than they were in Naples or Milan. Having assembled virtually all the provinces of The Netherlands under his control, in 1548 Charles set out to make fresh provisions for their future. Firstly he constituted them into the 'Burgundian Circle' of the Holy Roman Empire, taking them out of the main governmental structure. Although remaining part of the Empire, and in theory subject to taxation as such, they were no longer under the control of Imperial law. Having done that, he then decreed that in future all the seventeen provinces would follow the same principles and order of succession. These two edicts together gave The Netherlands for the first time a collective identity, similar to that which had been enjoyed by the Duchy of Burgundy. Unable to go their separate ways they had become, to all intents and purposes, a loose federal state with a considerable measure of independence. Charles was able to do this without provoking serious resistance because he knew The Netherlands, and its customs, and knew how far he could go. He refrained, for instance, from introducing any measures of centralisation, because he understood perfectly well the strength of the separate laws and customs which kept the provinces distinct. The Estates General was expanded to admit newly acquired provinces, but was itself a conservative force, unwilling to countenance a larger measure of integration. Each province was effectively governed by its own council and Estates, and Charles carefully respected the jurisdictional autonomy of each. He even permitted the privileges of certain jurisdictions to inhibit the work of the Inquisition, by which he set considerable store. For this reason, and quite against Charles's will, there were considerable differences of opinion on religious matters within the Netherlands as the reformation advanced. By the time that he abdicated in 1555, and handed over the government to his son Philip, the old Burgundian inheritance had become a quite different kind of political animal.

6. How absolute was Francis I of France?

The King of France owed his authority to God alone. In theory he was *legibus solutus,* above the law, because all the various laws of the kingdom were administered in his name, and all legislation was by royal edict. He was, however, answerable to the Pope for the safety and effectiveness of the church within his realm, and as *Rex Christianissimus* (Most Christian King), he was supposedly a champion of the catholic faith. In practice his responsibility to the Pope was very slight, because the Concordat of Bologna of 1516, which had resulted directly from his military victory at Marignano in the previous year, had given him the right to appoint to all bishoprics and other major ecclesiastical offices. His rights of patronage were consequently both extensive and profitable, and he was under no temptation to establish an English type of Royal Supremacy. His secular authority was greatly supported by the fact that he was entitled to raise taxes without any formal process of consent, the Estates General having surrendered that function in the previous century. The two principle types of tax were the *taille,* which was raised on both persons and property, and the *gabelle,* which was a tax upon the sale of salt. The king was bound by certain 'fundamental laws', such as the Salic law, and that which forbade the alienation of royal authority or property, but these were seen, understandably, as enhancing rather than limiting his power.

Appearances, however, could be deceptive. In theory the king paid for the normal expenses of government from the revenues of his lands and the profits of justice. This was what was meant by the king 'living of his own'. The *taille* was thus in origin a military tax, for war or defence. This meant that the nobility and clergy claimed exemption. The nobility because they contributed their services in person, and the clergy because they did not participate in warlike activities. The clergy paid their own taxes, known as *aides,* and these were subject to a process of consent, although refusal was both rare and difficult. The nobility did in fact serve, at their own expense in the first instance, and were often left unrecompensed except with honours and prestige. Exemptions from the *taille* could also be purchased, so that the weight of this burden was already falling disproportionately on the peasantry by the 1530s, and revolts against taxation were endemic.

When Francis came to the throne in 1514 the representative institution for the whole kingdom, the Estates General, was very nearly redundant. It consisted of three chambers, the nobility, the clergy and the townsmen, and was thus representative of every propertied interest, but it had no essential function. Unlike the English parliament, it had never played a part in legislation, and it had lost its right to vote direct taxation. In consequence it tended only to be convened when the realm, or the king, was in dire trouble and endeavouring to mobilise support. When Francis was captured after his defeat at Pavia in 1525, his mother, Louise of Savoy, who was acting as Regent, considered convening the Estates General, but did not eventually do so. Francis himself never felt the need for such an assembly. It was to meet several times during the civil wars of the later part of the century, but then went into complete abeyance from 1614 until 1789. Provincial Estates, of similar composition, still existed in those areas which had more recently been added to the royal domain; Normandy, Brittany, Burgundy, Provence, Dauphiné and Languedoc. These had no right to refuse royal taxation, or even to negotiate about its level, but they could negotiate about its assessment and collection, and thus had sufficient meaning to continue in existence upon a fairly regular basis. The provinces which had Estates, therefore, (the *pays d' états)* tended to be less obviously or arbitrarily burdened with the *taille* than *the pays d' élections,* which had no such protection and where the whole process was carried out by royal commissioners.

Legislation was a matter, not for any representative assembly, but for the *parlements.* These were both courts of law and corporations of lawyers, and thus consisted of the wealthiest and best organised interest group after the clergy and nobility. There were seven of them, of which by far the most important was the *parlement* of Paris. Their main responsibility was to enforce the law, but they also had the crucial function of registering the king's decrees, because without such registration these edicts did not have the force of law. Although all legislation had to originate with the king, he could not simply make laws in accordance with his whim. The *parlements* were privileged bodies, who appointed their own officials and enjoyed extensive powers, but their powers to impede the king's legislative will were limited. In the case of the provincial parlements he could suspend their functions, or abrogate their privileges. The *Paris parlement* was technically a part of the royal household, a status which reflected its remote origins, and this meant that if the king attended in person, then his will had to be obeyed. This was known as a *lit de justice,* and was occasionally resorted to for measures of the highest importance. The Edict of Nantes, for example, was to be so registered in 1598. Nevertheless, no king resorted to such sanctions lightly, because a prolonged withdrawal of good will and co-operation on the part of the *parlement* could cause great disruption and make the work of government infinitely more difficult.

The administration of the law consequently offered similar paradoxes to the process of legislation. Although the king was above the law in theory, and for most practical purposes, it nevertheless imposed a number of limitations on him. There was no common law in France. Most of the south was under Roman law, which was a written code, while the north had a patchwork of customary codes. More important, major issues, such as murder, which in England were Pleas of the Crown, and always heard in the king's courts, in France might well be heard in the court of a seigneurial franchise. It was where a crime was committed, rather than the nature of the crime, which determined whether or not it was heard in a royal court. The king therefore had much less control over the judicial system. He could not use it as an instrument of policy, and received only a small proportion of the profits of justice.

Administrative control by the Crown also showed two faces. At the top was the king's principle executive instrument, the *conseil du roi,* with numerous specialist sub-committees, also known as conseils; the *conseil des finances, conseil des affaires,* and so on. Theoretically the king appointed all these councillors, starting with a clean sheet at the beginning of his reign. In practice his freedom of choice was constrained, not only by considerations of political commonsense, but also by custom. Certain great offices of state, which carried automatic membership of the *conseil du roi,* were in the control of great noble families. These families were sensitive both of their honours and their interests, and quite capable of combining to defend both. The same was true of court offices, and consequently the king was not completely master, even within his own household. Below that level the king commanded an extensive professional bureaucracy - well beyond anything which the king of England could have afforded. On the other hand he had already begun to sell offices and reversions to offices, thus reducing his own control, and that of his successors, over future appointments. As offices showed an increasing tendency to become hereditary this became even more the case, but that process was not far advanced by the time of Francis's death. There was no French equivalent of the English Justice of the Peace, and the structures of local government showed a persistent tendency to fall under the control of the provincial nobility. This had happened first with the provinces themselves, then with the *senechaussées,* and finally with the *baillages.* Although in theory the king's servants as well as his vassals, and bound to him by ties of personal allegiance, in practice these nobles were the greatest restraint upon the king's power. The King of France might have no constitutional limitations, but in practice his power was by no means absolute. In 1523, for example, the whole of France was endangered because the Duke of Bourbon, the High Constable, considered himself to be aggrieved with the king over what was essentially a private issue of inheritance, and entered into an alliance with the Emperor, as though he had been an independent prince. Moreover, he had sufficient resources, and was thought to have sufficient control over those resources to be taken seriously. In the event he failed to make good his promises to Charles, but whether this resulted from incompetence, failure of nerve, or the inability to carry his own affinity against the king is not entirely clear.

There were two orders of nobility, and each presented a different type of challenge to the Crown. The *noblesse d'epée* were the old military aristocracy, and it was to this category that the greatest noble families belonged, The more wars the king fought, the stronger their position tended to become. Military services strengthened their clientage networks, because the lesser nobles naturally served under the greater, and tended to preserve that dependent relationship off the field of battle. At the end of Francis's reign, after almost thirty years of continuous warfare, the three major families of Guise, Bourbon and Montmorency were stronger than they had been at any time earlier in the reign, and the new king, Henri II, was to find them extremely difficult to control. The *noblesse de robe* were the civil service aristocracy, principally the upper reaches of the legal profession. Such men were the Presidents and councillors of the *parlements,* and they formed an indispensable link in the administrative structure. They were wealthy, but individually they were not powerful in the same sense as the military grandees. Their strength was collective, and lay in their organisation rather than in their individual resources. In normal circumstances the interests of both orders lay in co-operation with the king rather than in obstructing him, but each was jealous of its privileges, and could feel threatened by royal policy. The *noblesse d'epée* were deeply suspicious that increasing central control would erode their power base in the provinces; and the *noblesse de robe* feared that the continued sale of offices and reversions would cheapen their own status, and allow the king to circumvent the existing machinery. Francis used his court as the prime channel of communication with both orders. In so far as the court was the natural centre of government in personal monarchy, it was also a focus for the civilian nobility. In so far as the king was the fount of honour and the war leader of the kingdom, it was a magnet for the grandees. The court was itinerant, and extremely flexible, but offices in the household proper were comparatively rare, and were greatly sought after because they carried the privilege of constant access to the king. A household office was a key strategic position in the patronage network, and its holder use his influence, real or presumed, to very profitable effect. Ambition for such offices, which were exclusively in the king's gift, also gave him an additions means of control, so that all strong kings were able to use their courts to subdue independent ambition, and encourage the notion of an aristocracy of service.

The problem with the French monarchy was that it was only as strong as the incumbent for the time being. The unobstructed channels through which a powerful king could make his will effective, were equally open to reverse flow. The absolutism of the Crown was at least as much a source of weakness and instability as it was of strength.

7. The Constitution of the Holy Roman Empire

The Emperor was the senior and most prestigious of the secular rulers of western Europe; the successor of the Caesars and the secular head of Christendom. Throughout the middle ages his status had been challenged by his opposite number in eastern Europe, the Byzantine Emperor; but by 1400 that challenge had become largely academic, and in 1453 it disappeared altogether. In the eleventh century it had seemed likely that the Empire would develop into a powerful monarchy, on the same lines as the kingdom of France. However, a series of political disasters in the twelfth and thirteenth centuries, including a damaging struggle with the papacy, had left the Crown emasculated and the Emperor little more than a figurehead. There were Imperial institutions of government, notably the *Reichstag*, or Diet, which was a multicameral representative assembly on the lines of the French Estates General; and the *Reichskammergerichte*, or Imperial High Court. The Emperor had the right to legislate by edicts, which were called Pragmatics, and to collect Imperial taxes. As in England, ordinary revenues came from land, and from the profits of justice; extraordinary revenues had to be voted by the Diet. However, all this imposing facade was largely a sham, because the Golden Bull of 1356, which had settled the constitution of the Empire after a prolonged period of civil strife, had left the Emperor with no effective sanctions to enforce his theoretical rights. The office itself was elective, election being in the hands of a college of seven senior princes of the Empire; the king of Bohemia, the bishops of Mainz, Trier and Cologne, and the princes of Saxony, Brandenburg and the Palatinate. It was not normally in the interest of the Electors to choose one of their own number, or another major prince with extensive resources. So Emperors tended to the princes of the second rank (like Frederick III) who did not have sufficient leverage to move the cumbersome machinery which should have supported them. Not until the election of Charles of Spain in 1519 was that pattern broken, and even Charles found it difficult to impose himself. Effective power was in the hands of the autonomous princes, and neither the Diet nor the High Court could function unless they were prepared to be supportive. The Emperor could not even resort to the law to discipline a recalcitrant prince without the support of the majority of his colleagues.

Geographically, the Empire stretched from Calais to Vienna, and from Holstein to the papal states, but by the fifteenth century part of this extent was purely notional, the Swiss cantons, for example, and the city states of northern Italy barely recognising the most minimal suzerainty. Germany proper, which, never disputed its allegiance, was totally fragmented. Not only were there powerful principalities, such as the County Palatine of the Rhine or the Duchy of Bavaria, there were innumerable smaller states, such as Hesse and Wurtemburg, which broke up and reunited from generation to generation according to the customs of inheritance. The ecclesiastical states, such as the Bishopric of Bamberg or the Abbey of Fulda were not subject to the same hazard, but some of them were very small, and in many cases neighbouring secular princes had a disproportionate say in the election of incumbents. It was even debatable whether the Kingdom of Bohemia was within the Empire or not, in spite of the fact that its King was an Elector. Another major element in the make up of the Empire was the Imperial free cities, many of which, such as Strassburg, Augsburg and Frankfurt, were populous and wealthy, controlling their hinterlands, and often important trade routes. Other free cities were quite small, and survived either by the sufferance of their more powerful neighbours, or because of some quirk in the local balance of power. There were even Imperial free villages, and Imperial knights, each with his single castle and diminutive estate, the last remnant of a once numerous class. For all these small fry the decline of the Emperor and the rise of the princes was extremely bad news, but a surprising number managed to survive in the hostile political climate. The lands of the church were scattered throughout the Empire, and although no bishopric was a major power in its own right, several were important politically, like the three ecclesiastical Electors, or strategically, like Bremen, Münster or Liége. Ecclesiastical princes owed homage to the Emperor for their temporal estates, but their spiritual allegiance, which often took priority, was to the Pope.

As a result of all this, the resources of an Emperor lay much more in his own hereditary estates than in the elective office. In fact during this period the election became almost as much of a sham as the constitution. The title was virtually hereditary in the Habsburg family after the election of Albert II in 1438. Albert held the office for only one year, and was never crowned. He was succeeded by his cousin, Frederick III, who reigned from 1440 to 1493, and Frederick, by his son Maximilian (1493-1519). The election which followed Maximilian's death was a genuine contest, but resulted in the victory of his grandson, Charles. Charles was succeeded, not by his son Philip, as he wished, but by his brother Ferdinand (1558-1565), and Ferdinand by his son, Maximilian II. Albert was Archduke of Austria, but Frederick was mainly dependent upon his family lands in South East Germany, particularly Styria and the Tyrol, which were not wealthy. Maximilian in theory controlled most of the rich Burgundian inheritance, but in practice he exercised an intermittent and ineffectual regency for his son, Philip. Charles relinquished the Austrian lands to his brother, but enjoyed effective control over the Netherlands, and was in addition king of both Castile and Aragon, drawing great wealth from the Castilian Empire in the new world. In 1519, at least, the princes had not chosen to elect a weak king whom they could control. Charles's power extended to all corners of Europe, and came eventually to depend heavily upon Spanish money and manpower, but he was a lumbering colossus, who had great difficulty in focussing his resources. This was partly due to slow and poor communications, partly to the inefficiency of the revenue systems in each of his various dominions, and partly to the fact that he never made any attempt to create a unified system of administration. Unfortunately, no sooner had an Emperor been elected who had at least the potential to bring the Holy Roman Empire under control than he was confronted with religious strife on an unprecedented scale, and the separatism of some of the princes began to acquire an ideological tinge which made them even more intractable.

By 1530 several princes and cities had opted for the evangelical faith as expounded by Martin Luther and his followers, a faith which had been denounced as heresy, not only by the papacy, but also by the Imperial Diet, meeting at Worms in 1521. Charles never wavered in his allegiance to the catholic church, but he was compelled to accept that he could not overcome the Lutherans by force. Even with Spanish troops, he needed the backing of those Imperial princes who had also remained loyal to catholicism, such as the Duke of Bavaria. This was largely withheld, because the catholic princes had no more desire to see a resurgent Emperor than the Lutherans had. Once Charles had defeated the heretics in the name of orthodoxy, they feared that he would turn on them in the name of Imperial monarchy. Charles struggled with this problem intermittently for the rest of his life. In 1547 he actually won a decisive victory over the Lutheran Schmalkaldic League at the battle of Mühlberg, and attempted to impose a religious settlement, but was unable to exploit his victory, and was forced to compromise in 1555. By then he was already in process of abdicating his authority, and his method of doing so reveals that he had no long term ambitions for the establishment of a universal monarchy. As early as 1530 he had persuaded the Electors to endorse his brother Ferdinand as King of the Romans, that is, his designated heir, and Ferdinand would have no hereditary claim to the Crowns of Spain since Charles already had a son, Philip, born in 1527. When it came to the point, the Emperor regretted his decision, and attempted to persuade the Diet to accept Philip's claim, but they refused to do so, and the earlier arrangement stood. Frustrated in his purpose Charles then detached Milan and The Netherlands from the Empire, and handed them over to Spain, abdicating the latter to Philip in 1555. In 1556 he handed over the Crowns of Spain, and the Imperial fief of Franche Compté, but he did not abdicate as Emperor. It was only when he died in 1558 that Ferdinand came into his much diminished inheritance. Apart from the Imperial title, Ferdinand held all the Habsburg family lands within the Empire, and that remnant of Hungary which had survived the Ottoman conquest of 1526, so he was slightly, but only slightly, better off than his grandfather Maximilian. On the other hand, he did not have Charles's global problems. The French challenge, which had plagued the Empire throughout the early sixteenth century, faded away with the development of civil strife within France after 1560. The Balkan frontier with the Ottomans had also become stabilised by then, because the Turkish lines of communication were over-extended, and the sea war which Charles had endeavoured to sustain in the Mediterranean and North Africa was inherited by Philip. The religious peace of Augsburg in 1555 did not mark the end of the reformation, but it did signal a significant slowing down in the Lutheran advance, while the Peace of Cateau-Cambrésis in 1559 brought stability to the western and northern borders of the Empire.

Ferdinand had already succeeded, when he came to the throne, in persuading the estates of Hungary and Bohemia to elect his own son, Maximilian, to follow him in those realms. However, he continued to adhere to the Habsburg custom of dividing his hereditary lands between the co-heirs. As he had three sons, this meant that Maximilian's resources as Emperor were much diminished, and in spite of Hungary and Bohemia, he was not much richer, nor more powerful, than Frederick III had been a hundred years earlier. After 1565 the Empire consequently subsided into a period of weakness and inactivity. Maximilian could count upon the family support of his brothers, and indeed of his cousin Philip, in the event of real emergency, but for routine purposes such support could not be invoked. The power of the Imperial princes was therefore to remain unchallenged for another two generations. The Empire had gone from rags to riches, and back to rags again in four generations. It was not until the early seventeenth century that Ferdinand II's successful combination of hereditary lands, Imperial title and Bohemian Crown threatened a resurgence of Habsburg pretensions, and by then the parallel revival of France guaranteed a renewal of the early sixteenth century wars.

8. The Habsburg-Valois Wars

This struggle originated in the French invasion of Italy in 1494. Not only did Charles VIII challenge the Spanish control of Naples - which at that point had nothing to do with the Habsburgs - he also signalled his bid for the Imperial leadership of Christendom by announcing that his expedition was a preliminary to a crusade against the Turks. For the next twenty years the French fought with varying success against a shifting coalition of opponents, which included at various times the papacy, the Venetians and the English, but their most consistent opponent was Ferdinand of Aragon. In 1515 Francis I won the most comprehensive victory so far achieved at the battle of Marignano, and when Ferdinand died in the following year it appeared that the French supremacy would endure for many years. The Treaty of London, brokered by Cardinal Wolsey in 1518, was designed to stabilise that situation, because a French ascendancy in Italy had many advantages for the king of England also. However, this delicate diplomatic web was completely destroyed in the following year by the election of the young Charles I of Spain as the Emperor Charles V. Charles had no intention of accepting French control in northern Italy, and his many dominions threatened Francis with encirclement. It was at this point that the Habsburg-Valois wars proper began. After about two years of diplomatic sparring, during which both sides bid for an English alliance, actual fighting was resumed in 1521. In spite of Francis's high profile summit meeting with Henry VIII at the Field of Cloth of Gold, England eventually sided with the Emperor. Henry's contribution to the war effort was spasmodic and largely ineffectual, but Charles nevertheless won a total victory at the battle of Pavia in 1525, capturing his rival, who disappeared for several months into a Spanish prison. At first it seemed possible that France would be dismembered, as this disaster followed closely after the treason of Constable Bourbon in 1523, but a number of circumstances conspired to prevent so dramatic an outcome. Charles had also had a very difficult time over the previous five years. In Germany he had almost immediately been confronted by the Lutheran challenge, and in Spain by the revolt of the *communeros,* which had been ended by the king's victory at Villarlar in April 1521. In 1522 renewed Ottoman activity had been signalled by the capture of Rhodes; not a direct defeat for the Emperor, but a warning of renewed pressure on the Eastern frontier. In 1521 Francis had renewed his alliances with the Papacy and the Swiss Cantons, moves which had contributed significantly to the resumption of war. These allies may have been discouraged by the French defeat, but they were not likely to change sides because his victory made the Emperor the principle threat to everyone within his reach. In 1526 he therefore decided to free Francis on moderate terms, gaining some strategic territories on The Netherlands frontier and in north Italy, but not seeking to make any serious inroads into France itself. The Treaty of Madrid was a humiliation for the French, but it was not the disaster which Pavia had seemed to threaten.

The disaster which struck in 1526 did not overtake the French, but the Hungarians. For many years the Eastern bastion of Christendom, Hungary collapsed almost overnight following the defeat and death of King Lewis at Mohacs. Charles had already reduced his commitments in the south eastern part of the Empire by handing over the Austrian lands to his brother Ferdinand in 1521, and after 1526 Ferdinand also became the ruler of what was left of Christian Hungary, based on a dynastic claim which did not at all please the remains of the Magyar nobility. This put the Habsburgs in the front line against an apparently invincible Sultan, and ensured that the Emperor would have to buy support against these persistent foes with concessions in other directions, most notably to the Lutheran princes of Germany. There was no way in which Ferdinand could sustain the struggle without full Imperial backing, and Charles's attempts to limit expenditure in that direction were completely frustrated by his brother's inheritance. As though to emphasise the point, the Ottomans besieged Vienna in 1529. Thereafter Turkish pressure was intermittent, because the Sultan also had to wage war on more than one front, and by the 1540s the war in the Balkans was largely a matter of sieges, raids and counter raids; unglamorous and indecisive, but still expensive in both men and money. Following the siege of Rhodes the Ottomans also became an increasing threat by sea, and in an attempt to break down their alliance with the Muslim states of north Africa, Charles launched his navy successfully against Tunis in 1535, and unsuccessfully against Algiers in 1541. In the latter year, with sound political logic, although to the horror of many Christian rulers (including the Emperor), the Sultan and the King of France entered into a formal alliance, and the Turkish fleet wintered at Toulon.

Meanwhile, in spite of the Emperor's caution, the Treaty of Madrid brought its own nemesis. In order to secure his release, Francis had been compelled to surrender his two sons into Imperial custody. As soon as he was free he attempted to denounce the treaty as having been extorted under coercion, and the boys seemed destined for a long stay in Madrid. In spite of the circumstances, their continued detention provided the pretext for an anti-imperial alliance, which was known as the League of Cognac. The parties were the Papacy, Venice and France, and the real objective was the reduction of the Emperor's control over northern Italy, which threatened France with encirclement, and the papacy with the virtual loss of its diplomatic independence. In spite of its long tradition of alliance with the ruler of the Netherlands, England was sympathetic to the League, although not actually a member. Cardinal Wolsey succeeded in persuading Henry VIII that he ought to be apprehensive about Habsburg hegemony, and Henry was peeved with Charles for the unceremonious way in which the latter had broken his long-standing engagement to the Princess Mary, the daughter and heir of England. He can hardly have been genuinely surprised by this, because Mary was only eleven, and the Emperor urgently needed a mature wife. Henry, moreover, was already making it clear that he had doubts about his marriage to Catherine, the youngest daughter of Ferdinand and Isabella, who was Charles's aunt. Consequently the Emperor's marriage to Isabella of Portugal in 1526 enabled. Henry to denounce Charles's faithlessness before the compliment could be returned. In 1527 the war between the Emperor and the League took a melodramatic turn, at least as spectacular as the victory at Pavia, when an Imperial army ran out of control in central Italy, sacked Rome and made the Pope a prisoner. Ostensibly Charles was as shocked as his enemies by this unexpected consequence of his perennial cash-flow problems, but he was not slow to take advantage of it. Once the initial shock was over, and a seemly control restored, Pope Clement VII soon saw the advantages of 'living and dying an Imperialist', and English and French influence in the Curia were alike eclipsed. In 1528 England became briefly and notionally involved in the war on the French side, but this represented the death throes of Wolsey's foreign policy, as he sought desperately for some leverage at Rome to secure Henry the annulment of his marriage. So little attention did the other belligerents pay to Wolsey that he barely found out about the peace negotiations in 1529 in time to get included in the treaty.

In spite of the strength of his position, the Peace of Cambrai was no more than a draw in the Emperor's favour. Anything more would have been more trouble than it was worth, as the treaty of Madrid had shown. Francis renounced all his claims in Italy Charles gave up all his claims to the Duchy of Burgundy. The French king who was by this time a widower, also undertook to marry the Habsburg princess, Eleanor of Austria. The Peace of Cambrai had an almost unprecedented duration of seven years, but apart from that respite, it settled, nothing. When the duke of Milan died in 1535 without a direct heir, the Emperor, as suzerain stepped in and arranged the succession. Francis, unable to resist the temptation, promptly revived his own claim, and sent a large army to enforce it. They failed to take Milan, but on the whole the French had the better of the resulting war. The Emperor got into serious financial difficulties and was forced to borrow 200,000 ducats from the Fuggers (his Augsburg bankers), while Francis was able to seize and retain the Duchy of Savoy and about third-thirds of Piedmont. The war lasted less than two years, being ended by papal mediation at the Truce of Nice in June 1538, but it almost completely undid the Imperial advantages secured at Cambrai. For about two years the arch-enemies appeared to be reconciled, and the King of England, who survived by exploiting their feud, believed that the papal sentence against him was about to be enforced. These were crisis years in England, but by 1541 it was business as usual when two French agents returning from Constantinople were murdered near Pavia. Francis blamed Charles, and called upon the Ottomans for support. The resulting war lasted from 1542 to 1544, when it was ended by another inconclusive peace at Crespy. The Emperor gave up his claim to Burgundy (again), and Francis repeated his renunciation of Naples. More realistically, he also gave up his attempts to secure the northeastern provinces of Flanders and Artois. It was this peace which enabled the Council of Trent to be convened at long last, and freed the Emperor to take effective action against the Lutheran princes. In April 1547 at the battle of Mühlberg, he defeated the Schmalkaldic League, and imposed his own religious settlement, the Interim.

Francis died at about the time of Mühlberg, and for the time being his son and successor Henry II had no desire to renew the old feud, looking rather towards England, and Henry VIII's last conquest, Boulogne. But the Interim failed, and by 1552 religious revolt vas again stirring in Germany. This time there was no League, but the leader, Duke Maurice of Saxony, judged correctly that Henry would not be able to resist such an excellent opportunity. In return for the key border fortresses of Metz, Toul and Verdun, the ultra-orthodox King of France fought alongside the Lutheran rebels. Although the Lutherans were defeated, the Franco/Habsburg war soon became lethargic, expensive and unstoppable. In 1553 Charles, who was sick and aging, flickered into life to arrange the marriage of his son and heir, Philip, to Mary of England, who had succeeded on the death of her half brother, Edward VI, in July, but it was to be another four years before England became actively involved in the struggle. By that time the Emperor had retired to Spain, and it was Philip who sustained the Habsburg cause. By 1558, when the Imperialists had won a victory at St. Quentin, and the French at Calais, financial and military exhaustion was paralysing both sides, and six months of negotiations finally brought the cycle to an end at Cateau-Cambrésis in April 1559. On the whole Philip came out of this the better, as Henry was forced to give up Savoy and Piedmont, but the Habsburgs were unable to recover the border fortresses, or the English Calais. It was not, however, the terms of the treaty which signalled the end of an era, but the change of *dramatis personae*. Charles's departure broke up the Habsburg Empire, and Henry's death immediately after the treaty put France on the course to civil war. Neither the will nor the means for a large-scale revival of Franco/Habsburg rivalry was to exist again until the following century.

9. Spain from Ferdinand and Isabella to Philip II

As the Moorish conquest had been rolled back during the previous five hundred years, Iberia had emerged as a series of separate kingdoms; Navarre, Galicia, Laon, Castile, Portugal, Aragon, Valencia and Catalonia. By the middle of the fifteenth century these had been reduced through amalgamation and absorption to four. Navarre and Portugal remained independent; Galicia and Laon had become parts of Castile; Catalonia and Valencia of Aragon. In the far south the Emirate of Granada still remained in Moorish hands. Navarre was a largely mountainous kingdom, a small area wedged in between France to the north, Castile to the west and Aragon to the south. Portugal, covering about half of the Atlantic seaboard, was already looking to Africa and the Atlantic for its future. Towards the end of the fifteenth century Castile was a country of about five million people, with a mainly agricultural and pastoral economy. Much of the interior was semi-barren upland, grazed by huge numbers of sheep, and in spite of the extensive northern coastline, the kingdom was largely inward looking. By contrast Aragon, with a population of little more than one million, was commercially advanced, and traded energetically into the Mediterranean through its great ports of Barcelona and Valencia. The Castilian economy was dominated by the great monopolistic corporation of sheep masters, the *mesta*. The *mesta* was extremely wealthy, and frequently acted as a bank for the Crown. Not surprisingly, about 40% of its trade in raw wool was controlled by the Genoese, who operated one of the most sophisticated commercial systems in Europe. In 1494 a second monopolistic company was founded to operate that part of the trade which ran from Burgos and Bilbao to Antwerp. Before the discovery of the New World, the power of Castile was in the hands of those who produced or traded in wool. After about 1520, however, the Atlantic trade of Seville steadily overtook the wool trade in value, most particularly the import of gold and silver bullion from Mexico and Peru. Both the trade and the government of the colonies was a Castilian monopoly and during the sixteenth century Castile emerged from its relative seclusion to become a world power Meanwhile, Aragon was in decline, Barcelona was severely damaged by a civil war which lasted from 1462 to 1472, and further undermined by the establishment of the Inquisition there in 1487, which drove out the Jewish merchants who had previously played such a large part in its prosperity. Catalan trade with north Africa, Naples, Sicily and Egypt was reduced to a shadow during the sixteenth century, being constantly disrupted by Moorish and Ottoman pirates, and inadequately protected by a government whose priorities were elsewhere. In spite of repeated petitions, the merchants of Aragon were rigorously excluded from the lucrative New World.

When Ferdinand of Aragon and Isabella of Castile married in 1469, each was heir to the throne. Ferdinand was the son of Juan II, and Isabella was the sister and recognised heir of Henry IV. Henry was nicknamed 'the impotent', and his daughter Juana was generally believed to be a bastard, a view which he appeared to accept in recognising Isabella as his heir. The marriage agreement was a purely personal one, and did not envisage any substantial role for Ferdinand in Castile. However, when Henry died in 1474 a party among the Castilian nobility recognised Juana was queen, and they were supported by Alphonso V of Portugal, who regarded the marriage of Ferdinand and Isabella as a threat. Instead of simply supporting his wife, Ferdinand then advanced a claim of his own, based on his descent from John I, who had died in 1388. This claim was resisted, not by the *cortes* of Castile, but by a number of senior ecclesiastics, and never became clearly established. However, when the Portuguese were defeated in 1479 and Juana's party withered away, Ferdinand and Isabella were recognised as joint rulers of Castile, and Ferdinand's authority was not simply exercised in the right of his wife. When Ferdinand became King of Aragon on the death of his father in 1479, Isabella had no comparable position, and the joint monarchy was consequently never an equal partnership. Nor was it anything more than a loose confederation. Constitutional union was not contemplated, and the laws, customs, officers and *cortes* of the two kingdoms all remained separate. It was said later that 'The monarch who keeps these countries together is sovereign of each rather than king of all', a dictum which could be applied with equal truth to the whole Habsburg Empire. There was, therefore, no such thing as the kingdom of Spain. Each monarch was surrounded by personal councils, which travelled with them, and there was no federal structure of government.

The Council of the Indies was an entirely Castilian institution, corresponding to the monopoly of trade and settlement, and the same was true of the government of Granada after its conquest in 1492. This victory was of considerable practical significance, because the former Emirate was a prosperous land, but it was even more important symbolically. It represented the completion of the *reconquista,* and the final triumph of Christianity within the peninsula. It also represented the triumph of Castilian intolerance over the more relaxed traditions of Aragon, where the fourteenth century kings had been known as the 'lords of the three faiths', because Christians, Muslims and Jews had lived peacefully side by side. It was no accident that 1492 was also the year in which Jews throughout Spain were given the stark option of conversion or expulsion. The original terms upon which Granada had surrendered appeared generous. The preservation of Islam was guaranteed, and the preservation of Arabic language, law and custom. Whether Ferdinand and Isabella, who had already unleashed the Inquisition, ever had any intention of keeping their word must be open to question. In 1502 all Muslims who refused conversion were expelled. As with the Jews, there were mass conversions, and the Moriscos (Muslim converts), like the Marranos (Jewish converts) were placed under the supervision of the Inquisition to prevent backsliding. There then followed a century of sporadic persecution. In 1525 Arabic law and custom was prohibited, and in 1556 the Arabic language was banned. A massive Morisco revolt broke out in 1571, as a result of which tens of thousands were uprooted from their homes and resettled in other parts of Spain. As a result many fled to north Africa, where they reverted to their traditional faith and helped to spearhead the devastating attacks of the Barbary corsairs upon the Spanish coast.

In spite of its purpose, the Inquisition was a royal court, not an ecclesiastical tribunal and as such a clear expression of the intention of Ferdinand and Isabella to use catholic orthodoxy as a means of establishing a Spanish identity. The *reconquista* had already pointed in that direction, and a royal court which overrode all liberties and franchises was a means of expressing an ideological unity which had no constitutional equivalent. Apart from the Inquisition, the liberties of the various provinces survived almost intact down to the end of Charles's reign in 1556. Nevertheless, when Isabella died in 1504 there was a crisis, which must cast serious doubt upon the queen's whole attitude to the joint monarchy. In spite of the fact, that Ferdinand shared her rule in Castile, in her will she named her eldest daughter, Juana, as her sole heir and successor. Only if Juana were absent or incapable was Ferdinand to become 'governor and administrator' of the kingdom, and in no circumstances king. Juana's husband was Philip of Burgundy, and a strong aristocratic party immediately accepted a joint claim by Philip and Juana. So strong did their position become that in June 1506 Ferdinand withdrew to Aragon, and it seemed that the personal union was at an end. From Aragon he went on to Naples, where he systematically removed all the Castilians from high office, replacing them with Catalans, a further indication that he saw the two kingdoms going their separate ways. Ferdinand, however, did not give up easily. In March 1506 he had remarried, his bride being Germaine de Foix, the niece of Louis XII of France. Not only did he hope to get a son to replace Juan, who had died in 1499, he also hoped to enlist the support of his father-in-law to keep alive his cause in Castile. Neither of these hopes was to be fulfilled, but in the event it did not matter, because in September 1506 Philip died and Juana became (temporarily at least) deranged. The regency council, led by the great humanist reformer Cardinal Ciserños, then recalled Ferdinand as the only person who could cope with the situation. Having established his indispensability, the king was in no hurry either to return or to establish his exact status. He eventually arrived in Castile in August 1507, but it was 1510 before he finally took an oath as Regent for his daughter, a compromise situation which gave him effective control without alienating those (the majority) who continued to regard Juana as their lawful ruler. Once established, he abandoned his temporary friendship with France. His wife's brother, Gaston de Foix, was killed in battle in 1512, and Germaine inherited his claim to the kingdom of Navarre.

The events which followed show Ferdinand at his most successful and unscrupulous. Henry VIII of England was keen to re-open the ancient war with France, and Ferdinand persuaded him to send an army to Guienne ostensibly for a joint invasion. He then obtained from Pope Julius II a bull of excommunication against the d'Albret family who actually held Navarre. Faced with this threat, John d'Albret appealed to Louis XII. Ferdinand was aware of this, and used it as a pretext to invade Navarre 'in self-defence', using the English presence as a screen to deter French interference. Having successfully annexed the kingdom he promptly made a separate peace with France, leaving Henry VIII to continue the war on his own, and the Duke of Suffolk to get his army back from Guienne as best he could. By the time that Ferdinand died in 1516, Castile was well on the way to becoming a strong and centralised monarchy, and most people had forgotten that he was not actually king. The shadowy figure of Juana remained in seclusion, still ostensibly mad, to become theoretically joint ruler with her son, Charles, but in practice to be ignored by all except her minders until she died at an advanced age in the year of her son's abdication, 1556. There were a number of reasons for Ferdinand's domestic success during the last years of his 'reign'. One was that the opening up of the New World provided gainful employment for many restless *hidalgos;* another was that the lands of the powerful military orders had been annexed to the Crown, on the grounds that the king was *Rex Catholicus* and the true protector of the church. On the same basis he persuaded the pope to allow him to levy a regular tax upon the church, called a *cruzada,* the name of which is self-explanatory. A further reason was his good relations with the *cortes,* which as early as 1480 had addressed the problem of the royal revenues by passing an Act of Revocation, which recovered much of the royal land granted to the high nobility by Ferdinand and Isabella's predecessors. This gave the Crown an adequate income for ordinary purposes although, as in England, extraordinary revenue still had to be obtained by special grant. Charles did not at first make the most of this inheritance. Alienated by his habit of importing Flemish councillors, and irritated by his preoccupation with Germany after 1519, his subjects rose in revolt in 1521. The *communeros* were suppressed but Charles had learned his lesson. Thereafter he governed Spain through Spanish agents, and although there were endless complaints about the demands on Spanish money and manpower made by his Imperial policies, Spain in time became fanatically loyal to its Habsburg rulers. Castile prospered on the wealth of the New World, and both kingdoms gained by the rewards of Imperial service. The main story of his reign is one of the military and Imperial rise of Spain in Europe and America. At home the strength of the Crown was matched and reflected by the increasing omnipotence of the Inquisition, which progressively crushed every form of deviation, from Moriscos and Judaisers to Erasmian humanist intellectuals. By 1556 Spain's emergent sense of identity and special providence was unpleasantly reflected in the policy of *limpieza de sangre* or purity of blood; a policy which reserved all high offices (and many less high ones) to those who could prove unblemished Christian ancestry. It was a quid pro quo which the Castilians demanded in return for their loyalty, and which the king was willing to concede. He, after all, did not have to pay the price, and there was much to be said for a people who had such an exalted opinion of themselves when it came to governing an Empire.

10. Islam and Christendom

During the century from 1450 to 1550 Islam had three points of contact with Christian Europe. The Emirate of Granada was removed in 1492, leaving various residual problems; which left the so-called 'corsair' states of North Africa, such as Tunis and Algiers; and the Ottoman Empire. Both the corsair states and the Ottomans were aggressive, and the latter was a major power.

By 1450 the Turks had already entered Europe and overrun Bulgaria. The once powerful Byzantine Empire was reduced to a small hinterland around the city of Constantinople, already cut off from the rest of Europe, and a fragment of Thessalonika in northern Greece. In 1453 Mehemmed II became Sultan, an office which comprised military, civil and religious leadership, and immediately set out to consolidate the territories which his predecessors had acquired. In the same year he captured Constantinople, and converted it into Istanbul, the capital of his sprawling Empire. It thus became again the great Imperial city which it had been five hundred years earlier, but this was a small consolation to the now subjugated Orthodox Christians as they watched their great cathedral of St. Sophia converted into a mosque. In 1456 Mehemmed suffered a temporary check when the Hungarians defeated his siege of Belgrade, but three years later he overran the remainder of Serbia, leaving the Hungarian position untenable. Bosnia was added to the Empire in 1463-4 and (unlike Serbia) largely converted to Islam. Meanwhile the Turks had also continued to mop up the small independent Christian states of southern Greece, which had been created in the wake of the fourth crusade in the early thirteenth century. Athens and the Morea fell in 1458-60, and most of the Aegean islands, which were Venetian colonies, in a war which lasted from 1455 to 1462. By this time, as the Ottomans began to develop a naval capacity, the Venetians were sharing the frontline with the Hungarians. Another straggling war ensued from 1463 to 1479, which resulted in the loss of Negroponte to the Turks in 1470. Albania was conquered piecemeal between 1468 and 1479, and the last Byzantine fortress at Trebizond on the southern shore of the Black Sea, fell in 1461, giving the Ottomans complete control of that extensive coastline. Genoa lost its last trading post in the Crimea in 1475, and the Khan of the Krim Tartars became a vassal of the Sultan. Throughout the second half of the fifteenth century the feelers which Europe had been putting out towards the East, both by land and sea for the previous two centuries, were being systematically lopped off. At this stage the Ottoman priorities were almost entirely military. They had not yet learned to live alongside their Christian neighbours to the west, and had little interest in trade. This has to be understood when assessing the motives of the Portuguese, and later the Spaniards and Italians, in seeking outlets to the south and west. It is significant that Prester John - a mythic Christian Emperor of the far East - and the need to outflank the Ottomans, featured largely in the rhetoric of the early voyagers. The Sultan Mehemmed died in 1481. His career had been one of almost ceaseless military activity, most of it successful, but he did not leave the boundaries of his Empire stable or secure. Moldavia and Wallachia, to the north of Bulgaria, had been defeated but not conquered, while both the Hungarians and the Venetians remained strong enough to pose a threat to a less effective Sultan. At the same time there was tension with neighbouring states to the south and east. The Mamluks of Egypt and Syria were deeply suspicious of expanding Ottoman power, and a potential threat, while Persia had actually been in alliance with Venice during the long war of 1463-79. The Persians were also Shi'ite Muslims, while the Turks were Sunni, a difference analogous to that between catholic and protestant which later afflicted Christendom. The situation in 1481 was complicated by the fact that there was no law of succession to the Sultanate. Mehemmed had secured his own power by the traditional method of killing all the other male members of his family, but by some curious oversight he left two adult sons, Bayazid and Djem. Bayazid was supported by the elite troops of the army, the corps of Janissaries, and this enabled him to secure control. However, he failed to catch his defeated brother, and Djem escaped to the west, first to Rhodes and then, in 1482, to France. Complex negotiations then followed, in which the Sultan was compelled for the first time to do business with his infidel enemies on equal terms. Djem was placed in the custody of the Pope, and Bayazid paid a substantial pension to have him kept out of harms way. However, following his successful invasion of Italy in 1494, Charles VIII of France was strong enough to force Alexander VI to surrender the hostage. Charles probably intended to use Djem to confuse Ottoman resistance to his projected crusade, but his priorities remained elsewhere, and Djem died in 1495, before any serious action could ensue.

Djem's presence in the west had virtually paralysed Ottoman military activity for thirteen years, because the Sultan was unable to commit his armies in any direction as long as there was the possibility of a Christian coalition using his brother as a weapon. Skirmishing had continued along the Hungarian frontier, but the powerful kingdom of Mathias Corvinus (1458-1490) showed no vulnerability in these exchanges, and Bayazid could not risk a serious assault. After Mathias's death further probing forays were made, not only into Hungary, but also into the Habsburg lands of Styria, Carinthia and Camiola. Such attacks served to demonstrate the need for constant defensive vigilance on the Christian side, but made no substantive gains and peace was negotiated in 1495. A similar situation appertained in Moldavia, which might have encouraged further adventures if it had not been supported by Poland. No conquests were made, and a truce was patched up in 1494. Bayazid also fought a restrained and inconclusive war against Mamluk Egypt, during which both sides scored victories in battle, -but no major conquest or political advantage. Peace was agreed on that front in 1491. There was no immediate or dramatic change after Djem's death, and indeed the next initiative came from the Christian side when the Poles, possibly misunderstanding the relative Ottoman quiescence of recent years, endeavoured to break through to the Black Sea. This attack was beaten off, and Bayazid was content to make peace in 1499 rather than counter attack, because he had by that time decided that Venice was the weak link in the Christian chain confronting him. The Venetians had been at peace since 1482, but Bayazid had begun to build a Mediterranean fleet in 1496, and his plans had been given ample time to mature. Realising that the Christians had much greater experience in galley fighting than his own commanders, he began to look for reinforcements, and found natural allies among the corsair states of North Africa. In spite of Djem's death the Sultan seems to have feared a Christian crusade, and by 1498 he had decided to strike first, while the Venetians were preoccupied with the wars in northern Italy. As soon as he had settled with the Poles, Bayazid began to attack Venetian outposts. Lepanto and Modon fell in 1500, and in spite of help from both France and Hungary, the republic was forced into an unfavourable peace in 1503. This fairly low-key war served to consolidate Ottoman power on the Adriatic coast and among the islands. However the Sultan was unable to follow up this modest success because the Persians were again threatening. In the event that threat did not materialise because the Persians had problems of their own, which turned their armies eastwards rather than westwards in 1510; but a number of Shi'ite revolts broke out within the Ottoman Empire, and Bayazid also faced trouble from his own younger son, Selim. As the Sultan became older, and his health more suspect, it became a matter of life and death for his sons to secure their own interests. Selim went rather too far, and his quasi-revolt had to be suppressed, but he survived, thanks largely to the crucial support of the Janissaries. When Bayazid died in 1512 that same support enabled Selim to defeat his elder brother, Ahmed, and to execute his entire family. This led to a renewed confrontation with Persia, which had supported Ahmed, and in 1514 Selim attacked. The Shah was defeated and Tabriz taken in September 1514. Uninhibited by the kind of fears which had restrained his father, the Sultan committed all his resources to this war, and emerged with substantial territorial gains. This in turn altered the balance of power in the Muslim world, and freed Selim's eastern frontier from any threat for a number of years. As a result the Mamluks of Egypt and Syria were now no match for the Ottomans, and when the Syrians were unwise enough to offer some rather ineffectual support to Persia in 1516, Selim turned his attention to them. The Syrians were defeated outside Aleppo in August 1516; the city surrendered, and in a matter of weeks the whole country had been overrun. Seizing his opportunity, the Sultan then turned his attention to Egypt. A second Mamluk army was defeated in April 1517; Cairo was captured and the whole of Egypt added to the Ottoman Empire. There were several reasons, for these dramatic successes. Selim's resources were steadily increasing, and he could command more traditional fighting men than any of his rivals, but at the same time he was more willing than most Muslim commanders to learn from the technological developments taking place in Europe, particularly the use of firearms. By 1518 Selim was far stronger than any previous Sultan, although he till had to face rebellions, and a Persia which, although defeated could never be completely subdued. With the Christians there had been peace since 1503, but this was the result of accident rather than design. Selim was not at all reluctant to wage war in the north or the west, it was just that he had not had the opportunity. In fact he was building a massive fleet to launch into the Mediterranean when death unexpectedly overtook him in September 1520. He left only one son, Sulieman, so on this occasion the Empire was not disrupted by internecine strife, and the new Sultan picked up the threads of government and war exactly where his predecessor had laid them down. In 1521 he took the city of Belgrade from the Hungarians, and in 1522 the island of Rhodes from the knights of St. John. There is no doubt that Sulieman, who reigned from 1520 to 1566, aimed to do to the Christians what his father had done to the Mamluks and the Persians, and at first it seemed as though he might succeed. After a short delay, caused by Mamluk revolts in Syria and Egypt in 1523-5, he again launched his main army north west in 1526. The Hungarian host was destroyed at the battle of Mohacs, King Lewis was killed, and about two thirds of the kingdom conquered, including Budapest, which fell in September. In 1529 the Ottoman army briefly besieged Vienna, and prophets of doom saw its unimpeded advance into a Germany preoccupied with internal religious strife. The infidel at the gate was a very compelling image in the Christian rhetoric of the period, and was used as the symbol of Divine punishment, but in fact the Ottoman military machine had already reached the limit of its capabilities. Although it had a hard professional core, the main army consisted of a feudal array, which had to be summoned afresh for each campaigning season, and brought all the way from its rendezvous near Istanbul to the theatre of operations. Vienna was the limit of its lines of communication, and without a social and military revolution, further significant advance was impossible. So the Balkan front settled down to a long struggle of raids and sieges, in which neither side could secure a decisive advantage. In 1534 Sulieman's attention was again distracted to the east, where the Persian frontier had become unstable, and in 1536 Iraq was brought under Ottoman rule. Meanwhile a new pattern was beginning to emerge in the west. By entering into an alliance with the king of France in the same year, Sulieman became a part of the European political system, rather than outside force impinging upon it. This did not make him significantly less aggressive, but it did mean that the Ottoman Empire became an important element in the European balance of power.

11. The Pre-Reformation Church

The great schism of the western church had been brought to an end by the Council of Constance in 1417. That schism had originated in the withdrawal of the papacy from Rome to Avignon, a small independent enclave in the south of France, in 1309. However, Avignon was felt to be provincial, and too much under the influence of France, so that pressure steadily mounted for a return to Italy, and eventually, in 1378 Pope Gregory XI went back to Rome, where he immediately died. The election which followed confirmed the wisdom of the original move. The Roman mob intimidated the Cardinals into electing an extremely unsatisfactory Italian as Urban VI. Urban proved to be so insufferable that within a matter of months a group of French cardinals went back to Avignon, denounced Urban's election as invalid, and chose a rival Pope, who took the name of Clement VII. Clement also attracted a lot of Italian support, so much so that Urban was constrained to appoint what was virtually a new college of Cardinals from among his own supporters. The schism had quickly become political in the most obvious sense; France, Scotland, Castile and Aragon recognised Clement, while the Emperor, England, Hungary Scandinavia and most of Italy continued to accept Urban. Urban died in 1389, and the Roman cardinals elected another Italian as Boniface IX (1389-1404); Clement died in 1394 and was succeeded by the Aragonese Peter of Luna, who became Benedict XIII (1394-1423). The scandal was immense as the rival curias hurled anathemas at each other and competed fiercely for the taxation of their supporting churches. By 1395 political pressure was growing from the secular princes to force the resignation of both incumbents, but it was unsuccessful for many years. Eventually, in 1409 a General Council was summoned to Pisa with majority political support, but neither of the Popes would recognise it, and each summoned a council of his own, with enough support to make his assembly credible. The council at Pisa declared both the rivals deposed, and elected a new Pope, Alexander V. Neither Benedict nor Gregory XII, who by this time held the Roman position, would give way, and for about six years there were three popes. Alexander died in the following year, and was maladroitly replaced with a *condottiere* captain called Baldessare Cossa, who took the title of John XXIII. The last position was thus worse than the first, but the situation by this time was so close to farce that no one could seriously defend it, and for the first time a consensus of lay and ecclesiastical reformers was able to emerge. The Emperor Sigismund was able to use the political situation in Italy to manoeuvre John into calling a new Council at Constance in November 1414. There were other matters to attend to, not least the appearance of organised heresy in Bohemia, but the resolution of the schism was uppermost in everyone's mind. The papal office had been heavily undermined by the events of the previous twenty years, and a powerful school of thought developed at Constance in support of the idea that true authority in the church rested with the collectivity of its bishops, and not with any individual head. For the time being this was an unreal conflict, because power was in the hands of the secular princes, and particularly of Sigismund. It was he who ordered the execution of the Bohemian heretic John Hus, who had been given a safe conduct to attend the council, in July 1415. It was also he who captured and imprisoned John XXIII in the same year, and persuaded Benedict XIII's supporters to desert him. The respectable Gregory XII abdicated with dignity, and Henry V of England gave a lead to the other rulers in suspending his political partizanship. By 1417 the way was finally clear, and in November the council proceeded to make a new election, choosing an apparently safe and colourless Italian who took the name of Martin V Benedict XIII remained unreconciled but had virtually no support and was effectively ignored. The greatest problem was thus solved, but the issue of reform, which everyone agreed to be urgent, was hardly approached. A month before the election of Martin the council had passed a degree *(Frequens)* which laid down that General Councils should convene automatically at fixed intervals, irrespective of papal wishes. Since the new Pope was very much the creation of the council, it looked as though a new constitutional method of governing the church was being created, and that future Popes would be little more than Secretaries General. This did not happen because Martin showed unexpected skill and tenacity in defending the traditional prerogatives of his office. A council duly convened, in accordance with the terms of *Frequens* at Pavia in 1423-4, but circumstances had already changed. The Pope had been a consistent presence since 1417 and the council had not. Moreover the political will to co-operate did not survive the ending of the schism. In spite of an urgent agenda, therefore, the council of Pavia achieved nothing. Martin died in 1431, and in the same year another council convened at Basle. The new Pope, Eugenius IV, attempted to dissolve it, but the bishops insisted upon their right by the terms of *Frequens,* and refused to obey. Even if there had been no other urgent business, the continuing and dangerous Hussite revolt in Bohemia would have been sufficient to keep it in session. Eugenius backed down, and recognised the council in 1433. He did not, however, accept its pretensions, and was presented with an excellent opportunity to manipulate the situation when the Greek church of the expiring Byzantine Empire petitioned for re-union. The Greeks were not (of course) unanimous in seeking this solution to their problems, and the Latins were not unanimous in welcoming it. The council of Basle split, and the Greeks, not understanding the complexities of conciliar politics, opted to deal with the Pope rather than with the council. A minority of the bishops therefore left Basle for Ferrara, and joined the pope in negotiating what was ostensibly the end of the, Greek schism (1438-9). In spite of the unreality of this achievement, it swung the balance of power decisively in Eugenius's favour. The Council of Basle clung tenaciously to its life for another ten years, finally dissolving in 1448, but it had little political backing except as a means of putting pressure on the Pope, and became little more than a forum for debate. Although conciliar theory remained vigorous in some quarters, by 1450 the movement was dead as a practical method of resolving the church's problems.

The papacy was, however, unable or unwilling to take full advantage of its victory. Reform was desperately needed to redeem the credit of the church as an institution, but after the chequered history of the previous half century, the popes from Nicholas V (1447-1455) to Alexander VI (1492-1503) were in no position to seize a spiritual initiative. In addition to being the leader of the western church, the pope was also the ruler of a substantial central Italian state, the *Patrimonium Petri.* This had originally been created to protect the pontiff from too obvious a dependence upon secular princes - to give him a measure of political independence. However, it also had the effect of entangling him irredeemably in the relationships of the other Italian states. The *Patrimonium* not only had to be governed, it had to be defended. So successive popes became Italian politicians, and even military commanders, and their lifestyles approximated more and more closely to those of neighbouring princes. They became dilettantes, patrons of scholarship, the arts and architecture, and the monastic austerities occasionally practised by their predecessors disappeared. The Bohemian revolt was defeated, but small thanks to the papacy. The threat of a fresh council kept them amenable to political pressure, but the failure to tackle spiritual and theological problems also built up pressure for reform within the clerical establishment. It was not only the Hussites who believed that the church was failing to discharge its primary responsibility through a lack of leadership. In the north a movement called the Modem Devotion *(devotio moderna)* influenced both laymen and clerics with its semi-mysticial insistence upon personal piety and relative indifference to the formal offices of the church. The influence of a few genuine mystics, such as Tauler and Eckhardt, who pointed the way to a further interioration of the religious life, also served to undermine the power of ecclesiastical institutions. In Italy the campaign of the puritanical Florentine friar Savonarola, also indicated an attack from a different direction. There had always been criticism about the wealth and materialism of the church, and Christian history was littered with movements of protest, from the

Waldensians, who became heretics, to the Franciscans, who became a respected religious order. However, this reached new heights during the renaissance, and can be illustrated by the 'sacramental calculus'. Roughly speaking this meant a quantitative approach to salvation, based upon a flexible concept of good works. Every 'good work', from genuine acts of charity or compassion to going on pilgrimage, attending mass, or lighting a candle to a local saint, scored so much on the credit side of the believer's ledger, to set against the sins which constituted the debit side. Participation in the sacraments scored heavily in this calculation, as did gifts of money to the church, and the two could be connected. Consequently the impression arose that salvation was for sale. Indulgences, whereby remission of sins could be purchased, not only for the living but also on behalf of the dead, provided a classic example of the logical outcome of this mode of thinking. Nor was it lost upon critics of the church that the quasi-magical power of the sacraments gave the clergy the same kind of power as wise men or wizards. The age was much obsessed with magic, and the church chose to take witchcraft seriously because it realised the opportunity to provide the antidote - white magic needs black magic to combat. Humanist reformers, many of them clergy themselves, were deeply offended by this method of maintaining control over popular religion. In the north the Brethren of the Common Life, a fellowship of clergy and laity dedicated to practical piety and education, and in Italy the Oratory of Divine Love, a clerical and intellectual fraternity, were both set up to combat this type of corruption. The late medieval clergy were no worse than their predecessors, and abuses in the ordinary everyday sense were greatly exaggerated, but there was a deep seated malaise, caused by the fact that too many ecclesiastical leaders had been appointed for the wrong reasons, and were preoccupied with wealth and power rather than with the issues of their pastoral and teaching ministry. Only a few rigorous religious orders, such as the Carthusians and the Observant Franciscans, preserved their prestige. The main signs of hope were in Spain, where the zeal of the *reconquista* kept a higher standard of observance alive. In Spain, and particularly in Castile, the reforms of Cardinal Ciserños resulted in a purge of the religious orders, and the foundation of new educational institutions, such as the University of Alcala. Broadly speaking the more independent a church was from the papacy, the better chance it stood of being able to reform itself. It was partly because the German church was so poorly protected form papal priorities that the much more radical protestant reformation first began there.

12. Martin Luther and his Protest

Martin Luther was born at Eisleben in Saxony in 1483, the son of Hans Luther, a prosperous peasant turned mine manager. His relationship with his parents was good, and his local elementary schooling was effective. He soon developed bookish skills, and his father, who was very much a self-made man, was proud of him. To a man of Hans Luther's background the way to make a good living out of literacy was through the law, and Martin was originally destined to be a notary, not a cleric. He obtained his secondary schooling at Mansfeld, Magdeburg and Eisenach before enrolling at the university of Erfurt in 1501, at the relatively advanced age of eighteen. At Erfurt he absorbed the nominalist philosophy of William of Occam, which laid great stress upon the gulf which divided man from God, but nevertheless made man ultimately responsible for his own destiny. In 1505 Luther graduated with some distinction, being placed second out of the seventeen candidates for the degree of Master of Arts. However, instead of proceeding to the study of law as intended, he then outraged his father by withdrawing into the Augustinian friary at Erfurt. This cannot have been the sudden decision which he later represented when he was trying to mollify his parent, but little is known of the actual circumstances. He himself ascribed it to the fear of sudden death, and it may well be that, in spite of his formal education, Luther retained much of the peasant's proneness to supernatural terrors.

The Augustinian Eremites were a strictly reformed order, which constituted their attractiveness to such an earnest recruit, and provided him with the regular life for which he obviously yearned. Over the next few years, Luther developed significantly along two lines, professional and spiritual. His professional development took him back to the university, because the order was quick to recognise his ability, and in 1508 he was sent to the new university of Wittenburg recently founded by the Elector Frederick the Wise, to lecture in the Arts Faculty. This involved much exposition of the traditionally familiar texts of Aristotle, a classical Greek philosopher for whom he began to develop the liveliest distaste. He also commenced advanced study in theology, obtaining the degree of Bachelor of Divinity in 1510. He then returned to Erfurt to lecture in a very traditional vein upon the *Sentences* of the twelfth century biblical commentator Peter Lombard. While at Erfurt he was sent to Rome on the business of his order, and although he was probably not as scandalised as he later claimed by what he saw, nevertheless the visit left him with a lasting aversion to the papal curia. In October 1512 he proceeded Doctor of Divinity, and almost immediately went back to Wittenburg, to the chair of Biblical theology. Meanwhile, his spiritual life had been proceeding much less smoothly. He had taken his vows in September 1506, and been ordained priest in the following April. Both these steps were taken more in a desperate search for spiritual security than out of any positive sense of vocation. He continued to torment his confessor with endless recitations of sins which were mostly trivial or imaginary, and his first mass was a terrifying ordeal because he could not believe that such an unworthy sinner as he was could possibly perform the miracle of transforming the elements into the body and blood of Christ. Nor were his fears resolved by the experience, as they should have been according to his perception. God had not yet spoken to him. His revelation, when it came, was not sudden whatever he may afterwards have claimed. It came about through the convergence of his spiritual problems with his professional duties.

Between 1513 and 1518 he lectured on the psalms, and on the epistles of St Paul to the Romans, Galatians and Hebrews. As he did so he adopted the new humanist technique of direct literal exposition, as distinct from the older style of elaborate allegorical reconstruction. He also began to develop his own distinctive theology. His outburst in 1517 was consequently a result, not a cause of his changing doctrinal views. His great problem had been a sense of guilt and unworthiness, induced very largely by his training in nominalist philosophy, which posed enormous problems in the quest for salvation, and provided very few answers. All the conventional remedies suggested by the church had failed to provide Luther with the reassurance he needed. It was as though God had created man to be a sinner and then condemned him to hell for being one. It was this impossible dilemma which caused Luther to say later that he had come to hate the so-called justice of God as an arbitrary tyranny. Relief came through his biblical studies. In St Paul's first epistle to the Romans (a text upon which he was lecturing) he found the phrase 'the just shall live by faith'. in other words that man needed only faith to be redeemed by God.

In no sense therefore was he expected to 'learn' his salvation as Luther had hitherto understood, since only God himself could confer the gift of faith. Of course this insight was not original. As Luther himself soon came to realise, it had been propounded in the fifth century by St. Augustine of Hippo. However, it struck him with the force of revelation, and he developed his thought progressively through his lectures with a mounting and triumphant sense of relief. This revolution in his thinking had two important consequences. On the other hand it led him into a quasi-mystical contemplation of the sufferings of Christ, a course which brought him into contact with earlier German mystics such as Johan Tauler and Thomas à Kempis. Only by such contemplation could man fully appreciate the immensity of the gifts which God had bestowed upon him, and the love which had prompted the voluntary offering of such suffering. This was known as the theology of the Cross. And on the other hand it led to a diminution of every aspect of works theology - the traditional means of acquiring spiritual merit - including the sacraments of the church, and thus by extension the priestly office itself. Luther never pursued this train of thought to its logical conclusion and made the church redundant. He continued to believe in a visible church, and indeed in an ordained ministry, as giving faith and substance to the community of the faithful, and a means whereby they could testify to the faith which God had bestowed upon them. But it did mean that traditional forms of worship became at best an adjunct to the true appreciation of faith, more normally a distraction, and at worst a hideous distortion of the true message of the gospel. To treat salvation as a kind of commodity, to be purchased in the market place in return for a coinage of 'merit' was to blaspheme the purposes of God. The sacrament of penance expressed the heart of this contrast. It had originally been intended as a symbolic acceptance by the church of the contrition of the penitent sinner. The contribution was represented by an act of ritual self-debasement, and the acceptance by the form of absolution. However the form had largely replaced the substance. Confession, penance and absolution had become another method of acquiring 'merit', and the priority of contrition (which was so hard to assess) was commonly overlooked.

Into this developing theological consciousness in the Wittenburg of 1517 intruded the Dominican friar, Johan Tetzel, selling indulgences. The reason for this was that Albrecht of Mainz had purchased his archbishopric, and the Pope had granted him the right to sell indulgences in order to pay off his debt to the bankers. An indulgence had originally been obtained by going on crusade, and had waived the ecclesiastical penalties for which the warrior's sins would otherwise have made him liable, in acknowledgement of his zeal for the faith. Theologically this was entirely respectable. However, it soon became available to those who paid someone else to go on crusade on their behalf, presumably on the grounds that the benefit to the faith was no less. Thereafter it was available to anyone who contributed money to a suitably holy cause, and thus was perceived as being purchased. So far, however, the indulgence had not pretended to touch the guilt of sin itself, it remained a purely ecclesiastical device. However, in the early fourteenth century that limitation had been transcended. In 1343 the Bull *Unigenitus* had represented the indulgence as what can only be described as a form of bank draft. The saints, it was supposed, had acquired far more merit than was necessary to secure their own admission into paradise. The residue was deemed to have been deposited in what was explicitly called 'The treasury of merit', under the control of the Pope. The Pope could therefore allocate from that treasury for whatever reason seemed good to him, and the indulgence became a certificate entitling its holder to receive a benefit. The principle effect of this somewhat simplistic concept was to shift the emphasis of forgiveness from the penance due to the sin itself, thus transgressing the limits of theological propriety for the first time. Worse was to come, because so far the forgiveness had been theoretically dependent, not upon the payment but upon the penitence of the recipient. However, by the Bull *Salvator Noster* of 1476 Pope Sixtus IV shed all restraint and made the benefit of indulgences available to those already dead. The reason for this was that the souls of the deceased were deemed, reasonably enough, and with a few exceptions, to be neither good enough for heaven nor bad enough for hell. The vast majority of humankind were consigned to Purgatory where they spent a greater or lesser period expiating their sins in preparation for the kingdom of God. In that situation their souls were accessible to the solicitude of their living friends and kindred, who could by their prayers and other intercessions speed and ease their passage in various ways. One of these ways was by the purchase of an indulgence, which thus became a kind of gift voucher redeemable in purgatory. Not only did the indulgence so conceived remit sins, it was no longer conditional upon contrition, since there was no way in which the penitence of the dead could be assessed.

The indulgences which Tetzel was selling were thus the *reductio ad absurdum* of works theology, and a mere caricature of the sacrament of penance. They were, however, fully authorised by the highest ecclesiastical authority. Luther was not the only person to be outraged. The Elector Frederick banned Tetzel from his territories, but Wittenburg was close enough to the border for many citizens to travel to the market and take advantage of the friar's persuasive offer. Luther was not yet a popular evangelist; nor did he have any intention of challenging the authority of the church. Instead he couched his protest in proper academic form, drawing up ninety-five theses, or propositions, attacking the practice and theory of indulgence selling. These he then posted on the university notice board as a challenge to disputation. The response was to transform not only his position but the subsequent history of the church.

13. The Spread of Lutheranism within the Empire

As soon as Luther's theses were made public, the ecclesiastical authorities moved against him. This was not only because of the teaching which they contained, but also because of the manner of their dissemination. Luther had written them in Latin, as was appropriate for an academic debate, and the church had traditionally allowed a good deal of latitude to such discussions. However in this case, without Luther's consent, and probably without his knowledge, they were translated into German and anonymously published. From the point of view of the church, Luther had broken the rules which might otherwise have protected him by publishing suspect doctrine in the vernacular. Albrecht of Mainz also forwarded a copy of the Latin original to Rome, where it would have been easier to understand than the German. At this stage it seems clear that Luther had no intention of defying the church, let alone of causing a schism. His intention was to convince anyone who would listen of the necessity for reform, using this particular indulgence as a classic example of what was wrong. At first the assault upon him was led by Tetzel's order, the Dominicans, so that the chapter of his own order (their long-standing rivals) moved to support him. This caused Pope Leo X, when the matter was first brought to his attention to make the mistake of dismissing it as a 'monkish squabble'. In 1518 two important developments took place. Frederick the Wise, under the influence of his liberal Chancellor George Spalatin, showed himself to be sympathetic, although not yet openly supportive. This was partly because of his own dislike of Tetzel's mission, and partly because he tended to be possessive about the reputation of the university of Wittenburg. Secondly, in October, Luther was summoned to Augsburg to meet Cardinal Cajetan, who was both papal legate and General of the Dominicans. Cajetan was hardly an objective investigator, and he had no intention of conducting a debate. He simply demanded Luther's retraction and silence, having no opinion of so obscure an academic, and seeing no reason to take him seriously. When he found the German not only tenacious, but also quite able to get through his defences on the question of indulgences, he simply became angry, and Luther had made his first powerful enemy. By this time he was being driven reluctantly into open dissent, and before the end of the year had drawn up an appeal to a general council against the papal condemnation which he could foresee.

In December 1518, however, a fresh and decisive twist was given to the drama, when Frederick moved to Luther's defence, and refused to surrender him for trial in Rome. By an extraordinary coincidence of timing, in January 1519 the Emperor Maximilian died, and Frederick was the senior Elector. Until the election of a new Emperor had been completed, the pope urgently needed his co-operation and goodwill, so nothing could be done for at least six months; six months during which Luther's ideas were circulating freely all over Germany, and winning many supporters. Having no longer any reason to be reticent, Luther began to write other polemical works, and by the end of 1519 had several in print, in both Latin and German. As he became more explicitly unorthodox, the Augustinian order began to distance itself from him, but his colleagues in Wittenburg became increasingly enthusiastic. This was sometimes an embarrassment. As early as July 1519 one of his friends, Andreas Carlstadt, the professor of Hebrew, entered into a public disputation with the orthodox theologian John Eck. Eck successfully manoeuvred his opponent, and by implication, Luther, into agreeing that in some respects his opinions resembled those of the Bohemian reformer, John Hus, who had been condemned by the Council of Constance. Therefore, either Carlstadt was wrong or the Council of Constance had been wrong, and he found himself forced to argue that a general council of the church could err, which was heresy in itself. The issues had now broadened out far beyond the question of indulgences. Justification and freewill were in the front line, and Luther had been made to appear an open heretic. By the summer of 1520 his position had been transformed. Protected by Frederick, and supported by his colleagues, he wrote furiously, and his punchy direct German style in particular had a great appeal, even outside the circle of the literate, as his works were read aloud in market places and inns. He began to appear as a German messiah, a national hero who focussed all the powerful emotions of anti-clericalism and anti-papalism which had been building up for half a century. His *Appeal to the Christian Nobility of the German Nation* denounced both papal tyranny and clerical pretensions, teaching that all true Christians were priests in the sense that they enjoyed direct access to God in prayer. This was a natural conclusion from the premise that faith alone justified, and that the sacraments were not essential to salvation, but in making the threat to the priestly order explicit, it deliberately stoked the fires of controversy.

On the Babylonish Captivity of the Church, by contrast, was written in Latin for a clerical readership. This attacked, not the sacraments as such, but their effectiveness *ex opera operato,* that is to say that a sacrament was valid if it was properly executed by a validly ordained priest, irrespective of his intention, the intention of the recipient, or the state of grace of either. Again it was the authority of the priestly order and its unique intercessory position which was under attack. Luther also argued for a reduction in the number of the sacraments from the traditional seven to three, baptism, the Eucharist and penance. Later he also abandoned penance, and all the subsequent reformers followed him in accepting just two sacraments. A second German work, *On the Liberty of a Christian Man.* explicitly taught the liberating effects of the doctrine of justification by faith alone. This awakened a further powerful response, because Luther was by no means alone in finding the burden of having to earn salvation through good works impossible to sustain. There were many who felt that the confessional had become a tyranny, and that the church provided only mechanical remedies for spiritual anxieties. In July 1520 Luther was condemned by the papal Bull *Exurge Domine.* In December he burned a copy of the Bull and several works of canon law at Wittenburg, in a calculated act of defiance, which was also a declaration of ideological war. The new Emperor was therefore faced with an immediate problem, which showed every sign of turning into a political conflict. In spite of the papal condemnation, and much to the pope's annoyance, he decided to invite Luther to present his case to the Imperial Diet, under safe conduct. Ignoring the fate of John Hus at Constance, Luther came. Not surprisingly, his friends at the Diet were defeated and he was condemned, but the fact that he had friends at that level, and the nature of his popular reception on the way to and from Worms, spelled out a clear warning to the Emperor and his allies. On his way home, Luther was abducted by his chief protector, Frederick, who did not trust the Emperor's good faith, and he spent several months in the secure retreat of the Wartburg, where he devoted his energies to the vital task of translating the bible into German.

During his absence the reform movement in Wittenburg lurched towards radicalism under the impact of a group of preachers known as the Zwickau prophets. These men were not followers of Luther, but members of the extreme wing of the Hussite movement, the Bohemian Brethren. They desired to abolish the visible church entirely, as something hopelessly corrupted by the world. Hearing of their success, Luther abandoned his retreat. In March 1522 he returned to Wittenburg, and reasserted his control with a masterful series of sermons. His moderate and somewhat conservative programme of reform was then resumed, but some of his former followers did not return to the fold. Andreas Carlstadt in particular, remained wholly committed to a radical programme, and Luther broke with him decisively. However, it was not only in Wittenburg that events were developing a momentum of their own. All over Germany Luther's followers were looking, not just for a lead, but for a programme. What should a reformed church order consist of? What should be retained and what rejected? So far the 'movement' had been largely negative, directed against abuses and false teaching. Now it started to be positive and constructive. Luther and his chief ally, Philip Melanchthon, wrote a church order for Wittenburg, and other towns and parishes began either to adopt or to modify it to suit their own needs. It was a very confused period and the outcome in any particular place was usually decided by the attitude of the local magistrates. In 1523 the humanist scholar Franz von Sickengen and his allies tried to use Luther's teachings as a pretext for an anticlerical war, which was also aimed to plunder the ecclesiastical states in the interests of the Imperial knights, who were a much decayed and impoverished group. Luther repudiated the knights and they were defeated but his cause was seriously compromised in the eyes of some who had earlier been sympathetic. Nevertheless by 1524 a number of imperial cities (who were markedly more responsive to his teachings than the territorial principalities) had adopted an Evangelical church order, usually under the influence of a small number of reformed preachers; Erfurt, Magdeburg, Nuremburg, Strassburg, Constance, Basle, Danzig and Jena.   Meanwhile Luther's writings continued to pour off the presses, addressing themselves to every possible issue of theology, canon law or ecclesiastical order. Two dramatic developments in 1525 then helped to set bounds to what was still a rather formless movement. Luther quarrelled publicly and in print with the great humanist reformer Erasmus over the freedom of the human will. This quarrel exposed a fundamental difference between two men who had hitherto been thought of as allies, because Erasmus's grievance was with the practice of the church, while Luther's was with its doctrine. When this became clear, a significant part of Luther's humanist and intellectual support deserted him. Then came the traumatic events of the Peasant's war. The network of popular rebellions known by that title sprang from legal and social grievances going well back into the last century, when it had been known as the *bundschuh* (or peasant clog) movement. However, Luther's teaching also made its input, particularly the 'priesthood of all believers', which was interpreted in a radical and egalitarian manner never intended by Luther himself. Moreover some extreme radicals who had earlier been followers of Luther, such as Carlstadt and Thomas Muntzer, became deeply involved. Muntzer in particular urged an apocalyptic vision upon the peasants which appeared to threaten the whole established order in both church and state. Luther was alarmed and disgusted. However critical he might have been of the ecclesiastical establishment, he had no intention of undermining secular authority, which he regarded as Divinely ordained. He denounced the rebellious peasants in unmeasured terms. Unfortunately his tract, written when the rebellion was at its height and the danger appeared real, was not published until after its defeat, when it read like an exhortation to vindictive revenge. As a result Luther re-established his credentials with the princes, but cut himself off from much of his grass-roots support in the countryside, reinforcing the political and urban drift which was already noticeable. At the same time he broke decisively with the radicals, whom he had already denounced in his Wittenburg sermons. In his tract *Against the Heavenly Prophets* he stressed very powerfully the need to test the promptings of the spirit by the better or scripture, and made clear his extreme distrust of those who claimed a unique revelation.

By these actions he set the scene for the future. Evangelicalism was going to be magisterial in form, with a full commitment to the visible church, and a willingness to let the secular magistrates run the church's temporal affairs. It was to be predominantly a movement for the literate, with heavy emphasis upon the bible, and it was going to progress by political and territorial means, rather than by the spontaneous establishment of popular congregations. By 1529 several princes, including John George of Saxony (Frederick's successor) and Philip of Hesse had taken their states into the evangelical camp, and Lutheranism had become a part of the politics of the Empire. In 1530 the faith was defined by the confession of Augsburg, presented to the Imperial Diet, and in the following year a group of Evangelical princes and cities formed the Schmalkaldic League.

14.The Swiss and South German Reformers

The cities of Switzerland and South Germany provided a different context for the reformation from principalities such as Saxony or Hesse. Some were virtually independent city states, others controlled considerable hinterlands. In Switzerland the diocesan structure bore no relation to the political cantons. Basle had a resident bishop, and a university, and was a wealthy city. Strassburg was also wealthy, and had a cathedral chapter, but no resident bishop. Zurich had neither bishop, nor chapter, nor university, and was less wealthy but more independent. Ulrich Zwingli was the reformer of Zurich, and he was in many ways typical of the preachers who chose their own paths to reform. Born in 1484, he was a year younger than Luther, and his education was very different. From local schools in the vicinity of Zurich, he went to Basle and to Berne, and then to the university of Vienna. There he received a predominantly humanist training, including such modern subjects as mathematics and geography. From Vienna he returned to Basle, his studies probably having been terminated by some indiscretion, and completed his M.A. at the latter university in 1506. In the same year he became parish priest of Glarus, and combined further study with his pastoral duties. His humanist enthusiasm continued to grow, and he became a great admirer of Erasmus. He also made two trips to Italy as chaplain to mercenary contingents from the Canton, and what he experienced there turned him against the trade, which was one of the principle sources of wealth for a poor and numerous population. In 1516 he moved to the richer benefice of Eisiedeln where he (like Luther) had a brush with an itinerant indulgence seller. Unlike Luther, however, he did not fall foul of ecclesiastical authority in consequence. Indeed he received a papal pension for his service with the mercenaries, which he held for about four years. In 1518, in spite of an affair with the daughter of a local baker, he was appointed People's Priest in the great minster at Zurich, which gave him control of the most influential pulpit in the city.

Zwingli's intellectual progress towards evangelical conversion is much more obscure than that of Luther, and was probably more complex, but his spiritual crises were no less profound. Although not an academic he was well read in the scholastic theologians and commentators, and he took the Old Testament very seriously, in which he differed from Erasmus. Nevertheless he was deeply influenced by the Greek New Testament of 1516, and by two other events of that year, one public, one very private. The public event was the Concordat of Bologna between the Pope and the King of France, which resulted in the surrender of most of the papal power in France to the king, an abdication of responsibility which greatly shocked Zwingli. The private event was his illicit sexual relationship with the baker's daughter, which brought on a moral crisis similar to that which drove Luther into the cloister. The combination of these experiences seems to have driven him into an intense study of the scripture in an attempt to assuage his sense of guilt. In 1519 he nearly died of plague, and these mounting pressures finally drove him to the conclusion that 'You must leave all the rest, and learn God's meaning out of his simple word. Then I asked God for light, and light came'. The conversion experience was in many ways similar to Luther's, and the conclusion reached was the same, but Zwingli always denied that he reached it under Luther's influence, and the timing makes that plausible. The impact of this conversion upon his ministry was immediate. As soon as he had taken up his duties in the minster, Zwingli began to preach a systematic course of sermons on St. Matthew's gospel. He lacked Luther's oratorical force, but he had an appealing message, not only on personal salvation, but also on the nature of a Christian commonwealth - a theme which the German had largely neglected. His message appealed strongly to a city council struggling for greater autonomy, and in 1520, in the face of mounting conservative criticism, it specifically authorised him to continue with his scriptural mission.

One of the first consequences of this was a revulsion, against mercenary war. Zwingli was not a pacifist, and was to die in battle, but he regarded mercenary war as an affront to God. In 1522 the Canton refused to allow its men to take any further part, pioneering a new attitude, and sacrificing a lot of money. Zwingli was not a rebel by temperament, but his scripture based programme was much more radical than that of Luther. Roughly speaking, Luther said 'If it is not forbidden by scripture, you may do it', while Zwingli said 'If it is not commanded by scripture, you may not do it'. However, he proceeded very cautiously, creating a demand for change, which others then initiated with his support. The Lenten episode of 1522 was typical of his method. During the fast a group of his followers, all substantial citizens, deliberately and publicly consumed a meal of sausage. They were prosecuted in the ecclesiastical court and Zwingli, who had not partaken of the meat, immediately leapt to their defence with a hard-hitting pamphlet urging emancipation from unnecessary dietary restrictions. He also petitioned his ecclesiastical superior the Bishop of Constance for permission to marry - after he had already done so, but before he had admitted it. By the summer of 1522 the situation urgently needed clarification, because it was clear that the bishop had virtually no authority in the city, although all the existing ecclesiastical institutions operated in his name. In July the council set up a disputation between Zwingli and a rather obtuse Franciscan called Francis Lambert, and then proceeded to use the outcome as an excuse to proclaim its allegiance to the evangelical teaching. In 1523 Zwingli codified his teaching in sixty seven articles, renouncing the papacy, the mass, intercession, images, purgatory, and all the familiar rituals of the catholic faith. Two further disputations later in the year served to rally the whole city behind him. The authority of the Bishop of Constance was repudiated, the mass abolished, and a full evangelical church order established. By 1525 the religious houses had been dissolved, and a civil court set up to oversee matrimonial issues and public morals. In 1526 the council assumed the entirely ecclesiastical power of excommunication, so that for all practical purposes the church and the civic authority became synonymous. This assimilation became particularly significant when Zwingli was attacked from the radical side by anabaptists such as Conrad Grebel. The anabaptists regarded faith as an entirely individual matter, and would only admit adult members who had made their own profession. For this reason they rejected, not only the baptism of children, but also the whole idea of a Godly society or commonwealth, which was exactly what Zwingli's alliance with the council was intended to create. For that reason, rather than because he regarded them as heretics in the doctrinal sense, Zwingli caused them to be persecuted in Zurich. In spite of his lack of sexual continence, Zwingli was in other respects a puritan. Music was banned from the churches, along with all visual images, and the sacraments were given a very low priority. The liturgical emphasis was all on the word. This lack of sacramental content led to an open breach with Luther. In 1529 friends of both parties, such as the Strassburg reformer Martin Bucer, tried to bring them together at Marburg, but Luther rejected Zwingli's commemorative view of the Eucharist out of hand. Coolness turned into open hostility, and in the following year two separate confessions were prepared for the Diet of Augsburg, which presented the catholics with an immediate polemical advantage. By this time Zwingli was following political rather than evangelical priorities, and tried to place Zurich at the head of a league. In 1528 he had seven other Cantons and Strassburg with him, but his attempts to link up with the German princes failed, thanks to his feud with Luther. Consequently the league never had the stomach for the aggressive war which Zwingli wanted. In 1531 he at last succeeded in provoking conflict with the catholic Cantons, but Zurich was defeated and he was killed at the battle of Kappel. The catholic Cantons, however, had neither the means nor the desire to follow up their victory, and the reformation in Zurich survived. Zwingli's young successor, Heinrich Bullinger, adopted a completely different style, while maintaining the same doctrinal position. During his long incumbency of just over forty years, the city became, by entirely peaceful means, a major centre of international protestant influence, and it was the doctrine of Zurich, rather than that of Wittenburg or Geneva, which was to be so influential in England.

In Basle and Berne reform came more gradually, and rather later, between 1524 and 1528. Again disputations were used, but in Basle particularly there was tough catholic opposition because the bishop was resident in the city. The crisis there came at the end of 1528, and resulted eventually in victory for Oecolampadius, who was the Basle equivalent of Zwingli. Oecalampadius was a much more irenic and less aggressive figure than his Zurich counterpart, and although he also died in 1531, perilously soon after his triumph, the reformation in Basle also survived. In Strassburg the first reformer was Wolfgang Capito. He arrived in the city in 1523, accompanied by Conrad Zell, and they succeeded in creating an interest in evangelical teaching which the more substantial figure of Martin Bucer was able to exploit in the following year. So great had Bucer's influence become by the end of 1524 that churches were reorganised and an evangelical order introduced almost entirely by force of popular demand. The civic authorities were reluctantly persuaded to take a lead when it became obvious that if they did not do so the city would become ungovernable. However, Bucer was the most irenic of all the reformers. He valued peace almost as Luther valued faith. The mass was finally abolished in Strassburg, and the religious houses dissolved, in 1529. Bucer even experimented with tolerating the anabaptists, but they showed no sign of reciprocating his indulgence, and eventually Strassburg became as hostile to the radicals as any other city, catholic or reformed. By 1530 a distinct reformed tradition had emerged in Switzerland and South Germany, a tradition represented by the Tetrapolitan Confession, which was protestant but entirely separate from that of Luther, and which was to be given its final form over the following two decades by John Calvin.

15. Anabaptists and other Radicals

Radical heresy had existed within the church from very early days. It usually took the form of judging the institutional church by some subjective but absolute moral standard, and finding it wanting. This sometimes led to an open repudiation of the orthodox church, and the rise of separatism, as with the fourth century Donatists or the thirteenth century Waldenses; and sometimes to a retreat into the inner life of the spirit, as with the fourteenth century Fraticelli or the fifteenth century Lollards. Mysticism also created a grey area between orthodoxy and radicalism, but mystics were very seldom separatists, and non-separating radicalism was always seen as a minor problem. The Family of Love later came to occupy this position, and was an extremely elusive phenomenon. The most important radical sect in the period immediately before the reformation was the Bohemian Brethren, a group which had separated from the moderate Hussite, or Utraquist church before the middle of the fifteenth century. It was members of this sect, known as the Zwickau prophets, who appeared in Wittenburg during Luther's absence in 1521-2. Luther's protest, although it was not radical in intention, and was never so expressed by him, nevertheless triggered off a fresh round of radical responses. Andreas Carlstadt and Thomas Muntzer both began their reforming careers by responding to Luther's initiative, but both became impatient with his institutional and theological conservatism. Carlstadt joined forces with the Zwickau prophets to reject both transubstantiation and priestly orders. At Christmas 1521 he claimed to administer the communion in Wittenburg as a 'new layman', which was more of a gesture than an offence because, whether he liked it or not, he had been validly ordained. Carlstadt was non-violent but extremely anti-clerical. He took Luther's doctrine of the priesthood of all believers to a literal extreme, rejecting any ordained or professional ministry - a course which Luther never adopted. By this means Carlstadt gained a considerable following, but his teaching remained predominantly negative. Ultimately he developed a theology of suffering, in which the believer followed and sought to emulate the sufferings of Christ; a theology in which salvation came through suffering, rather as salvation came to Luther through faith. Rejected both by Luther and by the princes who supported him, he hovered on the fringes of the peasants' war, and eventually became a hunted fugitive. As such he earned his own salvation by suffering, and conferred the same upon his unfortunate wife, who remained the loyal companion of his misfortunes.

One of the reasons why Luther rejected Carlstadt was that he did not accept the ultimate authority of scripture, giving superior credence to the direct voice of the Holy Spirit. All the magisterial reformers insisted that the spirit must be tested by the letter, because the Devil was adept at imitating the voice of God. Many radicals however claimed that the scriptures were corrupted by human transmission, and shared Carlstadt's view. Among them was his contemporary, Thomas Muntzer. Both men also rejected infant baptism which, as we have seen, was one of the props of a Christian commonwealth. Carlstadt continued to accept adult baptism, but Muntzer eventually rejected baptism altogether, as just another meaningless sign. Muntzer also developed a theological principle which became his key to salvation, only in his case it was not suffering but poverty. The poor were the Elect of God, the meek who should inherit the earth. Whereas Carlstadt had been an academic, Muntzer was the parish priest of Allstedt, near Wittenburg. He was the first pioneer of a German liturgy, a development in which he anticipated Luther by some two years, and was also a fine and fiery preacher, attracting great crowds to his sermons. Between 1523, when he issued his first protestation, and 1525 when he became caught up in the peasants' war, his radicalism developed in two ways. On the one hand he became extremely anti-clerical, rejecting all the outward trappings of the church - including the bible and the sacraments - as part of a vast clerical conspiracy or confidence trick. And on the other hand he became increasingly violent. By 1525 he was not only preaching that the poor would inherit the earth, but that it was their right, and indeed their duty, to go out and take it. This was connected with his apocalyptic vision of the second coming of Christ, and made him a genuine social and political revolutionary, as well as a religious radical. This characteristic was not shared by Carltadt, nor by many other contemporary radicals, but in the paranoid atmosphere of 1525 they all became tarred with his brush.

The defeat of the peasants not only resulted in Muntzer's capture and execution, but also in a general retreat by the surviving radicals into a kind of sectarianism which increasingly withdrew into itself. Violent and apocalyptic groups did not disappear altogether (a particularly notorious one surfaced at Munster in 1533) but they ceased to be an important factor in the religious equation. More important after 1525 was the movement known as anabaptism, which had originated in Switzerland and been spread throughout South Germany by the persecution which had dispersed the original communities. In spite of their revolutionary reputation, these groups were mostly pacifist and quietist in orientation. Anabaptism probably originated in a tithe revolt among the peasantry of Zurich and Basle, who were supported in the first instance by reformed preachers such as Zwingli. To reformers it was legitimate to withhold tithes from the traditional clergy, on the grounds that they were not carrying out a true ministry. However, when it came to the point Zwingli could not oppose tithes on principle because he continued to believe in an ordained and 'called' ministry, and recognised the need for taxation to support it. So whereas Zwingli progressed to the idea of levying tithes as secular taxes, the radicals went on to deny the need for an ordained ministry at all. Conrad Grebel and Balthsasar Hübmaier denounced Zwingli as a 'scribe', and as a stooge of political authority. He fought back with the kind of effectiveness which partly justified the charges, and had his detractors either exiled or executed. Anabaptism then retreated to the peripheral villages of the Canton, where it became inextricably tangled up with political resistance to rule from Zurich. Grebel and Hübmaier were not sectarian in their intention. Unlike many later sectaries they were not deliberately withdrawing from an impure church. They would have been quite happy to have retained an established church of some kind in Zurich, provided they could have converted it to their own views. It was therefore Zwingli who turned the anabaptists into sectaries by rejecting them and driving them out. Once they had been rejected, however, they soon became both politically and ecclesiastically subversive, and invited forcible suppression.

This suppression came at the battle of Gniessen in November 1525, where the defeat of the radicals was followed by about seventy executions. The surviving preachers scattered all over South Germany and the Rhineland, creating the diaspora already referred to. Once uprooted from their political context, they quickly lost interest in revolutionary action, and their views had become largely pacifist when they were expressed by Michael Sattler in the so-called Schleitheim confession of 1527. These articles expressed what was soon to become the classic anabaptist withdrawal from the world, repudiating all office holding and the taking of oaths. No Christian could bear rule, and so there could be no such thing as a Christian magistrate, let alone a Godly commonwealth. A true believer would refuse to pay taxes, or contribute in any way to the life of the Devil's world. It is not surprising that the authorities became alarmed. We know now, with the benefit of historical research, that the holders of such views were not only poor and humble. for the most part, they were also relatively few. At the time, in spite of their abstinence from violent action, they seemed to threaten the dissolution of the whole social order. Paranoid fears of a great anabaptist conspiracy (equal to those of the Jews and the witches) were widespread among the princes and those who served them. The propensity of anabaptist congregations to appear and disappear with bewildering rapidity added to this nervousness. It now appears that this was mainly due to the restless wanderings of preachers who were always in danger of arrest, and whose influence, although charismatic, was also ephemeral. But that was not understood at the time, when there seemed to be anabaptists behind every bush. In fact the anabaptist communities seem to have developed in a number of different ways, when they endured at all. Some practised community of goods, others not; some revered the bible in the manner of fundamentalists, others thought it of no value. Predominantly they were a rural phenomenon, and went hand in hand with that social unrest which was by no means ended by the shattering debacle of the peasants' war. Indeed the defeat at Frankenhausen ushered in a period of apocalyptic visions and prophecies of revenge, which were to some extent a substitute for action. Hans Hut prophesied the end of the world for 1528, following an abstruse calculation of the number of the Beast in the book of Revelation. As often happens in such cases, his influence was not greatly reduced by the failure of his predictions to be realised. Although most of these groups expected God to act for them, and renounced violence, the authorities moved ruthlessly against them. Some 350 executions took place in the Rhineland alone in 1528 and 1529.

It is against this background that the bizarre events of the 'kingdom' of Munster must be seen. In February 1533 the city of Munster in Westphalia established the Lutheran reformation, and repudiated the authority of the Prince Bishop. However the leadership was theologically weak, and was moved sharply to the left by the appearance of Zwinglian preachers from South Germany. These men, who maintained that the Eucharist was purely a commemoration of the Last Supper, were known as sacramentarians, and effectively de-stabilised the insecure regime. Political weakness attracted still more radical preachers, anabaptists, who quickly established a following among the poorer townsmen. The divided magistracy needed all the allies it could get in the face of a counter attack by the Prince Bishop, but between November 1533 and February 1534 proved increasingly unable to control its allies. Finally, in February 1534, the council collapsed and a militant group of anabaptist leaders took over the city. News of this unexpected coup spread rapidly, and provoked an upsurge of anabaptism in the nearby Netherlands. A group of Dutch anabaptists then joined the leadership, and one of them, Jan Mathias, quickly established himself as the dominant personality. Jan then declared that Munster was the chosen venue for the second coming of Christ, which would take place at Easter 1534. The failure of this prophecy did nothing to weaken his authority. By this time most of the ordinary citizens had fled, and had been replaced by zealous anabaptist migrants, including a disproportionate number of women. By April 1534 the city was besieged by a combined catholic and Lutheran army, and Jan died leading a sortie which he had prophesied would lead to victory. He was promptly replaced by another Dutch fanatic, Jan of Leyden, who instituted an Old Testament kingdom, complete with polygamy and a sumptuous court, in the battered and starving city. Munster eventually fell after an heroic resistance, in June 1535, having made a fearful impression upon a world which seemed very vulnerable to such fantasies. The great anabaptist conspiracy had taken a visible and tangible form.

16. The Catholic Reformation before Trent

Every generation had seen movements of spiritual renewal within the church, and the late fifteenth century had been no exception. Both mysticism and Christian humanism had sought to escape from the suffocating worldliness of a religion dominated by materialistic imagery. Both had been denounced by conservatives who believed that the church must be accepted as it was because its evolution had been guided by the holy spirit. These movements had begun long before Luther, and indeed before Hus and Wycliffe, and for the most part contained no challenge to orthodox theology. Neither, however, had been capable of attracting a mass following, and there was a great need for a popular movement of renewal which was not doctrinally suspect. The orders of friars had twice before in their history responded to this sort of demand - when they were founded in the thirteenth century and when they were first reformed in the fourteenth. At that point each order had divided into Observants (who observed their rule strictly) and Conventuals (who were more relaxed). The Observants had succeeded in preserving their integrity down to 1500, when they were few in number but much respected. The Carthusians, Observant Franciscans and Carmelites had retained most of their original rigour, but what was lacking was high quality spiritual leadership to pull these rather fragmentary pieces together into a coherent movement. Part of the trouble was a legacy from the friars' success in previous generations. Because their services were so much in demand, particularly as confessors and preachers, they had been granted extensive privileges and jurisdictional immunities. This had not endeared them to episcopal and parochial incumbents, whose authority, income and prestige were alike threatened by these licensed intruders. The Lateran council of 1512, which was the most important attempt by the papacy to respond to the demand for reform before the advent of Luther, revealed that any attempt to use the existing orders as they had been used before would result in obstruction, frustration and failure. Moreover, just as a reform movement led by the mendicants would have been frustrated by the bishops, so a reform movement led by the bishops would have been frustrated by the pope, because of his fears of the revival of conciliarism.

There were promising initiatives, particularly the work of Cardinal Cisernos in Spain and formation of the Oratory of Divine Love, but no concerted strategy. In fact the official attitude towards the reformed religious orders was distinctly schizophrenic. On the one hand there was the revival of the strict Camaldolese order, which began about 1510 when they were joined by a group of devout Christian humanists led by Paolo Guistianini (a Venetian of noble blood); the foundation of the aristocratic Theatines in 1524 at Rome; and of the humble Capuchins, who were devoted to the care of the sick and destitute, in 1529. All of these were papally approved. On the other hand, however, reforming circles in Rome in the 1530s were more interested in suppressing orders than in founding new ones. Paul III, who became pope in 1534 accepted the need for a General Council, which his predecessor Clement VII had feared for largely discreditable reasons, and appointed reforming Cardinals such as Gasparo Contarini, Reginald Pole and Giacomo Sadoleto. Nevertheless he talked of suppressing all conventuals, amalgamating the observants into three or four large orders, and abolishing all immunity from episcopal jurisdiction. The report of his committee of enquiry into the state of the church, the *Concilium de Emendenda Ecclesia* had drawn up in 1536, which was undoubtedly a reforming initiative, was remarkably negative in tone, concentrating far more on abuses which needed to be corrected than on positive new spiritual initiatives. When it was leaked the Lutherans were delighted by what appeared to be a piece of self-flagellation which offered no challenge to their dynamic theology. Partly for this reason the reform movement in the Curia split. Most of Paul's new appointments were humanist intellectuals, keenly aware of the justification behind many of the protestant attacks, and anxious to resolve the Lutheran schism by negotiation. Some of them were even suspected of having heretic sympathies. Pole, as bishop of Viterbo, had gathered around him a very ambiguous group, several of whom later became open protestants. As a result a second reforming group developed, dedicated to fighting heresy with any weapon which came to hand, and to ending the schism by conquest and persecution. The humanist group came to be known as the *spirituali,* and the militants as the *zelanti.* The former were led initially by Contarini, and the latter by Gian Pietro Caraffa. It was to these highly placed leaders that the new rigorous orders looked for recognition, but until 1541 the *spirituali* were in the ascendant, and it was their ambiguity which was reflected in the contradictory signals.

Then, at about the same time, two important things happened. In 1540 a Basque nobleman named Ignatius Loyola was allowed to found a religious fraternity of a new sort, not strictly an order but a body of clerks regular. They called themselves the Society of Jesus, and almost immediately began to make an impression at the highest level. The second happening was the Colloquy of Regensburg (or Ratisbon) in 1541. At Regensburg a catholic delegation led by Contarini negotiated face to face with the Lutherans, led by Philip Melanchthon, Luther's trusted lieutenant. At the highest level there was a great will to succeed, encouraged by a shared humanist culture, and against all the odds a very complicated formula was worked out and agreed upon. However, its very subtlety defeated it. Suspicious hardliners on both sides conspired to reject the compromise, and the discussions ended in failure. Reconciliation had missed the tide, because there were by this time too many vested interests committed- on both sides. Cantarini died soon after the colloquy, and although the *spirituali* remained strong for another decade, they had lost the initiative. This at last solved the problem of leadership, because Paul III became increasingly sympathetic to a 'counter reformation' strategy, and allowed Carafa to re-establish the Roman Inquisition in 1542 to combat the growth of heresy in Italy. He also became increasingly determined to convene a General Council which would establish a firm doctrinal consensus on the disputed issues. He had made one attempt to convene a council at Mantua in 1536, but it had been aborted by a lack of political co-operation. However, the failure at Regensburg and the increasing aggressiveness of Henry VIII of England, prompted him to try again. The main problem was that a viable General Council required the participation of bishops from both the French and Imperial lands, and hence the co-operation of both Francis I and Charles V. Since each was concerned to checkmate the other this was extremely difficult to obtain. Charles had at first hoped for a 'German solution' and had pinned great hopes on Regensburg. It was only when that was disapp6lnted that he moved to support a General Council, and only when peace was signed at Créspy in 1544 that the right political climate existed.

The long awaited Council convened at Trent, which was an Imperial city but within Italy, in December 1545. By the time that the council met, the reformed orders were developing strongly, and the Jesuits provided some of its leading theologians. But the proliferation of these orders - Theatines, Capuchins, Bernardines, Sommaschi, Ursulines and many more - also had its negative side. Rivalry was intense, and sometimes took precedence over shared objectives. The defection of several zealous individuals from the Observant Franciscans to the Capuchins, for example, caused a bitter and protracted quarrel. In 1536 Paul III had agreed to disband the Capuchins, but his mind was changed at the last moment. In 1542 their Superior, Bernardino Ochino, defected to the protestants, and another acute crisis followed. Moreover, the success of the Jesuits was resented and envied by all the more traditional orders, old and new. This success was based principally on two things, effective educational practice and the Spiritual Exercises. The Jesuits were not originally a teaching order, and Ignatius was certainly not an intellectual. However, coming to learning late in life, he took it with the greatest seriousness, and the schools which the order established were soon favourites with wealthy and aristocratic patrons. This was not a happy accident, but the result of a carefully thought out policy, a policy which also made the

Jesuits the favourite confessors of kings and queens; that a major evangelical campaign will achieve much more working with the political grain than against it. For the same reason Jesuit universities such as Ingolstadt were among the power houses of the later Counter Reformation. The Spiritual Exercises were a unique blend of mystical contemplation and disciplined intellectual effort. Their effect upon those who experienced them was profound. However, in one very important respect all this intense reforming effort shifted the spiritual foundations of the catholic church from their traditional ground. Although the church had always recognised the individuality of the Christian soul, most of its emphasis had been collective; pilgrimages, rituals, celebrations, even sacraments, had all been shared experiences, involving the whole community. It had been the protestants who had concentrated upon the individual; his faith, his bible reading, his prayer. All the new catholic orders, however, based their success upon the spiritual prowess of the individual member, rather than upon collective discipline. Even the Jesuits, with their emphasis upon complete obedience and ostensible abnegation of self, built outwards from the inner man. What was needed, therefore, when the Council of Trent met, was a formula to convert this inwards spirituality, which was a reaction against institutional materialism, into a force which could control and lead a massive ecclesiastical organisation. By placing the emphasis of the Council upon the definition of doctrine (rather than the reform of practice), and the power of the Pope, these elements were successfully brought together

17. Exploration and Discovery

The renaissance at first contributed nothing to the widening of physical horizons. The rediscovery of the works of Ptolemy, the Hellenistic cosmographer, merely reaffirmed the fact that Asia and Africa were there, and extended far beyond their northern and western fringes, facts which had never been lost sight of in western Europe. The earliest deliberate voyages of exploration by the Portuguese in the fifteenth century seem to have owed nothing to intellectual curiosity in the abstract sense. The original move had been the capture of Ceuta on the north African coast, which was a direct result of a crusading impulse by then shut out of the *reconquista* by the expansion of Castile. Over the next forty five years the key figure was that of the enigmatic Infante of Portugal, Henry, known as the Navigator. It was he who was mainly responsible for sending ships south from Ceuta, down the African coast, and out into the Atlantic. His original motivation seems to have been that of the crusader; partly seeking infidels to conquer, and partly the lands of the legendary Prester John whose Christian oriental empire was to be the crucial ally against an expanding Islam. However, he became increasingly fascinated with discovery for its own sake, and by the time of his death in 1460 the Portuguese had settled the Azores and Madeira islands, which had previously been known but had remained uninhabited. They had also explored the West African coast to within about five degrees of the equator, establishing trading links with the Berber and other peoples of north western Africa. The Spaniards followed their neighbours' example only to a very limited extent. There was no royal interest or patronage, but Andalusian seamen, acting on their own initiative, occupied the Canary Islands. By 1460 'Prester John' had been approximately (and rather disappointingly) located in the ancient Christian empire of Abyssinia, and an Abyssinian mission had visited Lisbon in 1452. Henry was followed as the chief patron and inspirer of Portuguese voyages by his nephew Fernando, who completed the exploration of the Cape Verde Islands but made little southward progress. The rights and privileges of settlement and trade arising from future exploration were then leased out by the Crown to the Lisbon merchant Fernando Gomes, and the commercial priority became firmly established. The Gold Coast (present day Ghana)was reached and a trading fort established at El Mina. This had the immediate affect of opening up a direct gold trade by sea, bypassing the ancient Sahara caravan routes and adversely affecting the north African ports. In 1474 Gomes' lease expired, and these increasingly profitable rights reverted to the Crown.

By 1482 the Congo had been reached, and by 1487 Cape Cross in what is now Namibia. Forts were built at intervals down the coast to control access to the interior, and the curiosity of other Europeans was firmly discouraged. Meanwhile overland exploration was also being carried out. In 1486 an expedition set out from Benin in Nigeria, overland to Abyssinia, and thence to Persia and India. News of the success of this epic journey took some four or five years to reach Portugal, but one result was that the Portuguese already knew the locations of Calicut and Goa before Vasco da Gama set out in 1497. Bartholomew Diaz had discovered the Cape of Good Hope as early as 1487, rounding it by accident in bad weather, but his crews had mutinied and he had been unable to proceed further. Meanwhile, in anticipation both of further discoveries and of active competition, King John of Portugal had taken the precaution of securing the bull *Aeterni Regis* from the Pope, assigning all discoveries south of the Canaries and West of Africa to Portugal. That the king should have sought such a disposition, and that Alexander VI should have felt himself entitled to make it tells us a great deal about the contemporary view of the world. John's fear of competition at least was well founded, because although Diaz had returned in 1488, no further expedition was sent out until 1493, by which time Christopher Columbus had already sailed and returned in the service of Spain, claiming to have found the westward route to the Indies. Protracted negotiations then followed between Spain and Portugal, which resulted in the treaty of Tordesillas in 1494, establishing a line of demarcation 370 leagues west of the Cape Verde Islands. The zones of influence thus established eventually gave America (apart from Brazil) to Spain, and Africa and Asia (apart from the Philippines) to Portugal.

John died in 1495, and by the time Columbus returned from his second voyage in 1496, disillusionment had begun to set in. It was no longer believed that he had discovered Asia, and Spanish interest waned. However in 1498 Vasco da Gama reached India by sea. Trade links were immediately established, and by 1499 da Gama had returned with a cargo the richness of which aroused the cupidity of both countries and revived the flagging enthusiasm of explorers and patrons alike. King Manuel hastened to follow up da Gama's success with a much larger expedition, which started by finding (apparently by accident) the coast of Brazil, and then proceeded to India where a large cargo was obtained, mainly by force. Thereafter a regular annual fleet was established, and the Portuguese quickly became embroiled in the politics of India.

By1505 a pattern of alliances and hostilities had been established, a number of fortified trading posts set up, and a Viceroy of India appointed. Muslim rulers all around the Indian ocean fiercely contested the Portuguese intrusion into what had long been a peaceful and well ordered trade, but their ships were no match for the heavily armed Portuguese carracks, and the Egyptian fleet was decisively defeated at Diu near Aden in 1509. In the same year Alfonso de Albuquerque became Viceroy, and thanks to his aggressive policy over the next six years the Portuguese gained complete control over the Indian Ocean trade. In 1512 the capture of Molucca opened up the whole of Indonesia, the actual source of many of the most valuable spices, and in 1515 the strategic port of Ormuz unlocked the door to the Persian Gulf. The sheer volume of the trade was far greater than the Portuguese themselves could conduct with their limited manpower, so they established a licensing system which taxed the existing commerce, reserving only the long distance trade to Europe for their own ships. By 1520 Lisbon was one of the richest cities in Christendom. By contrast, Spanish exploration in the New World at first seemed unpromising. By 1500 everyone knew that the land mass which lay beyond the West Indian islands was not Asia. In place of teeming cities and a rich and ancient culture, it appeared to offer nothing but a few wandering savages. Effort was concentrated on getting round or through the land mass, rather than on attempts to discover what it really had to offer, because Asia was still the real target. Both the Portuguese and the French showed an interest in Brazil, and the former went to some trouble and expense to scare off interlopers, but they regarded the country mainly as a source of dyestuffs and hardwood.

Alexander VI confirmed the Treaty of Tordesillas, and protected the interests of Spain further north, but the first settlement on San Domingo was not a success. It required hard work to establish what was basically a farming colony, but the settlers were only interested in gold and slaves. Nor was Columbus a successful governor, and the only useful thing he did was to promote a programme of further exploration. The settlement moved to a healthier site in 1497, but proved extremely hard to govern. Over the next few years the Spanish colonist spread slowly over the islands of San Domingo and Hispaniola, converting the land into large farms, and the inhabitants into slave labour. The first effective governor was Nicholas de Ovando who ruled from 1500 to 1506. He established a ruthless discipline which gave the colony a modest prosperity, but his severity virtually extinguished the indigenous population, and from a very early date plantation slaves began to be imported from the Portuguese factories in West Africa. In 1509 settlement was extended to Jamaica, in 1511 to Cuba, and in 1512 to Puerto Rico. All this was achieved by encouraging the restless and dissatisfied to move on in search of fresh pastures, but the nature of the settlements did not change until the mainland was reached. A good deal of exploration had been carried out already, but the first colony on *tierrefirme was* established by Vasco Nuiiez de Balboa in 1509. Balboa founded the city of Darien, and established a viable farming community, imposing his rule upon the surrounding natives and exacting tribute from them. In 1513 he led an expedition across the isthmus to the Pacific side, and that encouraged further attempts to find a way to Asia. In 1513 also a royal governor of Darien was appointed, and although the first appointment was a bad one, the Crown had nevertheless made it clear that it intended to maintain control over these far-flung outposts, and not to allow them to become the possessions of private families. A royal court was established at San Domingo in 1511, and thereafter each colony was ruled by a governor and *audiencia*. At the same time in Castile the first Council of the Indies had been appointed. By 1519 a basic colonial administration existed covering Darien and the islands, but very little profit had accrued. The situation was a complete contrast to that which appertained in the only other European Empire, that of the Portuguese East. The Portuguese had established very small colonies of merchants, soldiers, clergy and administrators at strategic points to control a large and flourishing population. The Spaniards settled extensive tracts of thinly populated land, expelling or subjugating the existing inhabitants. The Portuguese grew rich by exploiting a society which was already rich, while the Spaniards stayed poor by farming the land.

However, in, 1519 that situation was dramatically transformed by the exploits of Hernan Cortes. Cortes was sent out from Cuba by the governor there, Diego Valesquez, to explore Mexico and establish a base there. However, Valesquez had made the mistake of allowing him to recruit his own force of 600 volunteers, and no sooner had he landed then he repudiated the governor's authority and set up his own private dominion, with the full support of his followers. He symbolically burned his ships, and founded the 'city' of Vera Cruz, writing directly to the Emperor for ratification of his actions and confirmation of his independent command. The dramatic rise of the *conquistadores* and the transformation of Spanish America was about to begin.

18. Money and People: financial and demographic problems

For reasons which are not entirely clear population levels all over Europe began to rise in the late fifteenth century. There was no revolution in the production or distribution of food, no dramatic changes in the climate, and no significant developments in medical science. However, there were some rather more elusive factors which may have been relevant. The incidence of plague seems to have diminished, probably because of some change in the numbers or distribution of the flea bearing rats. The mortality rate among the young and active, who were peculiarly susceptible to bubonic plague, may in consequence have fallen. At the same time the age of marriage was coming down, with a consequent improvement in fertility. This latter was a cultural change, which may have arisen because of improved living standards, or because of a recovery of optimism and confidence as a period of destructive civil and international wars came to an end. Overall population figures are very hard to reconstruct. Some estimates for the mid-fifteenth century have already been given, and city levels, which are better recorded, can be used as a rough guide. By 1500 six cities had over 100,000 inhabitants; Paris, Constantinople, Naples, Venice, Milan and Rome. A century later Paris and Constantinople had topped 200,000, and another seven or eight had joined the 100,000 + league; London, Amsterdam, Palermo, Marseilles, Messina, Lisbon, Seville and (probably) Moscow. Vienna, Nuremburg, Antwerp, Augsburg, Strassburg, Hamburg and Danzig all doubled their populations during the century, to end with between 40,000 and 60,000 in 1600. In 1500 there were about 150 cities with populations in excess of 10,000, amounting in total to about three million souls. By 1600 there were 220 such cities, and about six million city dwellers. Most of this urban population was in Italy, Spain and Portugal. North of the Alps, apart from Paris and London, only the Low Countries had a high urban density.

All large towns had a high mortality rate, because of overcrowding, poor hygiene and defective water supplies, so they were net consumers of population. Consequently the rural population must have been rising at a faster rate, in order to supply this migration. If the urban population rose by some 80%, the overall population must just about have doubled, and such an estimate can be supported in the case of England, where a figure of two and a half million in 1450 had become at least five million by 1600. The Empire probably rose from fifteen million to about twenty eight million over the same period. Increases of this order had a number of important consequences. Pressure on food supplies led to more specialised commercial farming, and helped to stimulate medium and short range trade. Pressure on the land brought marginal areas back into cultivation which had been derelict since the thirteenth century, and which was particularly vulnerable to crop failure. For the first time since about 1350 there was a surplus of unemployed young men. This partly fed the migration into the towns, but also provided the material for planned resettlement. The English 'planted' Ireland in this way in the late sixteenth century; the Spaniards Granada after the Moriscos were expelled in 1570. Both Spaniards and Portuguese colonised the new world and parts of the far East. The increasing size of armies was made possible by the same phenomenon, and on the other side of the coin there was a significant increase in vagabondage and brigandage, in Italy, France and Spain as well as in England. The constant dynastic wars of the early sixteenth century do not seem to have halted this growth, except perhaps in northern Italy, which was the principal battleground. Even there, there was nothing to compare with the devastation wrought in some parts of France by the English incursions of the fourteenth century, or in much of Germany by the Thirty Years War in the seventeenth. Another consequence of the pressure of population upon resources was the great price rise. By modern standards this inflation was not dramatic, some 2 or 3% per annum on average - but it went on for the whole century, and into the next, producing an overall rise of some 500%. Moreover it followed a long period of stable or declining prices, a stagnant economic situation which had become enshrined in the morality of the 'just price'. The idea that the value of every material object or substance was fixed and absolute, determined by some kind of Divine legislation, meant that inflation caused not only hardship and bewilderment, but also moral outrage. To make matters even more confusing, the price rise was not steady, but went by fits and starts, decades of relative stability being followed by rises of 20% or even 30% in a year. Moreover these rises were not always related to understandable causes, such as war or harvest failure. An English author in 1549 expressed particular indignation that the price of grain was rising when there was obviously no shortage.

Some contemporaries, however, were sufficiently emancipated from this culture to realise that prices reflect the relationship between supply and demand, and also the relationship between commodity supply and money supply. Thus when demand remains constant and supply falls, prices rise. This was known as 'dearth', and had been familiar for centuries; but in the past it had normally been a temporary phenomenon, corrected by the next good harvest. However, if supply remains constant and demand increases, prices will also rise, as they will if an increase in demand outstrips an increase in supply; and that, broadly, was the sixteenth century position. The steady upward movement of prices during the first half of the century can largely be explained in such terms. But from about 1540 another element entered the equation - American silver. Between 1540, when the great mines at Potosi in Peru were opened up, and about 1620, enough silver was imported to triple the existing supply. Significant quantities of gold also came in, mainly from Mexico, but also to a lesser extent from Africa, and the central European silver mines also increased their output. Much of this bullion was exported eastward to pay for spices and other oriental luxuries, but enough new coin was poured into the European exchanges to account for at least half of the inflation which occurred. Money being the sinew of war, the appetite for war increased with the cash supply, and every prince in Europe got into financial difficulties. In order to escape, most debased their currencies. This made the situation worse by making it appear that there was even more money in circulation than was really the case. There were sixteenth century writers who understood this situation, at least in part. The Spaniard Martin de Azpilcueta and the French man Jean Bodin both grasped the significance of the bullion imports, although neither seem to have seen the importance of population growth. However, the common reaction was to find immediate human scapegoats; rack renting landlords, grasping merchants, extortionate bankers, and so on. This was a reaction which sprang partly out of psychological need, and partly out of the moral imperatives already referred to. There were innumerable food riots, and the houses and businesses of bankers and money lenders were attacked. In England this linked up with the anti-enclosure movement, and led to widespread hedge breaking.

The demands of war, however, not only accelerated the circulation of money, and led to debasement; they also created what might be called credit inflation. Francis I, Charles V and Philip II particularly made huge demands upon their bankers. Each had very large revenue resources, but they were recalcitrant to mobilise, and armies could not be paid with promissory notes. The role of the bankers was to produce ready cash against the security of these resources. At first this led to a great boom in banking, the rise of the Fuggers, the Schetzs and other financial dynasties, and the flourishing of the great Bourse, or Exchange, at Antwerp. During the peak years from 1542 to 1557 well over a million pounds Flemish was being dispensed through that channel every year. However, financial exhaustion on both sides, and the virtual bankruptcies of 1557 led to soaring rates of interest and increasing instability in the money market. One result was that Spain became little more than a channel through which bullion passed on its way from the New World to the bankers of Antwerp or Genoa. By the early seventeenth century Spain had contrived both very high prices and an acute shortage of coin.

Another result was that heavy borrowers like Philip II were unable to service their debts, and further defaults by him in 1576 and 1597 forced the closure of a number of banks. The great inflation was not caused simply by money supply, nor by increasing population, nor by the demands of war, but by a combination of all three, together with some other factors which are even now difficult to locate. Why did the prices of grain and wool rise so much more steeply than those or either labour of manufactured goods? Why did the fluctuation of prices not correspond at all with the known fluctuations in the bullion supply?

Overall, the sixteenth century was a bad time for the wage earner. Wages approximately doubled between 1500 and 1600 in regions as diverse and far apart as Italy and England, but food prices rose as much as five times. Two factors made this possible without complete social breakdown. On the one hand, not all prices rose by as much as 500%, and on the other comparatively few people were wholly or mainly dependent upon wages. Servants, journeymen and soldiers, who were the groups most severely affected, each had perquisites or other methods of supplementing their incomes. A merchant seaman, for example, would be paid partly in kind, and partly in opportunities to trade his own goods. His wage might be insignificant, or even non-existent. In the countryside, wage earners were relatively uncommon; and even the poorest had some plot of land or common rights. The most adversely affected were those unable to work through sickness or age, and those forced to live on fixed rents or stipends, particularly the lesser clergy. Every country saw an increase in charitable provision, but the gap between rich and poor, between those who were able to benefit from inflation and those who were not, grew progressively greater In spite of the growth of the cities, the proportion of the population which was urban did not increase - three million out of about forty-five million in 1500, six million out of about 85m by 1600. Economic activity expanded greatly, and urban civilisation spread and developed, but the Europe of 1600 was no less rural than that of the middle ages, and that situation did not change until the industrial revolution.

19. The end of the wars, 1545-1559

Charles V had in a sense been 'setting up' the Schmalkaldic League for a long time. As early as 1542 Duke Maurice of Saxony had been persuaded to withdraw from the League, and had fought for the Emperor against the French in the war of 1542-4. In 1546 he signed a treaty of neutrality with Charles, and in October of that year received a secret promise that he would be granted the lands and Electoral title of his neighbour and kinsman John Frederick in return for his co-operation against the League. In June 1546 Charles also signed two other treaties, one with Duke William of Bavaria and the other with Pope Paul III, both of whom promised financial and military help against the protestants. On the other hand, the League was also preparing for war. Philip of Hesse, one of the original members who had been obliged to leave the League in 1541 following a scandal over his bigamous second marriage, rejoined in 1544. In the winter of 1545-6 several meetings were also held to prepare plans against an Imperial attack. When war actually broke out in November 1546, the two sides appeared to be fairly evenly, matched. The protestants had about 60,000 men, a good artillery train, and an excellent commander in the person of Sebastian von Burtenbach. However, the appearance was deceptive. The League did not have the financial resources to keep its army in being through the winter. Anticipating the usual 'close season', they disbanded their field army before the end of the year. The Emperor, however, kept his in being, and in a winter campaign which took his enemies completely by surprise, besieged and took a number of important cities, including Augsburg and Strasburg. In March 1547 the League struggled to regain the initiative, but its forces were raised in a number of different places, and could not easily be united. The Elector, John Frederick, attempted a pre-emptive strike against Duke Maurice, and found himself facing the full force of the Imperial army. His colleagues had no chance to join him, and he was defeated and taken prisoner at Mühlberg on the 24th April. His lands and title were duly transferred to Maurice. Martin Luther had died in 1546, and Charles's perpetual rival Francis 1 in March 1547. It looked as though the Emperor was victorious on all fronts.

However, his victory had been costly, both financially and politically. The Fuggers at last became exasperated by endless delays in the repayment of loans, and threatened to withhold all future credit. The Pope withdrew his forces from Germany, and endeavoured to move the Council from Trent to Mantua to escape from Imperial domination. He was also alienated by the appointment of Ferrante Gonzaga to be the Governor of Milan. At the same time, although the Schmalkaldic League had been destroyed, Lutheranism had not been suppressed. The new Elector of Saxony was just as Lutheran as the old. Also a number of other Evangelical states, such as Brandenburg, had never been members of the League in the first place, and had consequently not shared in its defeat. There also remained the problem of how to re-catholicise those protestant states, like Hesse, which had been defeated. In June 1548 the Interim was proclaimed so called because it was supposed to be a short term solution until the General Council at Trent had 'taken order' for the ending of the schism. Naturally it was a catholic order, although with a few marginal concessions, like communion under both kinds, hopefully intended to conciliate the moderate or the pessimistic. The protestants refused it wherever they were not immediately threatened by an Imperial army, and the Pope denounced it for making unnecessary concessions. Only a few cities, such as Strassburg, were constrained to accept it for a short time, and some leading protestant theologians, notably Martin Bucer and Peter Martyr Vermigli took refuge in England in consequence. In February 1550 a new protestant League came into being at Koenigsburg in East Prussia, and in 1551 Henry II of France set out to prise Maurice of Saxony away from his Imperial alliance. In this he was soon successful. In January 1552 by the Treaty of Chambord Maurice joined France and the new protestant League in alliance against the Habsburgs. In return for French men and money, the Germans agreed to surrender the border fortresses of Metz, Toul and Verdun. In March 1552 the French invaded Lorraine and helped themselves to the forts. Charles, who by this time was suffering from intermittent bouts of crippling gout which left him quite unable to attend to business, was taken by surprise, having trusted Maurice with uncharacteristic complacency, and was forced to flee across the Alps. The bishops assembled at Trent for the second sessions of the Council scattered in panic, and brought that august assembly to a premature end. However, neither Maurice nor Henry was able to follow up his advantage, and by the summer Charles had been given a chance to recover. With the support of Spanish troops commanded by the Duke of Alba, he laid siege to Metz. This was unsuccessful, but his armies won a victory at Sieverhausen in July 1553 and Maurice was killed. By this time the war had reached stalemate, and the Emperor was virtually crippled by his various ailments. His policies were continued with no less resolution by his sister Mary of Hungary, the Regent of the Netherlands, and her adviser Antoine de Perrenot, the Bishop of Arras, but the lack of his personal direction was nevertheless felt. It was in these circumstances that the opportunity for the English marriage alliance arose.

As long before as 1530 Charles had fixed the Imperial succession, persuading the electors to name his brother Ferdinand as King of the Romans. By 1545 he was regretting this move, and wishing to intrude his only legitimate son, Philip. However the Imperial Diet (that is, the princes) refused to consider any plan for introducing him, either instead of Ferdinand or after him. Relations between the two brothers and their families understandably deteriorated. Charles then concentrated upon detaching certain strategic parts of the Empire, so that he could bestow them upon Philip, who was his heir in respect of his Spanish monarchies and their dependencies. Much to Ferdinand's chagrin he converted the Duchy of Milan into an Imperial Vicariate, which he then granted to Philip for life, thus entrusting that key strategic territory in northern Italy to Spanish control. More importantly, by a Pragmatic Sanction (Imperial edict) of 1548 he constituted the seventeen provinces of The Netherlands into the Burgundian Circle of the Empire. The Pragmatic then went on to exempt the Circle from Imperial law, making its participation in the Empire merely one of shadowy allegiance. Having thus detached them, Charles then went on to decree that each of the provinces, which he himself held by a separate title, should follow the same order of succession, a succession which he settled on Philip. Philip thus became, for all practical purposes, heir to the Crown of The Netherlands, and some of the richest lands in Europe were transferred from the Empire to Spain. It is not surprising that, when Charles was attacked in 1552, Ferdinand and his sons did nothing to assist him, and were even suspected of complicity.

On account of his increasing incapacity, by 1553 Charles was contemplating abdication, and was very anxious that Philip should be able to hold The Netherlands against the hostility of his Austrian cousins. This problem was made more difficult by the fact that Ferdinand and Maximilian were popular there, whereas Philip, who had visited the provinces at his father's suggestion in 1549, was not. Having been brought up almost entirely in Spain, he was at ease only in that language, and his limitations as a communicator were taken for aloofness and arrogance. Mary Tudor was the Emperor's cousin, being the daughter of his mother's sister, and her providential success in securing the succession to the English Crown in July 1553 created the opportunity for a matrimonial coup. Philip was a widower aged twenty-six, with one son; Mary a spinster of thirty-seven, the good looks of her youth already fading and her health more than a little suspect. From a dynastic point of view such a marriage must be a very uncertain gamble, but as a solution to the short term problem, it could hardly be bettered. With England behind him, and the English fleet at his disposal, Philip would not need to fear challenges in the Low Countries, either from his cousins or from the French. Mary was known to be loyal to the old faith, and had a deep personal attachment to Charles which went back to the days when he and his ambassador, Eustace Chapuys, had afforded her a measure of protection against her father's unpredictable wrath. From the Habsburg point of view she was biddable. Philip had to be extracted from a negotiation with the Portuguese, at a cost of some embarrassment, but was willing, indeed eager, for an English marriage. The negotiations were conducted almost entirely by Charles's agents, and unfortunately father and son were not entirely frank with each other. Philip was looking first and foremost to complete the encirclement of France, and secondly to create a new dynastic power bloc in northern Europe by bringing England and The Netherlands under the same Crown. Charles could hardly be open about his misgivings over The Netherlands without making it clear that he lacked confidence in Philip's ability. Consequently, when he negotiated a treaty which gave Philip very little power in England, and excluded England from the French war, he was conceding nothing of importance by his own priorities, but his son was outraged, and almost withdrew. The French also did everything in their power to sabotage the negotiations, but they failed, and Philip swallowed his resentment. The marriage took place in July 1554, and Philip remained in England for just over a year.

There was no child of the marriage, and England did not at once become involved in the grinding war with France, but in August 1555 Philip was able to take over The Netherlands from his father without challenge or opposition. The war was stalemated, with both sides being stretched to the limit, and a truce was signed at Vaucelles in February 1556. This might have become a lasting peace but for the bizarre behaviour of Pope Paul IV. As Gian Pietro Caraffa Paul had long been the leader of the *zelanti,* the ultra orthodox reforming party in the curia. He was also an octogenarian and a Neopolitan. This combination made him fanatically hostile both to heresy and to Spain, and barely responsible for his actions. Elected in May 1555, he immediately set out on a course intended to provoke and antagonise the Habsburgs. In this he succeeded so well that Philip felt compelled to respond by invading the papal states in September 1556. The French could not resist the temptation to come to the pope's assistance, and the truce of Vaucelles broke down. In spite of French support, Paul was defeated in Italy and forced out of the war; but conflict was then resumed in the north in January 1557, and England was drawn in after a protracted political wrangle early in the summer. The French were defeated at St. Quentin in August 1557, but recovered Calais from the English in January 1558. Meanwhile Charles had relinquished all his authority, retaining only the title of Emperor, and had retired to the monastery of St. Yuste in Spain. Philip, left in sole command, did not take long to understand the impossible nature of the struggle which he had inherited. The war was again in stalemate on all fronts, and both sides were on the verge of bankruptcy. In October 1558 peace negotiations were resumed. In November Mary Tudor died, weakening Philip's hand, but freeing him from obligations to England. Thereafter it soon became apparent that Elizabeth's accession spelled no great advantage to either side, and a peace was eventually concluded at Cateau-Cambrésis in April 1559.

By that time a halt had also been called to the long-running religious conflict within the Empire. Frustrated of victory between 1548 and 1552, but unwilling to accept defeat, in 1555 Charles had handed over to Ferdinand the distasteful task of negotiating a settlement with the Lutherans. It was, in a sense, the first step in a process of abdication which went on for over a year. There was little that Ferdinand could do, other than accept the *status quo.* The Lutheran princes and cities were accorded equal rights with catholics within the Imperial constitution, and it was accepted that each autonomous authority had the right to choose the confessional allegiance of its subjects, enforcing that choice by whatever methods it wished. These concessions, however, extended only to the adherents of the Confession of Augsburg. Neither the Calvinists, who were already an emerging force by 1555 but who had failed so far to secure the allegiance of any Imperial territory, nor the various other South German groups who inclined to Switzerland rather than to Wittenburg, were included within the treaty. Ferdinand's only success was to insist that in future any territorial prelate who converted to Lutheranism must resign and be replaced by a catholic in the usual canonical manner. Unlike a temporal prince, he was not allowed to take his state with him. An attempt was also made to 'freeze' the confessional map at its 1552 configuration, but that was unacceptable to protestants who still felt that their faith was advancing, and could not be insisted upon. Had they been right, and had the Reformation continued to advance at the pace of 1525-50, the Peace of Augsburg would probably have been a dead letter within a decade. However, thanks to the development of the Counter Reformation, and the internal divisions of the Lutherans through much of the late sixteenth century, it remained more or less in force until the reappearance of religious warfare after 1618.

20. The France of Henry II

When Henry succeeded his father, Francis I in 1547, France had only partially evolved from a feudal kingdom, and was far from being a fully centralised state. The boundaries of the kingdom were better defined than they had been in 1515, but there were still uncertainties. The Duchy of Brittany, joined to France in a personal union when Charles VIII married the Duchess Anne in 1491, had been precariously retained until 1532, when it had been finally integrated into the kingdom, but many of its laws and customs were still distinctive. In the north east France still claimed suzerainty over Artois and Flanders. Theoretically surrendered by the Treaty of Madrid (1526) in fact the claims were maintained, on account of the dubious moral status of that treaty, until Cateau-Cambrésis in 1559. On the East, there remained considerable uncertainty over the exact location of the boundary between French and Imperial lands, and some noblemen owed allegiance to both king and Emperor. Provence and the Dauphiné in the South East were still not fully integrated, the king ruling them by virtue of separate titles, and controlling them through their own institutions. In fact, France still showed many signs of the piecemeal way in which it had been assembled. There were also many relics of the country's feudal past, both theoretical and practical. Towns, corporate guilds, and even individual estates, might function as autonomous franchises rather than subjects of a sovereign. The ancient system of customary law also supported such a concept, because although it was maintained and administered in the king's name, it had grown out of the community which it served, and that origin was still recognised. Codification of the customary law began in the late fifteenth century, and was largely complete by the time of Francis's death. But codification, although it helped everyone to know what the law was, and prevented major incompatibilities between one place and the next, was not the same thing as uniformity. Francis had encouraged the use of Roman Law, because it was more consistent with the absolutist theories which he liked to promote, but France was not to be subjected to a single code of law until the Revolution. Even language was an obstacle to unity. Quite apart from Breton, and some German speaking minorities in the East, two main tongues were spoken. In the north, the *langue d'oil,* the ancestor of modern French, and in the south the *langue d'oc,* or Provençal, akin to modern Catalan. As late as the end of the fifteenth century the division was fairly even, but during the sixteenth century the use of the *langue d'oil* by the royal court and by the king's officials altered the balance. By 1550 the *parlements* of Toulouse, Aix and Bourdeaux used it, and it was becoming increasingly common in ordinary use by the aristocracy only Gascony and Provence remained largely unaffected.

There was no universally accepted theory of royal government, and certainly nothing that could be called constitutional law - except possibly the Salic law which not only debarred women from the throne, but also barred claims transmitted through women. Strictly speaking, a king's heir was his nearest male kinsman, which would be his son if he had one, but could be a fairly distant cousin - which was how Francis had inherited from the sonless Louis XII. Absolutist theory was widespread and influential, particularly Guillaume Budé's *L'Institution du Prince,* but it was by no means universally accepted - and certainly not acted upon. The same was true of the centralisation of royal government. A complete machinery of royal offices existed, but the officers tangled constantly with local privileges and immunities, so that the actual practice of government was a network of pragmatic compromises. Nowhere was this better illustrated than in the case of the *parlements. The parlements* were courts of law, with jurisdiction over defined areas, and had grown out of the autonomous courts of the old fiefs. They also had extensive administrative functions. As we have seen, the *parlements* were ultimately amenable to royal control, but all kings recognised such actions to be of last resort and in practice the *parlements* could often be obstructive, and sometimes win important concessions. By 1550 the average number of councillors in each *parlement* was about seventy, making about 600 for the whole country. The judges employed by these courts numbered some 3000, at a time when the population of France numbered about fifteen million.

Below the *parlement* in the hierarchy of local government came the *baillage* (also called *sénéchaussee*, of which there were about a hundred. The *bailli or sénéchal* was rather like the English sheriff, and commanded the feudal levy (which was virtually obsolete). The main work of administration was conducted by the tribunal of the *baillage*, which was presided over by the deputy-bailli, or Lieutenant. In January 1552 Henry II introduced a new tier of jurisdiction between the *parlements* and the *baillage*, called the *prisidiaux*, of which there were sixty-nine. Opposition to this move by the *parlements* was tough and protracted (although ultimately unsuccessful) and for good reason. In fact Henry created the whole system, not in the interests of justice, or speedier administration, but in order to sell the large number of offices so created. Francis had made the creation and sale of offices a regular part of his fiscal system, and at the end of his reign it was estimated that he was receiving 900,000 livres a year from that source. In 1515 there had been some 5000 royal officials in the whole kingdom; by 1546 that number had risen to 20,000, and by the middle of the following century to 55,000. Many were unnecessary, obstructing the processes of government with bureaucracy, and making the whole system unwieldy and expensive. Such offices were, in effect, *rentes,* and could not be abolished without compensation, which subsequent kings could not afford. Nevertheless, both the administrative and fiscal systems worked with reasonable efficiency. The main problem was that regular taxation never produced enough to pay for the regular and expensive wars in which both monarchs engaged, hence the need to sell offices, and raise loans from foreign bankers, particularly in Antwerp. Francis had just borrowed the large sum of 6m livres when he died - equivalent to nearly 70% of a year's income.

The fiscal system was complex, revenues being divided into 'ordinary' and 'extraordinary'. The former consisted of the profits of the royal lands, and of the courts of justice, where these belonged to the king. The latter was direct and indirect taxation, particularly the *taille, gabelle* and *aides. The tailles* produced about half the 9m livres per annum which Francis's extraordinary revenue was bringing in at the end of his reign. The *gabelle,* produced about 6% and the various *aides,* which included both clerical taxation and duties on the sale of goods, about 17%. For the administration of ordinary revenue, France was divided into four regions, each supervised by a *trésorier de France,* with a team of subordinate officials. Extraordinary revenue was administered under two different systems, as we have seen. The *pays d'états* ran their own, and the rest of France was divided into four *généralises,* each under a *généraux des finances.* These in turn were divided into *élections,* each under an élu who was in effect a royal commissioner. Francis modified this traditional structure in two ways. In 1523 he created an official called the *trésorier de l'Epargne,* with responsibility for all casual revenues (such as loans); and in 1542 he introduced sixteen *recettes generales* as an intermediary layer between the *généralités* and the *elections.* The system which existed in 1550 was more centralised and more effective than that of 1515, but it still did not produce enough income for war Henry II, who started his reign deeply in debt, and got steadily further enmeshed, attempted in 1555 to set up a system of consolidated domestic loans, promising repayment at 20% per annum. This was known as the *Grand Parti de Lyons.* Not surprisingly, he defaulted after only two years, and when he died in 1559 was twelve million livres in debt and for all practical purposes bankrupt.

Financial embarrassment was not the only problem to have been created by the long wars. Prolonged war always worked to the political advantage of the major aristocratic families, whose high social status, military training and substantial private resources all made them indispensable to their kings. Francis, who himself enjoyed high military prestige, had managed to control this situation but his death revealed that this had been a personal ascendency. By 1551 Henry was allowing, and indeed, encouraging, the development of a situation which was fraught with potential danger, the emergence of three families whose clientage networks spread throughout France. The first of these were the Montmorencys, the family of his personal favourite Anne de Montmorency, the Constable of France; the second were the Guises led by the ambitious and able soldier Francis, Count of Aumâle, whom he created Duke of Guise; and the third were the Bourbons. This family had been virtually destroyed by Francis after the treason of the constable in 1523, but had then been rehabilitated, partly by the terms of the Treaty of Madrid. In 1550 they were led by Duke Anthony, who in 1555 became king of Navarre in right of his wife, Jeanne d'Albret, daughter of Francis's sister, Margaret of Angoulême; his son Henry was consequently a prince of the blood. As long as Henry lived, he kept these ambitious clans in a rough equipoise, but the defeat of Montmorency at St. Quentin in 1557, and the great victory of Guise at Calais six months later gave the latter an ascendency which he was quick to exploit. The marriage of his niece, Mary of Scotland to the Dauphin Francis in 1558 also brought him close to the royal family and encouraged further ambitions.

The dangers of this situation were increased by two additional factors. It was not only the king whose finances had suffered from the wars. Heavy taxation had damaged both trade and agriculture, and old economic centres such as Lyons were severely affected, leading to steep rises in unemployment and widespread social discontent. Only the west coast, open to the developing trade of the Atlantic, largely escaped the depression. At the same time many minor noblemen had served in the king's wars for honour, and in the hope of reward, rather than for regular pay. The disaster of St. Quentin left scores of them with heavy ransoms to find, and no prospect of recovering their losses. Disillusioned with the king, they naturally gravitated towards one or other of the great clientage networks, looking for an opportunity to escape from the heavy burdens of debt which the wars had landed upon them, and which the cessation of wars meant could no longer be lifted by a new twist of military fortune. More seriously still, economic and political grievances helped to create a welcoming audience for the Calvinist preachers who began to enter France from Geneva around 1555. Hitherto the reformation in France had lacked clarity, both of content and direction. In the early 1520s a humanist circle, led intellectually by Jacques Lefevre-d'Étaples, and politically by Guillaume Briçonnet, the bishop of Meaux, had enjoyed considerable influence at court. Marguerite de Valois, the king's sister was their chief patron, and Francis himself was sporadically interested. The extensive control over ecclesiastical affairs which the king had secured by the Concordat of Bologna not only meant that the French church was effectively his private domain but also that it was unusually corrupted by secular priorities. Had humanist influences been allowed to develop undisturbed, they might well have led to a major catholic reform movement under royal control. However, the prospect for this was ruined by the condemnation of Luther, and the almost simultaneous appearance of large quantities of his writings in France. The ultra-conservative theological faculty of Paris - the Sorbonne - took fright, and executions for heresy began in August 1523. When Francis was captured in 1525 his protection was withdrawn from the circle of Meaux. Some, including Briçonnet, were charged with heresy and forced to recant; others fled. For some time after Francis's return the *parlements* were hotter in their pursuit of heresy than was the king, but after 1534, when the so-called 'affair of the Placards' seems to have awoken him to the true implications of radical religious dissent, the king himself became a fierce, although sporadic, persecutor. It was this persecution that drove many reformers (mostly influenced by the South German preachers rather than by Luther himself) into exile. One of these was John Calvin, who eventually found refuge in Geneva, and issued from there in 1541 his *Institutes of the Christian Religion,* with a hopeful dedication to Francis. Henry II was a more consistent and committed persecutor than his father, and established soon after his accession an additional chamber of the Paris *parlement* - the so-called *chambre ardente* - to deal with cases of heresy. This did not last long, but neither the king nor the *parlements* flagged in their efforts. As so often in such cases, heresy appeared to thrive on persecution. Calvin and most of his fellow exiles in Geneva were French speaking, and their ideas soon became characteristic of French reformers. In 1555 Calvin established in Geneva the Company of Pastors, specifically to train missionaries for the French field, and within three years they were making a considerable impact. Protestant ideas spread rapidly among two main groups - urban artisans and the aristocracy. The latter, with natural qualities of leadership, soon became the protectors and patrons of the new churches. Unlike Lutheranism, Calvinism thrived in adversity, and new congregations developed rapidly; in 1556 at Blois; in 1557 in Bourges, Rouen, Caen, La Rochelle, Lyons, Aix, Bordeaux, Issoudun and Anduze; in 1558 at Dieppe, Le Havre, Tours, Saintes, Montargis, Marsellies, Bergerac, and several other places. The speed of the infection astonished everyone, and it reached to the highest aristocratic levels. Jeanne d'Albret, the Queen of Navarre and effective leader of the house of Bourbon, became a convert, as did several members of the Montmorency family, including Gaspard de Coligny, the Constable's nephew. Religion thus added its own potent ingredient to the fierce aristocratic rivalry which was surging up under Henry's feet by 1559, and which his death in that year unleashed upon the minority government of his son.

21. The Council of Trent

The General council had been an occasional method of resolving major problems in the church since the fourth century AD, Roughly speaking, it was an assembly of bishops, and the theory was that it represented the collective wisdom of the church, as informed by the Holy Spirit. Consequently the papacy had often found such councils difficult to handle, both in theory and in practice, especially since the development of the papal monarchy in the eleventh century. That problem had been particularly acute since the Council of Constance in the early fifteenth century. That Council had been called by the Emperor to put an end to the schism, and had done so successfully, but its success raised almost as many questions as it answered. Constance had failed in its secondary objective of reforming the church, and by burning the Bohemian reformer John Hus as a heretic, had created a national reform movement which was soon a thorn in the flesh of both Pope and Emperor. More important, however, it had left unresolved the question of the relationship between the revived Papacy and any future Council. Over the next 30 years a fully fledged conciliar theory had developed, which claimed that the representative nature of the Council, and the Divine origin of episcopal and priestly orders meant that the Council was the true and only vehicle of the Holy Spirit, and that in consequence the Pope was simply an executive officer, appointed by the church to provide unity and continuity of direction. This view had been effectively defeated by the Papacy after the Council of Basle in the mid-fifteenth century, not least because it was impossible to keep a council permanently in being, and no one could agree what its standing element might be. However, the situation remained precarious in the early sixteenth century. The renaissance popes made many enemies, and the calls for reform became loud and insistent well before Luther. In 1512 a Lateran Council had been called, but it had not achieved much. A Lateran Council was clearly a papal instrument, and by that time there were many who believed that the basic problem was at the top and could not be solved by such means. In 1520 Luther had appealed to a General Council against his sentence of excommunication, and by the time that Clement VII became Pope in 1523, the pressure was growing on all sides.

It did not succeed, because the Pope was determined that there would be no Council, and because the political circumstances were particularly unfavourable. Clement feared a council, not only because he feared another major challenge to his authority, but also because his own position was not entirely secure. Having been born out of wedlock, his ordination as a priest had depended upon a dispensation which could have been challenged; and there had been persistent rumours of scandal about his election, which he did not wish to have investigated. Quite apart from Clement's opposition, however, a General Council depended for its credibility and usefulness upon being genuinely representative of the church. With the Habsburg and the Valois perpetually at loggerheads, it was a hopeless prospect to get German, Spanish and French bishops together, to say nothing of those from French and Imperial controlled parts of Italy. The bishops could not travel without the consent of their Lords, and Francis and Charles took it in turn to be obstructive. At the same time, the Papal Curia formed a political battlefield as Valois and Hapsburg strove for ascendency. There were French and Imperial parties among the Cardinals, and each party brought pressure to bear upon the Pope to increase its strength. After the French defeat at Pavia, and even more after the inadvertent sack of Rome in 1527, it appeared that the Emperor's ascendancy was so complete that he could have forced the calling of a Council - indeed Ferdinand wrote to his brother urging just such a course. However, Charles had no appetite for a council at that point; he was still hoping to solve the Lutheran problem within Germany, and to have made his control over the Pope too blatant would have alienated the Italians and the English as well as the French. So Clement managed to evade a Council until his death in 1534, by which time the Schmalkaldic League had been formed in Germany, and the English schism had begun.

Another Pope like Clement VII, and the church might very well have fallen apart. However, the conclave following Clement's death elected Cardinal Alessandro Farnese at Paul III. Paul was by no means a saintly man. He was a humanist who had been brought up at the court of Lorenzo de Medici, a Roman aristocrat, and a man with many youthful indiscretions behind him. However, he was intelligent and energetic, and realised the urgency of the situation in which he had been placed. So, in spite of adding two adolescent grandsons to the College of Cardinals, he quickly announced his commitment to a General Council, and more tangibly, appointed a whole group of intellectually distinguished Cardinals of reforming inclinations - Contarini, Pole, Sadoleto, Caraffa, Morone. In 1536 Paul took two important initiatives; he appointed a commission of theologians to examine the state of the church, and he summoned a General Council to meet at Mantua. In the event, the latter move amounted to little more than an earnest of good intentions, because the summons coincide with a fresh outbreak of Franco-Habsburg war, and when only a handful of prelates turned up, the project was abandoned. The Commission, however, reported the following year, and its report contained a searching indictment of the worldliness, not only of the church at large, but particularly of earlier Popes. The sale of clerical offices and benefices was denounced as the 'Trojan Horse', from which all other abuses had sprung - a vice to which the renaissance papacy had been particularly prone. In the event, Paul did very little to cure fiscal and administrative abuses, probably because of the tough resistance of his own officials, but he did persevere with his efforts to summon a General Council. In May 1542 a second attempt was made, summoning the bishops to Trent, a city which was easily accessible from Rome but within the frontiers of the Empire. However, the experience of 1536 was almost exactly repeated. War broke out, both Charles and Francis refused their support, and the assembly date in November 1542 passed with hardly anyone present. Early in 1543 the Council was postponed. The Pope did not give up. Once the Peace of Crespy had brought an end to the war in 1544, he tried again, and at long last the Council opened at Trent on December 13, 1545. What followed was to be an extraordinary saga, because the Council of Trent was to stretch through three sessions, covering almost twenty years (1545-7, 1551-2, and 1562-3). It ran through five pontificates, and saw the Religious Peace of Augsburg (1555), the division of the Habsburg Empire (1555-6), the end of the wars (1559), and the beginning of the collapse of France. It also saw the ending and renewal of the English schism (1554, 1559), and the rise of Calvinism in France, Scotland and the Low Countries. Most of those who participated in the early sessions were dead by the time the Council closed, and it ended in a very different spirit from that which had prevailed at its opening. Nevertheless it was a single Council, and an extraordinary product of ecclesiastical statesmanship. The main problem throughout, except in the final sessions, was to maintain credibility by attracting a large enough attendance. At the beginning there were only thirty-one bishops, together with about fifty theological advisers and canon lawyers, who did not vote. The total number of bishops present at any time during the three sessions was only two hundred and seventy, and there can seldom have been more than fifty at any given time. Moreover their geographical spread was very uneven. Only a handful attended from northern Europe, and although England and Scandinavia were predominantly protestant, that was not true of Germany or the Low Countries. There the charitable explanation is that good catholic bishops were too busy fighting heresy at home to go gallivanting to Trent, but the true reason is more likely to have been inertia and secular preoccupations. Thirty-one Spanish bishops showed up at one time or another, and twenty French, but the vast majority - over one hundred and eighty - were Italians. There were several reasons for this. One was simply that they were nearer; another that there were far more of them to be available, since Italian sees were mostly very small. Because the sees were small, the revenues of Italian bishops also tended to be small, and many of them ran a profitable sidelines by acting as papal officials. It did not necessarily follow that all Italian bishops were amenable to papal pressure - that was certainly not true of the Venetians or Neapolitans - but it did mean that papal policy could usually count on solid backing whenever it came to a vote. This meant in turn that the pope's official theological advisers wielded a great deal of influence, and also that it would have been very difficult for any conciliarist pressure group to have attacked the papal leadership.

In fact one of the most significant features of the Council of Trent was the extent to which it remained amenable throughout to papal guidance and control - so much so that it was said at one point that when the Fathers at Trent sought the inspiration of the Holy Spirit, it was brought in a knapsack from Rome. This was not simply the result of 'rentacrowd' among the Italian bishops. The quality of the papal agents and advisers throughout was exceptionally high; in the first sessions Gian Maria del Monte, Marcello Cervini and Reginald Pole; in the second Marcello Crescenzi; and in the third Augustinian Scripando, Stanislaus Hosius and Giovanni Morone. Some of these men were reformers, and some conservatives, but all were men of exceptional ability and integrity. Such characteristics were not universal among the members of the College of Cardinals, so some of the credit must go to the popes themselves, who nominated them. A similar comment could be made about the *consultores,* or expert theological advisers. These were drawn mostly from the new order of the Society of Jesus, and from the Dominicans. The former were conspicuous for their spiritual and pastoral devotion, and the latter for the intellectual thrust and unity of the revived Thomist theology which they represented. The Council was never free from political interference, nor from internecine strife which occasionally descended to verbal abuse, and even to violence. So it is not surprising that when two hundred and fifty-five prelates and theologians subscribed to the final Decrees in 1563, there were many who declared that God had wrought a miracle on behalf of his church.

When the Council opened, there was immediate disagreement between the Legates, who represented the Pope's priority for doctrinal definition, and the Proctors of the Emperor, who called for the priority of reform. Officially the council compromised by deciding to deal with both together, but in practice it confined itself almost entirely to definition, and every definition was explicitly or implicitly hostile to Lutheran ideas. The most important (and longest) decree to be drafted during this period was that on Justification, asserting the freedom of the human will, and the validity of good works for salvation. This highly conservative definition was strongly opposed by many reformers, including Pole, who shortly after its passage in January 1547 withdrew from the council on the plea of ill-heath. The reformers were similarly, although less decisively, rebuffed over scriptural translation. Having reaffirmed the traditional view that both tradition and scripture were authoritative in the church, the Council then went on to reaffirm the validity of the Vulgate text, despite the numerous errors of translation which had been identified by humanist scholars over the previous century. This decision was less perverse than it might appear, considering that the church had always represented itself as being under the guidance of the Holy Spirit, but it was a grievous disappointment to the humanists, and another cause of Pole's chagrin. The council made no pronouncement on vernacular translations, but it gave no priority to scriptural studies, and clearly implied an endorsement of scholastic techniques - an endorsement which was to be repeated later in the decree on education. In another decree of the same session, the validity of all seven sacraments, and their *ex opera operate* character were also asserted, thus not only rejecting the Lutheran position, but also emphasising strongly the unique intercessory powers of the priesthood. By the time that the council was disrupted by war and plague in April 1547 only one gesture had been made towards reform - the condemnation of pluralism and non-residence - and it was perfectly clear that the church was not bent on reconciliation, but on victory.

The second session, held under Paul's successor Julius III (del Monte) was more politicised, and less productive. Upon the Emperor's insistence, protestant representations were invited. Few came, and their appearance achieved nothing but to demonstrate the pointlessness of such attempted dialogue. The only important decree to be prepared was that on the Eucharist, which reaffirmed the mediaeval doctrine of transubstantiation, but did not attempt to elaborate upon the scholastic philosophical propositions which supported it. This session was brought to an end by the rebellion of Duke Maurice of Saxony, which caught the Emperor completely by surprise, and sent the council scattering in undignified confusion. It did not reassemble for ten years, thanks largely to the hostile pontificate of Paul IV. As Cardinal Caraffa, Paul had been a zealous reformer of the conservative variety, but advancing age had made him increasingly fanatical and suspicious. He was responsible for the Roman Inquisition and for the Index of Prohibited books. By 1555 he was deeply suspicious of the Council, and wished to pursue a reforming programme by his own executive action. His successor, Pius IV, was rather like Paul III; his corrupt youth was followed by a reforming old age. He smashed the Caraffa faction in the Curia, and promoted his own saintly and distinguished nephew, Carlo Borromeo, who was to become one of the greatest leaders of the Counter Reformation. Pius realised that political interference was much less likely in the changed European situation, and took steps to reassemble the council. The final session opened at Trent in January 1562 and immediately embarked upon a fierce debate as to whether it was the same council as that which has dissolved so precipitately in 1552, or a new one. Since none of the earlier decrees had been ratified, the point was a substantial one. Should they carry on where they had left off, or begin again? The Emperor Ferdinand, who disliked the dogmatism of the early decrees, wanted a fresh start, but Pius was determined upon continuation, and his will prevailed. In spite of this decision, the atmosphere was quite different from that of ten years before. Firstly, the Spanish bishops (attending in strength for the first time) resurrected the old bogey of conciliarism, and were supported by some of the French, who were equally anxious for the continued autonomy of their national church. The issue was raised by the innocuous seeming question of whether the residence of bishops in their sees (which everyone wanted), was a matter of Divine law, or merely of ecclesiastical law. It took all Morone's presidential skill, and the voting strength of the Italians, to get the matter referred to the Pope for a decision, thus reaffirming the anti-conciliar position. The main theological achievement of 1562 was the reaffirmation and definition of the sacrificial character of the mass. Reforming proposals of heretical taint, such as communion in both kinds and clerical marriage, which were prompted by the anxious governments of Ferdinand and Catherine de Médici, who were struggling to reach accommodation with powerful protestant movements, were consistently rejected. As the session progressed the Pope's critics became increasingly divided among themselves, the French and Spanish falling out with particular violence, and the Legates' programme went steadily ahead. The most important of the late decrees were those reaffirming the doctrine of purgatory and establishing training seminaries in every diocese. If the former was backward looking, the latter was to prove one of the most positive and progressive decisions to emerge from these momentous debates. Finally, just before the Council dissolved in December 1563, it confirmed all the decrees of the earlier sessions, referred all outstanding business to the Pope, and asked for his ratification of its whole body of legislation.

Not only did the Council thus result in a redefined and reactivated body of catholic doctrine, and in an unequivocal declaration of war on all heretics, it also confirmed and gave increased substance to the role of the Pope. In the war which it was now determined to fight and win, the church needed unitary leadership, even if the price was high in some respects. Against all the odds the embarrassing and feeble Papacy of Leo X and Clement VII had become an agency for renewed spiritual drive and discipline. It would never again be the office of Gregory VII or Innocent III, but it was morally and theologically respectable, and its authority was recognised more fully than at any time since the beginning of the schism in the fourteenth century.

22. Portugal, Spain and the New World

The Portuguese had pioneered a massive expansion of European commercial and political horizons in the latter part of the fifteenth century. Having opened up the sea route from Europe to India, they set out to wrest control of the lucrative trade of the Indian Ocean from the Muslim merchants who had controlled it for centuries. Thanks to the military efforts of the second viceroy of the Indies Alfonso de Albuquerque, by 1520 Portuguese control of the whole of the lucrative sea borne trade of India was virtually complete, and for a few years the king of Portugal was the richest monarch in Western Europe.

However, between 1520 and 1550 the situation had slowly deteriorated. It proved virtually impossible for the Crown to enforce its monopoly, despite the fact that the government office which ran the enterprise, the Estado da India, remained a commercial rather than an Imperial department. The military burden of retaining the possessions and the supremacy which had been quickly if not easily won, proved too great for a country which was always short of manpower. The immunity which was enjoyed by Portuguese gentry from prosecutions for all minor crimes and misdemeanours encouraged the ill-discipline to which they were in any case prone, and stimulated corruption. It was not until 1544 that a High Court and a Chancery for India were established, and by then the administration had become chronically corrupt and inefficient. Part of the trouble was the pioneering spirit, which made local officials extremely difficult to control. In the early days their independent enterprise had often had beneficial effects, particularly in the spread of Portuguese interests into Java and Indo-China between 1510 and 1520; but such independence was much less valuable for a settled system. There was also a lack of resolute control on the part of the Crown. The king's interests were represented by a five man royal council, but no single official in Portugal had complete oversight until the appointment of an India secretary in 1569. The woes of the Portuguese in the mid-century were compounded by other factors. From 1540 the Levantine trade began to revive as Ottoman relations with Venice and France improved, and in 1548 the Portuguese base in Antwerp was closed down, thus reducing access to the main European money market. By the late 1560s half Europe's spice imports were again coming through the Mediterranean; in 1569 King Sebastian was forced to suspend payments in Antwerp, and in the following year the royal monopoly was abandoned. From 1575 the spice trade was farmed out, but the first farmer, Konrad Roth, a German, was bankrupt by 1580.

In that year the childless Sebastian died, and Philip II of Spain made good his claim to the inheritance. This should have meant that the struggling Portuguese empire in the far east could benefit from the successful Imperial experience of the Spaniards; but this did not happen because of Philip's undertaking to allow Portugal and its dominions to retain a large measure of autonomy under his overall control. Politically necessary in Europe, this undertaking was a handicap in the East, and Goa increasingly went its own way. The Viceroy raised and spent his own revenues, recruited local troops, and built his own ships. In one sense this led to a sensible *modus vivendi,* and the Portuguese became, perforce, much less of an Imperial intrusion in the area, but it also meant diminishing control over the trade routes. There was less strife from the numerous local accommodations which were worked out, but also much less profit. Only in one way did the Spanish connection make a major impact. Portugal became embroiled in Spain's wars with England and The Netherlands. The annual sailings of four or five large carracks from Calicut to Lisbon thus became subject to the depredations of English and Dutch pirates. Of the five which made the voyage in 1592, two foundered off the African coast and two were intercepted by the English. Of the latter, one ran aground and was lost and the other, the famous *Madre de Dios,* was captured intact. The Portuguese also provided one of the more effective squadrons in the Armada, and the English tried unsuccessfully to support the claims of Sebastian's illegitimate nephew, Dom Antonio, to the Portuguese Crown. In the early years of the seventeenth century both the Dutch and the English moved decisively into far eastern trade, and the Portuguese position was further undermined, as a number of their forts fell to the newcomers. At first the Dutch were much more successful, and that continued to be the case in the East Indies, although the English were eventually more successful in the sub-continent itself. Nevertheless the Portuguese hung on, even expanding their operations to China after 1545, and the residual impact of the Catholic church in the Portuguese territories was considerable, particularly that of the religious orders. In its prime the Portuguese far eastern Empire was a remarkable achievement, and the great cartographical offices which was established in Goa put the whole geography of the area upon a new level of knowledge and sophistication, but it proved impossible to retain control over such valuable information, and by the end of the century the maps which had given the Iberians such a decisive advantage were equally guiding their rivals and enemies.

The origin of Spain's interest in colonial expansion is too well known to need repetition. A first the Spaniards had shared much of the same motivation - a 'hangover' from the conquest of the last Moorish strongholds in Spain in 1492, and a desire to find a sea route to the east. However, what they found was central America, and when they signed the treaty of Tordesillas with the Portuguese in 1494, and accepted the papal division of the world into two spheres of influence, it seemed that they had received the rough end of the deal. The Portuguese had only been interested in colonies as a means to secure control of an existing trade and had never expanded them further than that control required. In the West Indies there was no existing trade to control, and settlement was essential to extract any wealth, agricultural or mineral, from the region discovered. Nevertheless, a dramatic change had come between 1519 and 1521 with the discovery and conquest of the Aztec empire by Herman Cortes. The Aztecs were not an ancient civilisation, and in some respects remained primitive, but they were wealthy, high developed in some arts and sciences, and militarily vulnerable. Most importantly, they controlled a well established system of tribute and labour services from a large population which was thoroughly accustomed to semi-servitude. What Cortes did was to replace one small warrior aristocracy with another, duplicating most of the features of the Aztec supremacy with conscientious accuracy. He destroyed the capital city, Tenochtitian, and built his own capital, Mexico City, on the site. Temples made way for cathedrals and monasteries. Above all, he took over the tribute and labour services, which formed the basis of the system of *encomiendas*. These were like great feudal estates, granted at first to the *conquistadores* themselves, and later to the Spanish colonists (most of them of hidalgo stock) who followed them out. Spanish society was urban in nature, and the colonists themselves mostly settled in newly founded cities, which formed the basis of government, and bore a striking resemblance to the cities of Castile. Here were based the *corregidors,* or royal officials who governed in the name of the king and the viceroy. So the Spaniards tended to live in the towns, and draw their income from the countryside, from agriculture or ranching. *Encomiendas* were often large - anything form 2000 to 20,000 dependent households. The system was simple, and reasonably effective, and was accompanied by a thoroughgoing missionary campaign, run mainly by the mendicant orders. Their principle was much the same as that of the *conquistadores,* to adapt as much as possible of the existing sense of the sacred to their own faith. They used the same sites, and many of the same festivals, producing a type of catholicism which was colourful, extrovert, and full of rather primitive symbolism.

However, neither the church nor the Spanish crown found the aggressive and avaricious colonial society easy to control. The colonists were more exacting taskmasters than their Aztec predecessors, and the Indian population declined steeply in the middle years of the century, thanks to overwork and European diseases. In the islands the labour shortage became acute, and by the 1560s the colonists were defying their government to purchase consignments of African slaves, which were being illegally imported by the Portuguese and the English. Elsewhere the colonists did their best to reduce the surviving Indians to slavery, especially those who had resisted conversion to Christianity, on the grounds that they were not proper human beings anyway. The church, and particularly the Dominicans, to their credit resisted this strongly, with the support of the Crown. Partly as a result of this restraint, and partly because of their own natural ambition and restlessness, the *conquistadores* were constantly in search of new lands to conquer. Between 1530 and 1533 Francisco Pizzaro repeated Cortes success by conquering the Inca empire in what is now Peru, while a series of other expeditions (often illicit in origin) opened up the whole of central America, from Columbia to California to settlement. The search was usually for gold and silver, and both were found in large quantities, particularly silver, but the most immediate result was the development of large new colonies. As the *conquistadores* spread, the government relentlessly pursued them - the lawyer treading hard upon the heels of the soldier. After what was often quite a short period of pioneering freedom, a new *audiencia* or royal court would be set up to control each settled region. By the end of the sixteenth century there were ten such courts in the new world; San Domingo (1526), Mexico (1527), Panama (1535), Lima (1542), Guatemala (1543), New Galicia (1548), New Granada (1549), Charcas (1559), Quito (1563) and Manilla (in the Philippines, 1583). The priest and the friar also trod hard upon the soldiers' heels, and a network of missions and dioceses accompanied the establishment of the *audiencias*.

By 1540, thanks partly to the impact of Las Casas exposure of 'human rights' abuse, the Spanish crown had determined to end the *encomienda* system, and in 1542 it was decreed that no more were to be created, and that existing rights should revert to the Crown on the deaths of the holders. They were replaced by a system of leases and temporary grants, and although forced labour did not cease it was brought under royal control and the worst abuses of the former system were remedied. At least, that was true in respect of agricultural labour, and the new *haciendas* or plantations were run with wage labour (or in some cases with African slaves). However, in the mining industry the situation was more recalcitrant, partly because the stakes were higher. Peru in particular, was almost entirely dependent upon the production of silver, which made it one of the most valuable provinces of the Empire. Mexico produced both gold and silver, and it had been Mexican gold which had first reflected the impact of the New World upon the economy of the old, but it was the discovery of the great silver mines at Potosi in 1540 which transformed the bullion trade. In 1520 bullion to the value of about 1000 pesos (mainly Mexican gold) had been shipped across the Atlantic). By 1545 this had risen to about 5000 pesos. By 1580 it had reached 30,000 pesos, before peaking at 35,000 in 1590, and then gradually falling back to about 8000 by 1650. The importance of this trade was very great even though, as is now generally agreed, it was not the only factor in producing the great European inflation of the sixteenth century. The mines consumed labour far more voraciously than the sugar or tobacco plantations, and attempts to improve the situation consistently failed. The crucial importance of the trade to the Spanish crown - it contributed about 15% of Philip II's total revenue by the 1580s - caused it to become a tightly controlled monopoly, exercised through the *casa de contratacion* in Seville. It also became an irresistible lure to Spain's enemies, both official and unofficial. The English successfully attacked Cartagena and other colonial cities in 1585-7, and captured some silver, but failed to take the heavily guarded flota. Thereafter the efficiency (and the cost) of colonial defence increased considerably, and when the English tried again in 1596 they were decisively repulsed. A decade later the Dutch were more successful, and on one occasion captured the entire fleet. But the main story of the Spanish New World in the early seventeenth century is similar to that of Spain itself - bureaucratic maturity, but economic and demographic decline. By about

1620 the Spanish American trade was largely in the hands of Italian, Dutch and English merchants, operating through sleeping partners in Seville, and Spain itself was deriving little benefit from it, while continuing to bear the costs of administration and defence. Nevertheless, unlike the Portuguese, it proved to be a remarkably durable Empire, which stamped its mark indelibly upon the whole continent.

23. Cateau-Cambrésis and its consequences

The treaty which ended the long Habsburg/Valois war was not satisfactory to any of its signatories. The French had little cause to be satisfied, because although they had retained Calais, and the three border bishoprics, they had lost most of Savoy, and with it any real voice in northern Italy. The English were disgruntled, and the advantage to Philip was mainly negative - he had managed to keep the French out of Milan and Lombardy. Most people at the time regarded it as little more than a truce, necessitated by financial exhaustion, and to be repudiated as soon as convenience served. In fact it kept the peace of central Europe until 1618. The main reason for this had nothing to do with the merits of the peace; it was the collapse of France into civil war, beginning with the death of Francis II in 1560 and lasting until the Edict of Nantes in 1598. Without France, the power of Philip II could only be challenged by a shifting coalition of opponents - the Barbary Corsairs, the Ottomans, the Dutch and the English -and the theatres of war became the Mediterranean, the Atlantic and the Low Countries. With each of these we shall be concerned in due course. My main purpose now is to look at the Empire in the late sixteenth century, in the lull between two storms caused by the Imperial ambitions of Charles V and Ferdinand II. From the accession of Ferdinand I in 1558 to the death of his grandson Rudolf in 1612 ambition was scarcely the order of the day - it was more a question of keeping the show on the road - but it was nevertheless an important period of development. In spite of losing the Netherlands and Milan to Philip, Ferdinand deployed an impressive range of titles when he succeeded to the Empire (by election, although that was a formality) on Charles' death. Most important in terms of resources were the family lands of Upper and Lower Austria, and the Alpine provinces of Tyrol, Styria, Carinthia and Carniola. Less important, except strategically, were the remaining Habsburg lands along the Upper Rhine, such as Alsace. His remaining possessions, the kingdoms of Bohemia and Hungary, sounded most impressive, but in practice added little to his power. Most of Hungary was in the hands, either of the Ottomans or of the Princes of Transylvania who owed allegiance to them. What little remained was dominated by a fractious aristocracy - and the same was true of Bohemia. Apart from these somewhat shadowy crowns, Ferdinand held no more than his grandfather Maximilian had inherited from his great grandfather Frederick. He was the victim of family custom as much as of his brother's Imperial policy, but it was a custom which he showed no inclination to repudiate. In spite of making a number of rather feeble attempts to introduce a centralised system of government for his scattered patrimony, on his death in 1564 he divided his lands between his three sons. The youngest, Charles, received Styria, Carinthia and Carniola; the second, Ferdinand, received Tyrol and the lands in South West Germany; which left the eldest, Maximilian, only Upper and Lower Austria. Maximilian duly succeeded to the Imperial title, and Crowns of Bohemia and Hungary, but was able to do little even to combat the Ottoman threat, let alone pursue any effective Imperial policy in his relations with the German princes. The Habsburg family alliance, although it was real enough, could not begin to supply the defects of such a ramshackle political system.

This situation should warn us not to think of the sixteenth century Habsburgs, in spite of their policy of matrimonial conquest, as bureaucratic monarchs of an eighteenth century type. Had Charles, or Philip, left more than one legitimate son, their territories might have been even more quickly fragmented. Although they had a strong sense of dynastic unity and purpose, they seem to have had little sense of the political integrity of states. This was no doubt partly the result of the way in which the patrimony had been assembled, and partly of the recalcitrant political realities with which they had to deal. The career of Philip II, both in Spain and the Low Countries, suggests that his attitude may have been different, but he was not put to the ultimate test of having several heirs. With the death of Maximilian II in 1576 a *reductio ad absurdum* was threatened, because he left six sons. However, common-sense at last prevailed, and instead of reducing them all to the level of petty counts, he converted to primogeniture and left his whole estate to his eldest, Rudolf. Nevertheless in 1578 Rudolf was compelled to buy off the claim of his five brothers, who were by no means anxious to see the political sense of what had happened. At the same time there was another side to this dynasticism. From 1568 when his eldest son Don Carlos died, until 1578 when the future Philip III was born, Philip of Spain had no direct heir, and had he died during that period, Maximilian or Rudolf would have succeeded him. They were strongly aware of that possibility, and for that reason did not allow their policies to stray too far in any direction which might have jeopardised their acceptability in the peninsula.

Two conflicts dominated Imperial policy over these sixty years, and determined most of the internal politics of Germany. The first was that against the ever-threatening Turks, and the second the strenuous efforts of the catholic church to recover the ground which it had lost between 1520 and 1555. Ferdinand I inherited a war on his eastern flank, which he was able to bring to an end in 1562, largely because Sulieman was preoccupied with other problems, but only at the cost of confirming all the latter's conquests, and paying a tribute which left him at the mercy of the Diet and his various provincial estates. Nor did such humiliation lead to any real security. In 1566 Sulieman was back in Hungary at the head of an army, the pretext having been provided by some double dealing on the part of the Prince of Transylvania. On that occasion the situation was saved by the Sultan's death, and the treaty of 1562 was renewed in 1568. It soon transpired that Sulieman's successor Selim II (known as 'the sot' for obvious reasons) was not the man his father had been, and the formal peace lasted until 1593. However, the distinction between war and peace on that frontier was hazy, as the local Ottoman commanders kept their own forces happy with constant raiding, no matter what the official situation. This meant that Maximilian and Rudolf had to bear the expense of a constant, if fairly low key, state of military preparedness, along with the burden of the tribute which they were supposedly paying to keep the peace. This meant that the Emperor never appeared without his begging bowl, and although the efforts of his Spanish cousin on the Mediterranean front took a little of the pressure off him, Philip had no funds to spare for direct subventions. He was consequently left in the same position that Charles V had often been in, of having to make political and religious concessions in return for funds. It was not until 1606 that the treaty of Sitvatorok brought some relief by bringing the tribute system to an end. The Turks were not as strong as they had been, and were operating at the limit of their communications system, but there was still no question of recovering territory and indeed a little more was lost.

The second major conflict of the period was far more complex, and its importance within Germany can hardly be overestimated. It took its form, and much of its bitterness, from the settlement which had ended the previous round of religious wars - the Peace of Augsburg. In the first place, that treaty had been between the catholics and the Lutherans - no protestants who did not subscribe to the Confession of Augsburg were entitled to benefit from it - and the Calvinists were the most dynamic and fast growing protestant group after 1550. Secondly, the principle of territorial autonomy, *cuius regio, eius religio,* created a permanent breach in the Imperial constitution. And thirdly the 'ecclesiastical reservation' (which was a part of the Recess of the Diet, but never accepted by the protestants) declared that no further secularisation of church property was to occur, and that any catholic prelate who became converted must automatically resign his see. In view of the fact that three of the seven Electors were bishops, and that three of the four secular Electors were already protestants, the point of this is not far to seek. It should also be remembered that when the Grand Master of the Teutonic order became a protestant in 1525, he had converted the lands of the order into an hereditary Duchy for himself and his family - the Duchy of East Prussia. Because of these factors, the whole pattern of religious conflict was different after 1555. Instead of armed conflict between states, it took the form of social and civil conflict within states. In Hungary, for example, little attempt had ever been made to stop the spread of protestant views, although the ruling Habsburgs remained consistently loyal to Rome, and were supported by a section of the nobility. In 1606 Rudolf was at last forced to concede full toleration, not only to Lutherans, but also to Calvinists. Similarly in Bohemia the German townspeople were mostly Lutheran and the Czech nobility mostly Hussite, in spite of the missionary efforts of the Jesuits the catholics remained a disorganised minority.

Within the Empire proper, however, the story was rather different. The Habsburg heartlands of Austria, Carinthia and Carniola had been heavily infiltrated by the reformers, both townspeople and nobility being affected. However, imperial authority was somewhat more effective in these lands, and although as late as 1571 the Austrian nobility were able to insist upon the freedom to use a Lutheran liturgy, by the 1590s the tide had turned, and such concessions began to be withdrawn. One reason for this was that a bloodthirsty peasant revolt, provoked by taxation for the Turkish war (1594-7) drew the government and the nobility strongly together; another was the exceptional energy of the revived catholic church, under such leaders as Melchior Khlesl and Peter Canisius. Starting with the foundation of the *Collegium Germanicum* in Rome to train clergy for the German mission, successive Popes gave a high priority to the recovery of the Imperial lands. In 1573 the *Congregatio Germanica* was also established as a headquarters for the same campaign, and within Germany itself the main centre was the University of Ingolstadt in Bavaria, which was strongly under Jesuit influence. It was men trained in these institutions who began to found new catholic schools and seminaries in the last quarter of the century, and effectively turned the tide in those lands which had remained under catholic political control. The caveat is an important one. No state which had been converted to protestantism in the first half of the century was recovered, and wherever the government remained protestant, both within the Empire and outside, the Counter Reformation was rebuffed. But in those lands, such as Austria and Bavaria, where the ruler was favourably disposed, the threat of heresy - very real down to the 1570s - was finally defeated. This process was aided by the protestants themselves. Unity had never been their strong point, and after 1555 there was not only strife between Lutherans and Calvinists, but also among the Lutherans themselves. Martin Luther had been a charismatic leader, not a man who had created systems and organisations, and his death in 1546 was immediately followed by disruptive disputes. These arose naturally from the disagreements which had existed during Luther's lifetime between himself and his leading disciple, Philip Melanchthon, which only their mutual respect and affection had held in check. Melanchthon was a humanist and an eirenicist - Luther was neither. 'Philip proceeds in charity, and I in faith', he had once said. Melanchthon had been willing to make further concessions, both at Augsburg in 1530 and at Regensburg in 1541, but Luther had restrained him. Part of the problem lay in the inherent contradictions of Luther's own thinking. Justification by faith alone, and the total dependence of man upon the will of God lead logically to anti-nomianism, a position which he strongly repudiated. Luther was a predestinarian, whose dictum was 'God saves whom he wishes', but Melanchthon was more inclined to say 'God saves him who wishes to be saved', and Luther did not attack him; so the two positions, inherently contradictory, remained side by side in the Evangelical church after 1546. Melanchthon outlived Luther by 14 years, dying in 1560, and was thus a central figure in the protestant response to the Interim of 1548, and in the negotiation of the religious peace of Augsburg. The key figure in the drama over the Interim was Duke Maurice of Saxony, who had supported the Emperor in 1547, and tried to create his own settlement, the so-called 'Leipzig Interim' in December 1548. Melanchthon and his friends supported this in the interests of peace, to the outrage of such hard-line Lutherans as Amsdorf and Flaccius Illyricus. In the event, Maurice broke with the Emperor in 1551, the Leipzig Interim became a dead letter, and Melanchthon had compromised himself with his co-religionists for nothing. The split within the Lutheran ranks which resulted was bitter, and lasted until 1580, depriving them of much of their force in the face of the counter-reformation. Illyricus attacked Melanchthon fiercely as early as 1549 on the issue of *adiaphoira,* or 'things indifferent', a dispute in which, somewhat paradoxically, John Calvin intervened on Melanchthon's side. Melanchthon did not eventually persist in his defence of *adiaphora,* but he did become much more willing to talk to the Calvinists on the issue of the Eucharist, and that became another bone of contention between himself and the 'Wittenburg' party. Disputes raged particularly at the University of Jena in Prussia, where for a time all the leading protagonists were imprisoned. More seriously, the Lutheran princes also took sides, with the Duke of Saxony supporting Flaccius, and the Elector the Philippians. As the latter drew closer to the Calvinists, they were persecuted in those lands which adhered most strongly to the original Lutheran doctrine. Partly as a result of this unseemly strife, the Rhenish Palatinate converted to Calvinism in 1583.

Efforts started to be made in 1576 to heal this damaging breech, when the theological advisers of the Elector Augustus of Saxony produced the Formula of Maulbronn. The Philippians responded to this initiative with their own formula of Torgau, and the negotiations which then followed produced the Formula of Concord in 1580. The schism was formally healed, but by then the damage had been done. Not only had the Lutherans lost their chance to evangelise the rest of Germany, and found themselves checked by the catholic revival, they had also begun to lose ground to the Calvinists. As their theology had become more contentious, it had also become more legalistic and - a style which has been appropriately described as 'protestant scholasticism'. By the end of the, century Lutheranism was politically and theologically on the defensive, and was being manoeuvred into a position in which it would soon have to defend itself from a new wave of catholic and Imperial aggression.

24. The Rise of Calvinism

The Swiss Cantons had successfully broken away from the Holy Roman Empire during the fifteenth century. They had no constitutional unity, but only a customary and loose confederation. Some, like Zurich and Basle, were ruled by substantial cities, in the same manner as Pisa or Mantua; others, like the so-called 'forest cantons', were rural communes without any obvious focus. The only outside authority which still existed in the cantons in the early sixteenth century was that of the church, and the early development of the reformation has to be seen at least as much in terms of removing that authority as in terms of positive evangelical drive. The first canton to embrace reform was Zurich, where the lead was given by the People's priest at the Minster, Ulrich Zwingli. Zwingli was a native of the canton (although not of the city), and had been strongly influenced by the humanism which he had encountered at the University of Vienna. His vision, almost from the first, was that of a 'Godly Commonwealth', in which church and state were united under a 'Godly magistracy'. Eventually Zwingli's zeal overcame his discretion, and having prompted the Zurich council into war against the catholic forest cantons, he was killed and Zurich defeated at the battle of Kappel in 1531.

Zwingli's successor in charge of the 'state church' of Zurich was Heinrich Bullinger, whose doctrine was the same, but whose personality and tactics were completely different. Bullinger was not at all aggressive, but spread his influence by innumerable friendships and a vast correspondence. During the 1540s a number of English protestant exiles arrived in Zurich, of whom John Hooper was the most notable, and when they returned to England after Henry VIII's death in 1547, they took his influence with them. Consequently the English protestant settlement, which was shaped between 1547 and 1553, owed much more to him than it did to Luther - the only major church in Europe to follow the Zurich teaching. The neighbouring cantons of Basle and Berne also embraced the reformation under Zurich influence, before the battle of Kappel, and thereafter went their own ways to some extent, but continued to acknowledge Bullinger's influence. Meanwhile a separate reformed tradition was being established on the fringes of Switzerland, in the city of Geneva, and in 1549 (thanks largely to Bullinger's diplomatic skill) the two churches united in the *Consensus Tigurinus*. Bullinger lived until 1570, and his personal influence continued to be great wherever the reformed tradition spread, but it is significant that the united church became known, not by his name but by that of the reformer of Geneva - John Calvin.

Calvin was a Frenchman, born at Noyon in Picardy in 1509, the son of a lawyer. His father acted for the Cathedral chapter of Noyon, and in consequence was able to secure a benefice for John (who was well below the canonical age) to support his education. He entered the University of Paris in 1523 and followed the arts curriculum, which by then included instruction in good humanist Latin, and began to study theology. This latter he did surreptitiously, because his father (like Luther's) was insistent upon him becoming a lawyer. In 1528 he took his M.A., and went to Orleans to study law. But by this time his official studies were becoming distasteful. He spent some time learning Greek, and moved to Bourges in order to have access to better humanist teachers. In 1531 his father died, and he abandoned his legal studies altogether, being apparently set upon an academic career in the humanities. However at this point - somewhere in 1532 - he underwent a religious conversion. Unlike Luther, he never described this process, but it seems to have been an emotional rather than an intellectual experience. When it happened, he immediately began to associate with the reformers who were already numerous in Paris, and incurred the suspicion of the Sorbonne and of the Paris *parlement,* which were then orchestrating a campaign against heresy. In November 1533 his friend Nicholas Cop, the Rector of the University, who was more an Erasmian than a Lutheran, stirred up a hornet's nest with an ill-timed attack upon the policy of persecution, and Calvin, along with many others, went into hiding. After a discreet interval he retreated to Orleans, where his earliest theological writing was produced in 1534, a short tract of no great importance, which shows him struggling to integrate classical and biblical influences. After the furore over the Placards in October 1534 he left France altogether, visited Italy, and spent some time in Basle where in 1536, he published the first edition of the *Institutes of the Christian Religion.* Written in Latin, and somewhat amateurishly printed, this small book made no impression at all. In the summer of that year he seems to have returned secretly and briefly to Paris, because it was in endeavouring to return from Paris to Basle that the second momentus event of his life occurred. The long smouldering conflict between Francis I and Charles V had flared up, and he made a long detour to avoid the hostile armies. This brought him to Geneva, where he was intercepted by a fellow Frenchman, Guillaume Farel, and asked to assist in the task of evangelising the city. Geneva was not a Canton, and had never been a part of the Holy Roman Empire. Theoretically it was an independent Prince-Bishopric, wedged in between the Canton of Berne and the lands of the Duke of Savoy. In practice it was dominated by Savoy, because the duke nominated the bishops. By 1530 the council of the city (which was only of modest size and wealth, numbering about 6000 citizens), was showing signs of wishing to emulate Zurich, an ambition in which it was encouraged by Berne for its own reasons. Farel was one of a group of exiled French reformers who had already taken refuge in French speaking Switzerland, and he had successfully converted the small territory of Neuchatel when, in October 1532, he arrived in Geneva. His first efforts were not successful, but some of his friends were able to make a start, and in December 1533 Farel returned. This time he did better, winning a significant disputation and attracting considerable support within the council. The bishop then made a major error. He gathered a small army and attempted to occupy the city. This was frustrated with Bernese help, and the reformation immediately became associated with political independence. In June 1535 the celebration of the mass was suspended, and in May 1536 the Council swore to live 'in accordance with the word of God' - that is, to embrace protestantism. The Duke of Savoy was unable to intervene, as he was at this point in process of being dispossessed of his territories by the French, and Bernese protection was sufficient guarantee against any renewed attempt on the part of the bishop. But Farel knew perfectly well that this political conversion was skin deep, which was why he solicited Calvin's aid as soon as the opportunity presented itself. Although he was not well known at this time (and was still under 30 years of age), Calvin had already begun to show those characteristics which later earned him his reputation. He had a phenomenal memory, and a logical, incisive mind - partly the result of his own inherent qualities, and partly of the legal and classical studies which he had pursued. He also had a tough and inflexible sense of purpose, which after his conversion took the form of a vocation. He had, he later declared, not the slightest desire to stay in such a place as Geneva, but he recognised in Farel's well-timed intervention the authentic voice of God; so he accepted the call.

His ministry in Geneva began quietly, but soon ran into difficulties which arose from its political origins. Both the city Council and their Bernese protectors wanted an Erastian church in Geneva, following the Zurich model, and consequently saw ecclesiastical discipline as a matter for the secular magistrate. Calvin objected. To him it was essential that the church should control its own discipline, without reference to the state. To his opponents this suggested a new clericalism - the re-introduction in another disguise of that priestly authority which they had expelled the bishop to remove. After a sharp struggle, Calvin and Farel were dismissed, and the former retreated to Strasburg. He remained there for three years, from 1538 to 1541 as pastor of the French congregation, and wrote a number of important treatises which substantially increased his standing among the reformed theologians. In 1539 he issued a second Latin edition of the *Institutes,* and in 1541 the French version which was to make him the most influential of all

French speaking leaders. In the summer of the same year he was invited to return to Geneva, and negotiating from a position of strength, was able to insist upon the adoption of a new church order as a precondition of his acceptance. This was the order which he published as the *Ordonnances Ecclésiastiques* in November 1541, and which became the model for reformed congregations throughout Europe. The order of pastors, doctors, elders and deacons which was thus established provided a disciplinary structure through which Calvin and his supporters were able to impose their moral authority upon the city, but it did not solve all the problems. In the first place, not only did Calvin hold no civic office, he did not even become a citizen until 1555, and the resentment of many of the established bourgeois families against what they saw as the arrogant interference of the French exiles always provided a potential threat to his ascendancy. The chief bone of contention was the power of excommunication, which, although it was an ecclesiastical sanction, carried many secular implications in a community where church and state were coextensive. The Consistory, the ruling body of the church, claimed the exclusive right to wield this sanction, but for many years the Council would not agree, and citizens could only be excommunicated with the agreement of the magistrates. Nor was Calvin's extreme puritanism universally acceptable, and coalitions of opponents (known to his supporters - most unjustly - as the 'libertines') regularly threatened the control which his friends exercised in the Council. The last major crisis occurred in 1553, when the libertines were very close to an electoral majority. Both sides were unscrupulous, but Calvin was the more ruthless. He had always been as severe as his authority would permit towards those whom he regarded as heretics, and in 1544 the Italian eirenicist Sebastian Castellio (who objected to persecution on principle) was expelled from Geneva. In 1553, in the middle of the tense political struggle, Miguel Servetus arrived in the city. Servetus was a Spanish unitarian, whose views had long since been condemned by both protestants and catholics. He had been in the prisons of the inquisition, and had quarrelled with Calvin many years before. Why he came to Geneva, knowing Calvin's views, is a mystery, but he may have had some intention of overthrowing him with the aid of his political enemies. Whatever his motivation, he soon drew attention to his presence, and was imprisoned. The 'libertines' then most unwisely espoused his cause, accusing Calvin of tyranny. Since just about every reputable theologian in western Europe was opposed to Servetus, it was not difficult for Calvin to win the day. Servetus was burned, and the 'libertines' were defeated and discredited.

Two years later, in 1555 Calvin at last became a citizen, and the Council gave way to the Consistory on the question of excommunication. Having won the domestic battle, and made his local authority virtually unassailable, Calvin then began to turn his face outwards, and to use the protestant powerhouse that Geneva (most improbably) had become, for the wider purposes of evangelisation. His first instrument for that purpose was the Company of Pastors, which provided theological and pastoral training, particularly to exiles from France, who were then sent back to preach the word. The first missionaries from this source entered France in 1555, and by 1559 they had made so much progress that a National Synod of reformed congregations could be held, in spite of the fierce hostility of the king, Henry II. His second instrument was the final and mature version of the *Institutes,* issued both in French and in Latin in 1559. Calvin's thinking, both theological and ecclesiastical, had a sharp and systematic quality that neither Luther nor Zwingli could match. Above all it gave his converts a total conviction of Divine favour (not strictly justified) which enabled them to survive under the most adverse circumstances, and to organise themselves both for administration and for war. As a church 'under the cross', the Calvinists were to prove far tougher than any other reformed tradition. The third instrument was the Geneva Academy, modelled on that of Strasburg, and founded under the Rectorship of Theodore Beza in 1559. The Academy, which was not a university because it studied only theology, gave Geneva an academic status which it had hitherto lacked and which the Company of Pastors could not supply. By the time that Calvin died in 1564 Geneva was known as the protestant Rome, so great had its ascendancy become. By that time, not only had reformed preachers established over 2000 congregations in France, they had won control of Scotland, and begun to appear in significant numbers in the French speaking southern provinces of The Netherlands. In France religious war had already commenced, and in The Netherlands iconoclastic riots (which were a peculiarly Calvinist phenomenon) had begun to undermine civil order, and were threatening to combine with other circumstances to form a highly explosive mixture.

25. The Jesuits and the Counter Reformation

The Society of Jesus was founded in 1540, and is traditionally regarded as the most important of the Counter Reformation orders. This was largely because it represented the most successful adaptation of the traditional religious life to the changed spiritual and political climate of the sixteenth century. Some reformers felt that the regulars, and particularly the friars, were a liability rather than an asset in the battle against a rapidly developing protestantism. However, a small number of very zealous men had already begun to see a revival of the regular life as the best means of revitalising the spirituality of the church. Such men as Paolo Guistiniani, who with a number of other young Venetians of aristocratic family entered the Camaldolese order between 1510 and 1512, and within fifteen years had turned it into a small but powerful centre of the strict observance. Or Matteo de Bascio, a simple priest fired by the example of St. Francis, who set out to restore the primitive virtues of the Franciscans. By 1529 his community had been recognised, and by 1535 it had acquired the name Capuchin, by which it was to be known thereafter.

Neither the Camaldolese nor the Capuchins were innovators. Rather, they represented the philosophy 'when threatened, return to first principles'. Consequently, although they represented a positive response to the problems of the church, they did not represent a distinctive response to the problems of that particular situation. The Theatines, on the other hand, pioneered a fresh approach, just as the friars had done in the thirteenth century. They arose out of the Oratory of Divine Love, which was not an order but a voluntary community of priests and laymen, dedicated to personal sanctification and to works of charity. The Oratory had been set up before 1500, one of several such experiments in Italy inspired by a general awareness of ecclesiastical malaise. The Theatines were formally established in 1524 by Gaetano da Thiene and Gian Pietro Caraffa. They were not monks, nor friars, nor canons, but clerks regular, that is pastoral priests living together under a rule. Like the friars, they worked in the world rather than in the cloister, but unlike the friars they were not great preachers, specialising rather in what we would now call 'personal counselling', and in the administration of the sacraments. The Theatines were ever numerous, partly because of their low profile, and their influence was damaged by an enforced flight to Venice after the sack of Rome in 1527, but they became in time a major source of reforming bishops, partly because of their largely aristocratic recruitment. Clerks Regular became in due course the characteristic religious of the Counter Reformation, adaptable to a wide variety of worldly circumstances. Another group, the Clerks regular of St. Paul, later known as the Barnabites, were established at Milan in 1533. They specialised particularly in education and youth work, had a reputation for great strictness of life, and developed their rule gradually until it took its final form in 1579. The Somaschi, another group set up near Bergamo in 1532, worked particularly with the sick and with orphans. They did not become a full order until 1568, but were highly regarded in the later 16th century for their devoted work among the destitute of the great Italian cities.

There is no reason to suppose that religious vocations were more common among men than among women, but the *genre* of the clerks regular did not translate easily into a female form. The tradition had always been for women religious to retreat from the world rather than to engage with it. There were (for example) no female friars. The nearest parallel had been the Franciscan Tertiaries, but they had been more concerned with their own spirituality than with works of corporal mercy. However, in 1535 in Brescia a group of young unmarried lay women took the unprecedented step of forming themselves into an organised company dedicated to St Ursula. The members were to remain living with their families, but under a strict rule of obedience, and were to devote themselves to works of charity, particularly the Christian education of young girls. By the end of the century the Ursulines had become a regular teaching order, running their own schools, but that had not been the intention of the founder, St. Angela Merici, and merely served to demonstrate how difficult it was, and profoundly unconventional, to organise sixteenth century lay women in the manner of modern social workers. Indeed the Council of Trent laid down a principle of strict enclosure for all women's orders, and it was not to be until St. Vincent de Paul founded the Sisters of Charity in the seventeenth century that the situation even began to change.

All these new orders pioneered, in their various ways, the direct involvement of professed religious with the pastoral problems of daily life, and with the desperate physical and spiritual needs of ordinary men and women. All were successful, although in differing degrees, but all were eclipsed by the Society of Jesus - an order which concerned itself, from an early stage in its existence with the pastoral problems, not of the humble but of the great. The Jesuits became to the royal and aristocratic houses of Europe what the Barnabites or the Somaschi were to the sick and poor of Naples - spiritual advisers, comforters and friends.

It was a relationship which served both parties well, although it carried from time to time the penalty of too much success -jealousy and political hostility. In one very obvious respect the Society of Jesus differed from all those which have been mentioned so far. Neither its founder, nor any of its original members was Italian. Six out of the original group of ten were Iberians, and the order was from the beginning far wider in scope and purpose, transplanting readily, not only into other parts of Europe, but to every corner of the world. Inigo Lopez de Loyola was a Basque of aristocratic family from the hills above Bilbao. Born in.1491, until he was about thity he followed the natural calling for a man of his status - that of soldier and courtier. But in 1521 he was seriously wounded at the. siege of Pamplona in nearby Navarre. After the battle he endured an agonising journey across the mountains in a litter, and a long period of enforced idleness at home. Like most gentlemen of his generation, he was literate in the vernacular, but had no Latin and was not a natural reader. Having soon run out of the secular romances which were his normal taste, he turned to Spanish translations of the lives of the saints, and of the *Life of Christ* by Ludolf the Carthusian. A combination of this unaccustomed literature and of the circumstances in which it was confronted produced in him a religious conversion of a profound and lasting nature. It was as though the content of his mind was completely changed, while the form remained the same. He still aspired after heroism and high adventure, but now in the service of God rather than of his Prince. Nor did he cease to be dashing and dramatic in pursuit of his new vocation. As soon as he was able to travel he went to the shrine of Our Lady of Montserrat in Catalonia, symbolically exchanged his aristocratic clothing for that of a beggar, and swore himself to penitence and service. He then retired to the neighbouring town of Manresa, and by inflicting upon himself a regime of extreme austerity, induced a series of profound mystical experiences. He also read the *Imitatio Christi of* Thomas à Kempis (again presumably in a Spanish translation), which was to have a profound influence upon his spirituality. His mind, which was still unconfused by learning of any kind, then began to assume that extraordinary blend of the mystical and the military which was later to provide the unique strength of his contemplative system, the 'Spiritual Exercises'.

At this stage his only conscious plan seems to have been to join one of the *corps d'elite* of the church militant. After leaving Manresa in 1523 he went on pilgrimage to Jerusalem, and there sought to join the Observant Franciscans. Rejected for some unknown reason, he returned to Catalonia, and there decided that the lessons which God had taught him at Manresa could form the basis of his own unique mission in the church. With characteristic self-discipline he set out to prepare himself for this by the painful and unaccustomed route of academic study. He learned Latin at Barcelona, and then moved first to Alcala and later to Salamanca. everywhere the power of his personality and the nature of his spiritual insight brought the troubled to seek his help and advice. As a mere layman, he had no right to offer such guidance or counsel, and he was industriously pursued by the Inquisition. By this time he knew enough theology to defend himself against charges of heresy, but he was twice imprisoned before deciding to seek the freer (if no less orthodox) atmosphere of Paris. There he studied for seven years, from 1528 to 1535, and laid the intellectual foundations of his future life. He also gathered around him a group of six like-minded friends with whom, in 1534 he took vows of poverty and chastity. The expressed intention of the group was to serve God in the Holy Land, but, failing that, to place themselves at the disposal of the Pope - a humility bordering upon arrogance which was never to be far from the attitude of the Society in its later years. In 1537 the group reconvened in Venice with three additional members, and all those who were not already priests (including Ignatius) were ordained. War between Venice and the Turks blocked access to Jerusalem, and the group turned instead to their second declared purpose. Ignatius went to Rome to offer his own and his companions services to Paul III. As we have seen, it was not a propitious moment to propose a new extension to the regular life, and two years of argument and investigation followed before, in June 1539, the whole group met in Rome, where they added an oath of obedience to a superior and drew up a constitution for their proposed society. Finally, by a, Papal Bull of September 1540 the Society of Jesus was formally constituted as an order of clerks regular, and Ignatius was elected as the first General (as the superior was significantly called).

The new order quickly demonstrated both its usefulness and its appeal. To a greater extent than any other order of clerks regular, the Jesuits abandoned all the traditional features of the corporate life, neither singing high masses, nor reciting the offices, nor indulging in collective fasts or other mortifications. Everything was subordinated to the work to which the order was dedicated, spiritual counselling and the education of boys. The Jesuit was supposed to keep his will and mind concentrated upon the job in hand, and not to be side-tracked by the alluring but self-indulgent delights of contemplation and spiritual introspection. The note struck exactly matched the needs of the reviving catholic church, and both Paul III and Julius III backed the order strongly the former with a confirmatory Bull of 1544 which removed the original maximum of sixty members, and the latter with an expository Bull in 1550 which amplified the constitution and made it more explicit. This constitution, with a carefully graded membership, was one of the Society's great strengths. It provided for a long probationary period (two years novitiate, a 'scholasticate' of indefinite length often about five years) followed by a second or 'spiritual' novitiate, and then three grades of full membership, culminating in an elite of 'spiritual coadjutors'.

When Ignatius died in 1556 the order had about 1000 members, of whom only five were Spiritual Coadjutors, and a further forty-three had reached the second grade of the 'fourth vow'. This complex structure ensured the very highest quality at the top, and guaranteed the fullest indoctrination before membership was reached at all. The other strength was the Spiritual Exercises, which were at the same time a highly disciplined system of meditation and the nearest thing possible to a deliberately induced mystical experience.

By the time that the Council of Trent ended in 1565 the Jesuits had developed a remarkable range of activities all over Europe. Some of them were moral and dogmatic theologians and controversialists of the highest calibre, such as Lainez and Calderon. Others were private tutors and confessors to royal and aristocratic families. Others again ran schools and university institutions. They preached, organised retreats and wrote on every conceivable subject in which the interests of the church could be served. Canisius in Germany, Hosius in Poland, Norvegus in Sweden and Persons in England became almost synonymous with missionary activity in those countries. By 1556 the order had over thirty colleges for lay youths, devoted almost entirely to the wealthy and influential of the next generation. They may have lacked the purely pastoral appeal of the Barnabites or the Ursulines, but they did the job that most urgently needed to be done if the catholic church was to recover its ascendancy, and they did it with extraordinary effectiveness and success.

26. The French civil wars to 1572

Henry II's death in July 1559 could hardly have come at a worse time for France. Not only was there widespread economic discontent caused by the heavy war taxation, and aristocratic discontent caused by the abrupt ending of the wars, but French protestantism had completely changed its nature over the previous decade. At the time of Francis I's death in 1547 it had been widely dispersed, but unfocussed in doctrine and almost entirely lacking in organisation. As late as 1551 the records of the *juges des presidiaux,* established in that year to try heretics, reveal that the problem was still one of scattered individuals and small groups, mostly of urban craftsmen and small traders. By 1558, however, there was already a network of organised congregations, each with its own pastor and elders on the model laid down in the *Ordonnances Ecclésiastique,* and following the lucid and dynamic theology of Geneva. Fewer than fifty such congregations can be identified in that year, but the number was increasing rapidly, and was largely determined by the number of trained pastors which the Genevan Company could produce. The movement had also become markedly more aristocratic, and had acquired an important rural dimension. Many of the new pastors who returned to France from Geneva between 1555 and 1560 were from aristocratic families, and they brought with them habits of leadership, established connections, and above all respectability. By 1561 it could be plausibly claimed that there were 2150 congregations, and in some areas, particularly in the south west, they had become numerically and politically dominant. Despite its proscribed status, and the active hostility of both the king and the *parlement,* the Reformed church had been able to hold its first national Synod in Paris in May 1559 under the noses of both. Nor was it only moral and spiritual leadership that was contributed by the aristocracy. By 1562 the majority of Calvinist congregations were under the protection of their local *seigneurs,* and organised for their own defence. The hierarchical nature of Calvinist organisation also facilitated this, with local and provincial synods assuming military functions of mobilisation and co-ordination. In May 1560 it was claimed that the reformed congregations of the Rouen area alone could raise 20,000 men. In November 1560 the Synod of Clairac divided the province of Guienne into seven *colloques,* each with its colonel. By 1562 organisation of this nature was fully developed in Guienne, Languedoc, Provence and Dauphiné, and was coming into existence elsewhere. It is not surprising that this military potential should have appealed to one of the major noble families who had climbed to power at court under Henry II. With the bulk of their estates in the south of France, and the Queen of Navarre as a genuine convert, the Bourbons were the natural leaders of the Reformed party, and the Duke of Conde (the king of Navarre's brother) who was not noted for his evangelical zeal, nevertheless became protector-general of the churches.

This dangerous situation was made worse by the fact that the new king, Francis II, was fifteen years old - too old for a minority, but not old enough to exercise effective power himself. Instead he became almost immediately dependent upon the kindred of his wife, Mary of Scotland, whose mother had been Mary of Guise. The Guises were a formidable combination, Mary's two brothers being Duke Francis, the victor of Calais, and Charles, Cardinal of Lorraine, the senior prelate of the French church. The Guises became, naturally and willingly, the champions of the catholic faith and the heirs to Henry II's policy of persecution. The young king's personal commitment to his formidable kinsmen gave them a complete ascendancy which inevitably drove the other major family, the Montmorencys, into alliance with the Bourbons, and consequently into a relationship with the reformed church. This was made easier by the fact that the Constable's nephew, Gaspard de Coligny, like Jeanne d'Albret, was a genuine convert. By the spring of 1560 the religious and political temperature was rising steeply. The government was over forty million *livres in* debt, and resorted to the desperate expedient of calling the Estates General, which had not met since 1484. The Duke of Condé used his widespread influence to make this assembly as difficult as possible, and the third estate refused to provide any financial assistance unless the government abandoned its official policy of religious coercion and allowed the Estates General a share in the executive power. Francis gave ground on the first point, but not on the second. A series of edicts were issued, granting liberty of conscience but prohibiting armed assemblies. This was enough to get some money, but not to defuse the political situation. By this time both religious parties were aiming for full control, and neither was prepared to be satisfied with toleration, even if the government had been strong enough to make a serious attempt at enforcement. The Huguenots then made a serious mistake. Impatient in spite of their rapid progress, and fearing a military initiative from the Guises, they decided upon a pre-emptive strike to seize control of the court. This so-called Conspiracy of Amboise in March 1560 failed completely, and led to the arrest of the Duke of Condê. Nevertheless the Guises were shaken, and sought to stiffen their supremacy by entering into an alliance with the Queen Mother, Catherine de Médici.

Catherine was an Italian princess, a niece of Pope Clement VII, who had been an exemplary queen in the sense that she had borne Henry four sons, but she had never been popular, and during her husband's lifetime had been eclipsed in political influence by his mistress, Diane de Poitiers. In the summer of 1560 she grasped her opportunity, and rapidly emerged as a politician of energy and resource. Francis II was never in robust health, and in December 1560 he died. This changed the political situation in a number of ways. In the first place Mary of Scotland became queen dowager at the age of seventeen, and came under immediate pressure to return home, where her mother had recently died and the English backed protestants were in the ascendant. At the same time the Guises lost their blood-link with the Crown. Secondly Charles IX, who succeeded his brother, was only nine years old, and consequently a regency was unavoidable. In the circumstances a Bourbon regency would have led straight to civil war, and Catherine's recent emergence to prominence was therefore a welcome relief to everyone except the Bourbons. She took the initiative herself, and by becoming Regent began that tenacious but unsuccessful defence of her sons' position which was to last until her death in January 1589. Her main problem was that, because of the accumulated debts of the crown, she was fighting virtually without resources, and therefore had to rely upon her innate skill at playing off one faction against another. Court intrigue took the place of constructive policy making, not only because Catherine was a natural intriguer, but also because she had no option. Starting with the support of the Guises, and the hostility of the Bourbons, by the summer of 1561 her attempts to reconcile the religious factions had almost reversed that situation. The so-called Colloquy of Poissy failed because both sides hoped for government support, and neither was willing to accept it as a mediator. Given the complete Guise ascendancy of the previous summer, this was a measure of the degree to which Catherine had asserted her independence by moving towards the protestants.

However, as the Bourbons became partly reconciled, not only the Guise but also the catholic part of the Montmorency faction (headed by the Constable himself) became totally alienated, and withdrew from the court during the autumn. By the end of the year both catholics and protestants were arming and mustering troops, clashes began to occur, and the Crown had neither the prestige nor the force to control the situation. In January 1562 Catherine tried to stave off conflict by issuing an edict of toleration, permitting Huguenot assemblies outside of walled towns, and protestant services in private houses. The main result was to outrage hard line catholics, without winning much by way of gratitude from the protestants. In March the Guises took their own remedy, attacking a (legal) assembly at Vassy, and killing thirty people. Huguenot forces under the Duke of Condée occupied Lyons, Tours, Blois and Rouen, while Guise and Montmorency occupied Paris. The fighting was sporadic but bitter, and Condé brought in English help, giving Le Havre to Elizabeth as a cautionary town for the return of Calais. Unable to suppress the conflict, Catherine negotiated constantly with both sides, and in March 1563 managed to secure enough backing to arrange a settlement at Amboise. This was not so much the result of her skill, as of good luck. Anthony of Bourbon had been killed in the fighting, the Duke of Guise assassinated, and both the Constable and Condé taken prisoner. The death of Guise temporarily weakened his party, and Condé's, imprisonment made him a flexible negotiator. So he settled for 'household toleration' for protestant nobles, to the outrage of both Coligny and Calvin. By this time the Genevan reformer had become convinced that in the circumstances of France his supporters had no option but to fight. Calvin himself had long denied (as had Luther) that there could be any circumstances in which resistance to legitimate authority was permitted. But in the light of the French situation (and in response to specific questions) he had declared that it was possible for a 'godly' (protestant) inferior magistrate to resist an 'ungodly' (catholic) superior. It was thus legitimate for the Bourbons, as princes of the blood, to resist a persecuting policy on the part of the French crown, but not permissible for private citizens, no matter how godly, to take the law into their own hands.

For about four years Catherine managed to maintain the precarious peace which she had achieved at Amboise, but the issuing of the decrees of the Council of Trent, and her own meeting with the Duke of Alba at Bayonne (mainly for the purpose of seeing her daughter Elizabeth, who was Philip II's third wife), both of which occurred in 1565, convinced many protestants that an all-out counter attack was coming. Events in The Netherlands heightened that fear, and when Alba established the Council of Blood in that country in 1567, and began a policy of fierce repression, the Huguenots again became convinced that a pre-emptive strike was called for. In September 1567 Condé and Coligny attempted another coup against the court - and failed again. The protestant war machine by this time was efficient, but missionary progress was flagging as catholic resistance stiffened, and the Huguenots were still no more than a small proportion of the population - although stronger among the aristocracy. This time both sides brought in foreign help, although Elizabeth had been bitten once, and did not venture again. The Elector Palatine sent troops to help the protestants, and the Duke of Alba supported the catholics (who were both the Crown and the Guise this time). Thanks largely to these foreign mercenaries, the fighting was more savage than before, and atrocities on both sides were numerous. It was also inconclusive, and after a few months Catherine managed to patch up another truce at Longjumeau, on the same terms as before. But Longjumeau was even more fragile than most of the truces which broke up this long crisis, because the Guise ascendancy was now supported by the king's younger brother, the Duke of Anjou, and the protestants, unsuccessful in formal operations, were continuing to infiltrate the royal service. Within a few months war had broken out again. The Duke of Condé was killed, and the Huguenots suffered a number of reverses, but Coligny kept a formidable army in being, and took advantage of the constant disputes between the royal and Guisard commanders. Moreover, the Crown still had inadequate resources to keep large armies in being, or to follow up the victories which were won.

By August 1570 Catherine's persistence had again overcome the warlike zeal of the rivals, and the pacification of St. Germain once again restored the *status quo*. This time, however, the advantage lay with the Huguenots. They secured four garrison towns as security for the treaty, and Philip of Spain's consistent support for the catholic cause was neutralised by the effect of the Morisco risings in Spain. Catherine began to move cautiously but positively towards a rapprochement with the Bourbons. In the summer of 1571 Coligny returned to court, and quickly established a personal ascendancy over the king. As Philip's difficulties multiplied, both at home and in The Netherlands, the idea of pulling his distracted country back together by a war against the ancient Habsburg enemy began to appeal to Charles. This would have meant linking up with both the Dutch and the English, and a long step in that direction was taken by the Anglo-French treaty of Blois in April 1572. This has been described as a 'diplomatic revolution', and it represented the end of the long-standing Anglo-Burgundian association, but it was more important in that connection for England than for France. Coligny's ascendancy at court was fragile, and bitterly resented by the Guises, who blamed him (without any real evidence) for the death of Duke Francis. By the summer of 1572 Catherine was also thoroughly alarmed by the prospect of a war against Spain, and had slipped back into the duplicity which she always called upon when other resources failed. By the middle of August she had arranged to marry her daughter Margaret to the young Huguenot leader Henry of Navarre (Jeanne d'Albret's son), and at the same time plotted the assassination of Coligny with his Guise enemies. These two events were to be linked through the presence of many Huguenot leaders (including Coligny) in Paris for the wedding. On 22 August, immediately after the marriage, a Guisard assassin wounded Coligny, but did not kill him. The Huguenots demanded justice, and Catherine panicked - as the Guises had probably calculated that she would. On the following day, by what means is not known, Catherine convinced the king that a general massacre of the Huguenot leaders was the only remedy to prevent a massive scandal of royal complicity. The Guises were willing, and prepared, to act as agents, and the notorious massacre of St. Bartholomew's eve followed, almost certainly far exceeding anything which either Catherine or the king had intended. Thousands were killed in Paris alone, and the massacre soon spread to those provinces where the catholics were still in a large majority.

One immediate result was that many of the surviving protestant aristocracy in northern and central France abjured, leaving the pastors once again in control. Another was that the territorial division between catholics and protestants became more marked as Huguenot minorities were wiped out. Civil war broke out again, as protestant areas rose in revolt against the crown , and the pretence of royal impartiality was finally destroyed, leaving the Huguenots to find another theory of their relationship with the state. Finally, all prospects of French assistance to the Dutch rebels disappeared, and the Treaty of Blois came under severe strain. By the end of 1572 Catherine was back where she had started, under firm Guise control, and the fourth civil war had crystallised into an unsuccessful siege of La Rochelle.

27. The first phase of the revolt of The Netherlands

The area collectively known as The Netherlands consisted in the early sixteenth century of seventeen separate provinces, linked together only by Habsburg overlordship, and by the Estates General in which thirteen of them were represented. All were theoretically within the boundaries of the Holy Roman Empire, and the bulk of them had come to the Habsburg family by way of the Burgundian inheritance, brought by the marriage of Mary (daughter and heir of Charles the Bold, the last Duke of Burgundy) to Maximilian, the son of the then Emperor, Frederick III. Charles V thus ruled most of The Netherlands by a double right, both as Emperor and as head of the Habsburg family. Charles had been born in Ghent, and was well aware of the sensitivity with which the provinces cherished their separateness and jurisdictional autonomy. His rule had consequently been very traditional, in spite of major confrontations with some of the cities, such as Bruges, which had been stripped of its privileges after carrying defiance of Imperial authority too far. Only in one respect had Charles transcended the limits of tradition, and that was in issuing a series o proclamations or 'placards' of increasing severity, culminating in the 'Edict of Blood' of 1552. These 'placards', aimed at curbing heresy, resulted in thousand of executions (mainly of Anabaptists) over a period of thirty years. Even in this respect, however, a matter on which he felt strongly, Charles did not attempt to transgress the jurisdictional autonomy of the provinces, with the result that a number of refuges survived and the placards were very unevenly enforced. The Netherlands were worth taking trouble over, particularly the southern provinces of Flanders and Brabant, because they contained some of the wealthiest and most commercially advanced cities in Europe. After the severe blows suffered by the north Italian cities in the wars of the late fifteenth and early sixteenth century, Antwerp (in Brabant) emerged as the unchallenged financial capital of Europe, and the great Bourse (built in the 1530s) took over the functions and prestige of the Venetian Rialto. In the normal course of events The Netherlands would have been transmitted along with the Austrian lands of the family (and the Imperial title) to Charles's younger brother Ferdinand. However, by 1545 relations between the brothers were strained, and Charles decided that his son Philip should receive The Netherlands, along with the territories of the Crowns of Spain. There was not much logic about this arrangement, except that Charles clearly wanted his son to have the plums. In these circumstances it is not surprising that Ferdinand felt cheated, or that Charles felt it necessary to arrange an English marriage for his son in the hope of strengthening his position to hold on to his northern inheritance. By 1553, when this marriage was arranged, the situation had been made more urgent by Charles's declining health, and by Philip's disastrous tour of the southern provinces in 1549-51. Intended as a public relations exercise, this two-year residence produced only mutual suspicion and ill-feeling. The omens were not, therefore, particularly good when Philip eventually took over control on his father's abdication in 1555. The four years during which he resided there, from 1555 to 1559, were marked by tension over a number of issues. The Estates General resisted demands for taxation which they (rightly) believed was intended to finance a war in which they had no interest. Eventually a grant of 800,000 florins a year was made conditional upon collection and supervision by the Estates' own agents, a humiliating condition which Philip was forced to accept, but neither forgot nor forgave. The nobles, many of whom (including the Prince of Orange) had distinguished records of loyal service to Charles, complained bitterly of being excluded from positions of real authority in favour of foreigners (mainly Spaniards). However, after the signing of peace in 1559 Philip withdrew to Spain and left behind him a government of apparently impeccable traditionalism. The Regent was his half-sister Margaret, Duchess of Parma, and all the leading nobles, including William of Orange and Counts Egmont and Horn, were named as members of the Council of State. Unfortunately, these arrangements did not represent the reality of Philip's intentions. He left secret instructions that the Regent should take important decisions only with the advice of a hard core of trusted administrators, of whom the chief was Antoine Perrenot, Cardinal Granvelle. Nor did Philip leave The Netherlands in a prosperous or stable condition. The collapse of the English cloth market after 1550, and the disruptions caused to trade by the war had reduced the prosperity of the southern provinces, and the resistance of the Estates General to taxation had left the government in a state of virtual bankruptcy. At the same time the religious situation was becoming more and more troubled. As we have already seen, both Lutheran and radical ideas had attracted a considerable number of adherents, and the radicals had been executed in large numbers. Lutherans (who were mostly middle or upper class townsmen) had found it much easier to escape persecution, partly because of the privileges of the towns in which they lived, and partly because their wealth and status distanced them from those social revolutionary aspects of radicalism which were particularly feared. It was also true that the nobility of The Netherlands, and the Burgher oligarchies of the big cities had a tradition of enlightened humanism which made them very reluctant persecutors. It was not only that persecution was bad for trade (which it was) but also that the reforming ideas of the 'new learning' had taken a strong hold. Wealth had meant improved education, and improved education had brought reforming ideas. Moreover the ecclesiastical institutions of The Netherlands were more than usually inefficient and worldly. In 1559 the seventeen provinces were divided into no more than four bishoprics, divided between the metropolitan archbishoprics of Rheims and Cologne (neither within Philip's territories). Appointments to these bishoprics were controlled by their wealthy and aristocratic chapters, which, like their counterparts in Germany and France, provided 'outdoor relief' for the younger sons of the nobility. In 1561 Papal Bulls instituted a drastic and much needed reform of the ecclesiastical structure, providing for three new archbishoprics (Utrecht, Mechlin and Cambrai) and fourteen bishoprics (of which twelve were new), under the primacy of the Archbishop of Mechlin. This scheme not only had the immense advantage of bringing the ecclesiastical and secular boundaries of The Netherlands into line, but also recognised the linguistic divisions, since the Province of Utrecht was Dutch and Frisian speaking, Mechlin Dutch speaking, and Cambrai Walloon. However it aroused bitter resentment and was only slowly implemented. One of the reasons for resentment was that Granvelle was immediately named as primate; another was that the transfer of patronage from the aristocracy to the Crown was not only a loss to the former, was but also (rightly) seen as a critical step in a royal policy of imposing more centralised control. Even worse was the proposal to finance these new sees by appropriating the revenues of several of the wealthiest and laxest of the religious houses, which would also have severely damaged the patronage of the nobility. A concerted campaign in the provincial estates in which the nobility (most unusually) joined forces with the burghers, eventually forced the abandonment of this latter plan. The new bishoprics scheme was thus a major bone of contention, just at the time when the dynamic new force of Calvinism was entering The Netherlands for the first time. There had been a centre of radical protestantism at Emden in Friesland for some time, which had disseminated its influence throughout the poorer northern provinces, but what was now happening in the south was very much more dramatic. When the borders with France were re-opened in 1559, French speaking Calvinist preachers began to cross into Hainault and Flanders, and enjoyed rapid success. There were two reasons for this; one was that economic depression in the cloth towns had created hardship and unemployment, which gave the preachers a willing and volatile audience among the urban poor; the second was that the intellectual appeal and orderliness of Calvinist doctrine gave it a 'respectability' which the earlier radicalism had not had and enabled the preachers to make a small but significant number of aristocratic converts. Margaret's government was therefore operating under great strain, and this strain first came to the surface in a concerted campaign by the nobles to get rid of Granvelle. Philip at first seems to have believed that he could gain the co-operation of most of the nobles by sacrificing his minister. In 1564 Granvelle was withdrawn, but at the same time the king sought to sow discord among his opponents by fostering intrigues on the part of the Walloon nobles (particularly the Duke of Aerschot) against the Dutch, led by William of Orange. William was *persona non grata* with Philip because he had repaired his declining fortunes by, marrying (in 1561) Anna, the immensely well endowed daughter of Duke Maurice of Saxony. Maurice had been a leading opponent of Charles V, and a Lutheran. If the king had been inclined to distrust the powerful Prince of Orange before, he now regarded him with undisguised hostility, and in spite of William's early aversion to the intolerance of Calvinism, believed him to be a leading promoter of heresy. Within the Netherlands William and his friends took over the position vacated by Granvelle, but found themselves opposed, not only by Aerschot but also by the Provincial Estates, which demanded an end to extraordinary taxation and the relaxation of the religious persecution. Philip was bombarded with complaints from all sides, which only confirmed him in the opinion that the Netherlanders were incorrigible and incompetent. However, in 1565 Orange and the Estates found enough common ground to agree upon a demand for the Estates General to be summoned, and for the pursuit of a more liberal religious policy. In October 1565 Philip flatly rejected both demands, and appointed Aerschot to the Council of State. The result was a movement known as the Compromise - a league of about 400 nobles (mostly minor), to force concessions from the Regent irrespective of the King's embargo. They might have succeeded had their gathering not coincided with a number of serious outbreaks of Calvinist iconoclasm in the southern cities, and had one or two extremists among their own number not sought to back up their demands with an appeal to arms. Thoroughly alarmed, the moderates and *politiques* made common cause with the catholics to put down these dangerous threats. William of Orange led the forces of law and order, and at the same time Margaret promised some relaxation of the religious persecution, at least against Lutherans. By August 1566 the crisis appeared to be over. Philip, however, was not prepared to leave well alone, and in order to understand why, we need to grasp one or two essential points about Philip's character In the first place he had a strong sense of his own inferiority to his father, for whom he retained an exaggerated respect. Everything that his father had bequeathed him thus became a sacred trust - both the territories themselves and the defence of the catholic church. This meant that compromise and surrender were alike out of the question, no matter what political reality or wisdom might dictate. In the second place he had a genuine, almost pathological hatred of heresy, and would no more have considered tolerating it than signing a pact with the devil. His reaction to political defeat in 1566 was consequently to resort to force. In August 1567 the Duke of Alba arrived with a large army, and took over the government of The Netherlands. His instructions were simple and far reaching; to punish the leaders of the recent insubordination; to destroy the autonomy of the towns and provinces; and to extract enough money from the country to pay both for its own government and for his army. The Netherlands was to be ruled explicitly for the benefit of the king's imperial policies, without regard for their own wishes or interests.

28. Civil war and settlement in France, 1572-1598

The fourth religious war which followed the massacre of St Bartholomew consisted mostly of an unsuccessful siege of the Huguenot stronghold of La Rochelle. In 1573, the Duke of Anjou was most improbably elected to the throne of Poland, and another peace was patched up. The situation, however, could not now return to the status quo. As soon as the massacre was over, Catherine found herself saddled with the responsibility, and decided to make the best of a bad job by claiming the credit in her dealings with the catholic powers. This meant that she could no longer act as an honest broker with any chance of Huguenot consent; and the Huguenots were forced to abandon the (rather threadbare) theory that they were really fighting for the Crown. The Huguenot party was again dominated (at least for the time being) by its pastors, and developed explicit theories of resistance and covenant. The other main effect of the massacre had been to peg the Huguenots back to their areas of main strength, in the south and west. Elsewhere the expansion, so noticeable right up to 1572, was checked and never began again. Although the protestant party was still strong, and well organised, it was becoming localised. If any chance of ultimate Huguenot victory had ever existed, it disappeared in 1572.

Considering the severity of the blow which had been dealt them, the Huguenots recovered with remarkable speed. This was partly because of the toughness of the clerical leadership; partly because Henry of Navarre escaped from custody at court in 1575 and renounced his recantation, and partly because of their alliance with the politique party which emerged in the wake of the massacre. These politiques were a party of the centre. Some were catholics who were revolted by the massacre, some were pragmatists who simply wanted peace and a chance to trade, some were enemies of the Guises (like Montmorency Damville). They ought to have formed natural allies for Catherine in her search for peace, but because of her association with the Guises, they allied with the Huguenots. They also attracted the support of Catherine's youngest son, the Duke of Alençon, who was trying to establish a separate political identity for himself. Charles IX died in 1574, and the militant Duke of Anjou returned from Poland to succeed him as Henry III. The throne gave Henry a dramatically different perspective on the struggle. He was now able to see the disastrous damage that the fighting was doing to the authority and finances of the Crown, and the extent to which it was overshadowed by the power of the Guises. As a result of these insights, in 1576 Alençon was allowed to negotiate the Peace of Monsieur, which granted the Huguenots freedom to worship everywhere except Paris and the Court, eight security towns, and mixed commissions to try disputes. The immediate result was a resurgence of catholic extremism, directed this time as much against the king as against the Huguenots. Since the early 1560s catholic extremist associations had been in existence. These local leagues, consisting of clergy, nobles and bourgeois, had devoted themselves to counteracting the influence of the Huguenots in their immediate locality. In 1576 on Guise initiative, these unions were brought together into a single Catholic League. Not surprisingly, in view of the leading role of the Guise clientage, this swiftly emerged as a politically reactionary movement, as well as a militant religious one. Its aims included the restoration of traditional rights and powers to provincial estates and nobility, and the confirmation of traditional liberties and immunities. In other words the undoing of all the progress which the monarchy had made towards centralisation and absolutism during the previous century. The monarchy was to be confined within its ancient feudal limitations. With a programme like that (quite apart from its religious tone) it is not surprising that the League found immediate favour with Philip II. With a mixture of manipulation and intimidation the League dominated the Estates General of Blois in 1576, and Henry decided to act against it. Ostensibly praising its religious aims, he declared his sympathy, and in 1577 placed himself at its head, instead of the Duke of Guise. If he hoped to use it for his own purposes, he was disappointed. Deprived of its real function, the League suspended its activities (but not its organisation). In a sense it broke in the king's hand, but in another sense it remained in being awaiting the hand of its true master, the Duke of Guise.

Nevertheless, this was a period of success for the king. As nominal head of the League, he renewed the war against the Huguenots and politiques, and the disagreements between those two parties allowed him considerable military progress. By the Peace of Bergerac in 1577 he cut back the Huguenot's concessions, and declared all leagues dissolved (unavailingly, as it turned out). There then followed a period of uneasy peace at the national level, and sporadic small-scale fighting in the localities. This enabled a partial economic and financial recovery to take place. Alençon (now, confusingly, Duke of Anjou) sought adventures in England and the Netherlands, while the Duke of Guise plotted restlessly and rather futilely with Philip on behalf of Mary, Queen of Scots. Catherine de Médici worked constantly to defuse the tense situation, but the whole logic of events was against her. No one was satisfied, and the economic recovery was sabotaged by enormous increases in the *taille* and the *gabelle* as the king strove to rebuild his ruined finances. Then in 1584 the Duke of Anjou died without heirs. Since the king was also childless (as had been Francis 11 and Charles IX), the next heir was the protestant leader, Henry of Navarre. The dramatic possibility of a Huguenot king immediately resurrected the Catholic League. The initiative this time came from an extremist group among the bourgeois and clergy of Paris; they quickly entered into alliance with the Guises, and the old League of 1576 reappeared all over France; but there was never complete community of interest between the Paris League and the rest, as was shortly to be demonstrated. At first, however, this Guise-led movement appeared to carry all before it. In many parts of France royal officials were replaced by Leaguers, and royal taxes went into the League coffers. Organisation apart, there was clearly a deep and widespread antipathy in the country to the thought of a heretic king, and the League had much tacit support outside its own ranks. In December 1584 the Duke of Guise, acting like an independent sovereign, signed the treaty of Joinville with Philip of Spain, whereby the latter was to subsidise them in return for the secession of French Navarre. That so blatant a betrayal of French national interest should have aroused so little protest is a measure of the strength of feeling in the country. In the face of this power, Henry III was virtually helpless; he renounced all concessions to the Huguenots, and the civil war resumed. The fighting was protracted and inconclusive, which suited Philip very well, since it prevented France from interfering in his campaigns against the Netherlands and England. In order to make doubly sure, Philip prompted the Duke of Guise to seize Paris from royal control in May 1588, at exactly the time that the Armada sailed. This *coup* did not help the Armada, but it made Guise all powerful in France, and drove the humiliated king to the desperate expedient of having him murdered. His brother the Cardinal was assassinated the next day (24 December 1588) and Catherine de Médici died (probably of despair) a few days later. Far from restoring Henry to power, these crimes produced a revulsion of feeling which left the Catholic League stronger than ever under the leadership of the Duke of Mayenne, and in control of virtually every town in France. In Paris the radical Leaguer clergy set up a revolutionary regime 'The Sixteen', which foreshadowed the Committee of Pubic Safety. The only option left to the king was alliance with Henry of Navarre, but this merely meant an exchange of masters, and he had ceased to have any independent authority by the time he was in turn assassinated in August 1589. In dying, he recognised Henry of Navarre as his successor, and he was duly proclaimed as Henry IV; however, there was no chance of his being acceptable to most of catholic France. The League proclaimed his aged uncle Charles, Cardinal of Bourbon, as Charles X, and the war went on. The end was now, however, in sight. Henry made conciliatory statements, and announced his willingness to accept instruction in the catholic faith. In 1590 'Charles X' died, and the League had no plausible alternative. In 1591 Mayenne fell out bitterly with the Paris Sixteen, who had executed two judges of the Paris *parlement,* and the League began to fall apart. In 1593, with extremely good timing, Henry announced his conversion to catholicism, and immediately began to conciliate his former co-religionists. He was able to do this because, after a series of pro-Spanish Popes, Clement VIII (elected in January 1592) was willing to reconcile him in defiance of Philip's wishes. With the League demonstrating its political bankruptcy, and the ostensible cause for its existence removed Mayenne found his support crumbling. Henry IV was crowned in July 1593, and entered Paris in March 1594; the last League resistance was not eliminated until 1598, but by then the movement had long since been broken. The final problem, like the first, was the Huguenots. Still well organised and intractable, they had to be bought off, which the king was by no means unwilling to do. By the Edict of Nantes of 1598 they were accorded a guaranteed minority status, with garrison towns and rights of access to office. Although the *parlement* of Paris fought a rearguard action against the edict, it marked the end of the religious wars, and the re-emergence of France as a great power.

29. The Creation of the United Provinces

In the short term, the Duke of Alba's policy was extremely successful. The Council of Blood rounded up and tried almost 12,000 people of all ranks and conditions, many of whom were executed. The Counts of Egmont and Horn, once loyal servants of Charles V, and more recently campaigners for noble privileges, were beheaded in a deliberate exhibition of 'frightfulness'. A feeble attack from Germany by the exiled William of Orange was easily beaten off and all overt opposition was completely crushed. However, when it came to implementing the more positive side of his instructions, the Duke found himself in immediate difficulties. Not even the loyalest and most catholic of The Netherlands nobles had any use for Philip's centralising policies, and had no intention of assisting in the dismemberment of their provincial liberties. For the time being, Alba could browbeat them, but in the long run it would be impossible to govern the country without some measure of co-operation from what was ostensibly the royalist party. Almost equally serious was the frustration of Alba's intention to make the government of The Netherlands pay for itself by taxation. Curiously enough, this was brought about as much by Philip's legalism as by the Netherlanders themselves. The rulers of The Netherlands, like those of England (but unlike those of France) had never established a right to tax without consent, and in spite of the nature of his regime, Alba was not permitted to usurp that right. Consequently, in March 1569 he was compelled to summon the Estates General, and to put his demands before them. The first, for a one-off, 1% tax on all real property, presented no difficulties, but the second, for a 10% tax on all commercial transactions (the 'tenth penny') ran into immediate difficulties. It was modelled on the Spanish *alcabala,* and was in fact a totally unrealistic tax for a commercial society; to have granted it would have meant bankrupting the whole Netherlands economy, and the Estates General turned it down. Alba resorted to piecemeal coercion of the Estates of particular provinces, with some success, but failed to budge the representatives of the wealthiest areas, Flanders and Brabant. Popular opposition to the tax was almost unanimous, and belated attempts to collect it without consent were everywhere unsuccessful. Eventually it had to be abandoned, and with it went any chance that The Netherlands would cease to be a drain on the Spanish exchequer. The logic of the situation was inexorable; if The Netherlands were to be governed in the interests of Spain, then Spain would have to pay. The king, however, was never willing to make the concessions necessary to alter that situation. The abandonment of the tenth penny was not a concession but a recognition of the inevitable. Alba was aware of this *impasse* long before it dawned on his master; his power had no other base but unchallengeable military control, and by 1570 that control began to be threatened by events outside The Netherlands. One of these was the increasing hostility of protestant England, signalled by the seizure of the Genoese treasure galleys in 1568 as they were bringing the pay for his army. Another was the increasing Huguenot influence at the French court after the Peace of St Germain had made possible Coligny's return. The third (and probably the most important) was the emergence of the Prince of Orange as a statesman of great ability, and an implacable enemy of Spanish rule. Orange, from his exile in Germany, built up a network of diplomatic contacts, both inside and outside the Netherlands; and became progressively more protestant in his alignment. His own position also changed. From being primarily a defender of provincial and aristocratic liberties, he had become by 1572 possessed of a vision of The Netherlands as some sort of a united and autonomous state. 1572 was a crucial year. In May William's brother, Louis of Nassau, invaded from France and captured the town of Mons; at the same time William himself was mustering a force in Germany. Negotiations with the French promised a full scale invasion, and in the summer the Duke of Alba had all his resources deployed in the south to counter such a move. It never came, of course, thanks to the massacre of St. Bartholomew; but what did come was, if entirely

96

unplanned a remarkable coincidence. In 1566 the radical wing of the aristocratic 'compromise' - minor Calvinist nobles - had gone into exile, and had taken to the sea. Calling themselves the 'Sea Beggars' they lived by plundering (mainly) Spanish shipping. What distinguished this from mere piracy was that the Prince of Orange, as an independent sovereign, was able to issue Letters of Marque. Until 1572 they had operated mainly from England, but that summer, in what was ostensibly a gesture of conciliation towards Philip, Elizabeth had expelled them. They immediately descended upon the coast of Holland and seized the small port of Brill. From this base they quickly fanned out, meeting with a mixed reception but very little effective resistance. The reason for this was partly that Alba's troops were down south, and partly that the burgher groups which governed these relatively poor northern towns had been much more heavily infiltrated by the Calvinists than was the case in the great southern cities. In places like Bruges and Antwerp, Calvinism was mainly the religion of the poor and was associated with violence and social revolution. In the north, it was usually possible to establish a Calvinist ruling clique without having to look outside the existing burgher class, and this was of crucial importance. Some towns, such as Middleburg and Amsterdam, resisted the Beggars, but in the majority of cases they entered by agreement. Once established, they frequently behaved in a high-handed fashion, imposing Calvinism upon the reluctant by force; but by the time that Alba was free to disengaged his forces and deal with this attack from the rear, the Beggars' grip upon the provinces of Holland and Zeeland had become unshakeable. Despite the most strenuous efforts, and a fair measure of success, by the Spring of 1573 Alba had conceded that he could not re-take the maritime provinces because of his lack of naval power; he asked for, and obtained, his recall, being replaced as Governor by Don Luis de Requesens. Requesens clearly wished to be conciliatory. He issued a general pardon, and abandoned financial pressure, but was unable to negotiate a settlement because Philip would not countenance any religious concessions. Holland and Zeeland were not merely under Calvinist control, but becoming more Calvinist month by month. Before 1572 the overwhelming majority of protestants in The Netherlands were in the populous southern provinces. In the north, despite their crucial importance, they were a small numerical minority. But as the policy of persecution continued in the south, and it became increasingly clear that the north could not be easily conquered, an extensive migration began to take place. This not only gave the Calvinists a more secure grip on Holland and Zeeland, thus strengthening their determination to resist, it also brought an industrious population of artisans and small traders to increase the prosperity of the towns. At the same time the resistance of the *politique* nobles in the 'loyal' provinces became more overt once Alba's formidable presence was removed. Requesens had to rely almost entirely upon his polyglot army and upon Spanish money to keep his unpopular regime in being and to maintain some kind of pressure on the rebels. In the autumn of 1575 the financial constraint of fighting on two fronts, as well as sustaining the costs of an Empire which had not yet begun to be hugely profitable, proved too much for Philip and he went bankrupt. The unpaid armies in the Netherlands mutinied, and in the midst of the confusion Requesens died, in March 1576. Before he could be replaced, and justifying their action by the urgency of the situation the *politiques* led by the Duke of Aerschot, seized control of the Council of State and summoned the Estates General. They were, however, quite unable to cope with a mutinous army, and in November 1576 the troops sacked the city of Antwerp, causing untold damage and over 7000 deaths.

Within days of this horrifying event, the Estates General had come to terms with the Prince of Orange and published the Pacification of Ghent. While professing continued allegiance to Philip (a concession on Orange's part) the Pacification stipulated that all foreign troops were to be withdrawn, government was to be conducted with the consent of the Estates General, and the edicts against heresy were to be suspended. When the new Governor, Don John, arrived at the beginning of 1577 he had no resources, and was forced to accept this situation in the so-called Eternal Edict. Philip, however, remained as intransigent as ever on the question of religion, refusing to accept any concession, and this served to split the united front. The majority of the Estates General accepted the maintenance of catholicism. Holland and Zeeland would not, and the war resumed. It was a confused struggle, as most of the *politique* lords at first adhered to the Pacification and fought against the Governor. In the autumn of 1577 they tried unsuccessfully to bring in the Archduke Matthias (the Emperor's brother) against him, being unwilling to accept the authority of Orange. Gradually Spanish military power revived, in spite of the death of Don John in 1578 and his replacement with Alexander Farnese, Duke of Parma. In 1579 the uneasy alliance of anti-Spanish forces fell apart; partly because of jealousies between the nobility and the Estates General, and partly because of the revolutionary upsurge of Calvinism in the southern cities, which alarmed the politiques as much as the earlier outburst had done in 1566. In 1579 the Walloon nobles formed the Union of Arras, and came to terms with Parma, who was permitted to make sufficient political concessions to give the settlement some chance of stability. The nobles were strong enough to carry the southern provinces with them, and ten of the seventeen states ceased to be a factor in the conflict. This was a major blow to Orange, who had hoped to preserve a united front against Spain, but he was compelled to salvage what he could by accepting the strongly Calvinist Union of Utrecht, whereby the seven northern provinces presented their own interpretation of the Pacification of Ghent. By this agreement political power was divided between the Estates General and the House of Orange, and Calvinism was established. A bitter pamphlet war followed, as the northerners sought to justify themselves, and Philip sought to condemn them as traitors and heretics. In 1581 the northern provinces formally renounced their allegiance to Spain in the Act of Abjuration, and began to seek an alternative sovereign. Their main need by that time was for military aid, as Parma began to gain one victory after another, but an attempt to call in the Duke of Anjou was a fiasco, and Orange was already looking to England when he was assassinated in 1584.

By the time that this happened, the religious distinction between north and south had become absolutely clear. Not only had there been much voluntary migration, Parma had also expelled the Calvinists from the south and many, although not all, had gone to the north. As the counter reformation strengthened its grip on Flanders and Brabant, commercial prosperity shifted to the north, with Amsterdam in particular taking the place of a virtually ruined Antwerp. With so much trade depending upon protestant countries such as England and Denmark, whose merchants did not care to venture within reach of the inquisition, this is not surprising. What is surprising is that, even when the north was militarily *in extremis,* as it was by 1585, these ports continued to flourish. The struggle could certainly not have been carried on without them. In 1585, unable to prevaricate any longer, Elizabeth grudgingly came to the assistance of the United Provinces, sending a small army under the Earl of Leicester. Leicester became embroiled in the internal quarrels of the Regents against the Ultra-Calvinists, did little good and deeply offended his own queen. However, as a result of her move, Philip launched the Armada against England, and that took some pressure off the Dutch at a critical period. In spite of all the quarrels and blunders the United Provinces survived; this was partly because of their prosperity, partly because of the toughness of the sea defences of Holland and Zeeland, and partly because of Philip's overstretched resources. Philip lived up to the last penny of his income, and even when the silver of the Indies was at maximum flow (1580-1590) he never had enough for all his projects. By 1590 Parma's offensive had slowed to a crawl, and he could ill afford a diversion to relieve Paris in 1592. Parma's death in the latter year, and the emergence of Maurice of Nassau (William of Orange's son) as a brilliant general, shifted the balance of power in the Netherlands again. Between 1592 and 1598 the Spaniards were finally driven out of the north, but the northerners could make no significant inroads into the now solidly catholic south. By the end of the century stalemate had been reached, although it was to take another nine years to bring the Spaniards to negotiate, and nearly half a century and another war to acknowledge the *fait accompli* of the independence of the United Provinces.

30. Spain as an Imperial Power

Unlike his father, Philip II had no imperial ideology Only the Holy Roman Emperor himself could claim the temporal headship of Christendom - the *Imperium*. What Philip exercised was *Monarchia,* and the fact that he exercised it over many lands did not alter its nature. He rejoiced in his title of *Rex Catholicus,* and saw himself as the natural champion of the church; but for that very reason his relations with the papacy were constantly strained, because his championship inevitably favoured Spanish interests, and successive popes reacted with mounting suspicion. Philip's Imperial practice was also different from that of Charles V in a number of significant ways. Charles had been a restless traveller, polyglot and cosmopolitan. After his early unhappy experiences in Spain, where the arrival of his Flemish councillors had provoked revolt, he had tended to rule each of his numerous dominions through its own natives, committed to his service. Philip spoke only Castilian, resided in Castile for the last forty years of his life, and preferred Castilians to all his other subjects in positions of power. The New World was also a Castilian monopoly. Even other Spaniards were not in theory allowed to trade there, and were not appointed to office. The justification for this was that Castile was the backbone of the Empire. Its taxes contributed nearly 70% of Philip's ordinary revenue, and its manpower provided most of the dreaded *tercios,* the most effective soldiers in the world. Much of the country was upland pasture, economically dominated by the *mesta,* a sheep ranching consortium, and over-populated in the early sixteenth century, like many upland regions. But Philip effectively killed the goose which laid so many golden eggs. By the end of the century the *mesta* had been ruined by the *alcabala,* which was siphoning off the equivalent of £500,000 a year into the royal coffers, by the demands of the recruiting sergeant, and the rival attractions of the celibate religious life. But if the Empire was bad for Castile, Castile was also bad for the Empire. Castilian pride and intolerance were notorious from England to Naples, and from Portugal to Brabant. The Marquis of Ayamonte, the governor of Milan wrote to Philip in 1570 'I do not know whether there is anyone in the world who is subject to the Spanish Empire and nation...who does not abhor their name...' The Italians, wrote one Castilian, were as bad as the Indians of the New World, and had to be shown who was the master. It was Castilian *conquistadores* who justified their inhuman treatment of the indigenous peoples of the New World on the grounds that they were not proper human beings anyway, and who invented the purely racial criterion of *limpieza de sangre* (purity of blood) as a qualification for office and power.

The strengths and weaknesses of Castile were closely related. The crusading zeal, growing out of the *reconquista,* which motivated so many of her soldiers, seamen, nobles and explorers, also provoked a paranoid fear of the slightest deviation from a rigidly defined doctrinal orthodoxy. The discovery of a handful of humble *alumbrados* in Seville and Valladolid in 1559 provoked something approaching a national panic and gave the Inquisition overwhelming popular support. A decade later the constant harassment of the remaining Morisco population of Granada, an industrious and downtrodden people, not only drove them into revolt but provoked large numbers into escaping to north Africa. There they joined the Barbary corsairs, and not only wrought a terrible revenge upon the Spanish coast, but also took service with Spain's Ottoman enemies, a course of action which would probably otherwise never have occurred to them. The Inquisition was a symbol of Castilian solidarity. It had been set up in 1478 as an ecclesiastical tribunal, staffed mainly by the Dominicans, but had always been in substance a royal court. In the later sixteenth century it acquired a somewhat undeserved reputation for 'frightfulness', as a part of the Black Legend built up by English and Dutch propagandists. Its procedures were never particularly cruel, but they were secretive and arbitrary. The accused was never informed of the charges in advance, nor of who had brought them, and both hearsay and circumstantial evidence was accepted. Consequently malicious prosecutions, arising out of private disputes and personal grudges were numerous; and no one who had been arrested by the Inquisition was free from the taint thereafter, even if they had been acquitted. Nevertheless, its popularity remained high, and in the middle of Philip's reign it was said to have been served by 20,000 informers. This was largely because Spaniards in general, and Castilians in particular, took ideological subversion very seriously. The Inquisition had been established to deal with those who had been forcibly converted from Judaism or Islam (Marranos and Moriscos) and who were suspected of backsliding. Assimilation had never been particularly successful, particularly of the Moriscos, because of language difficulties, and because there was never any effective policy of Christian education. Moriscos could not become priests, or enter any professional employment - so they clung to their traditional ways, and were increasingly persecuted. By contrast protestantism was never a great problem, and the *luteranos* were little more than bogey men - like the demonic figure of Anna Boleyna who started to figure in Spanish carnival processions. To be a wholehearted Castilian patriot, one had to be a pure blooded 'Old' Christian a sentiment much stronger among the peasantry and minor hidalgos than it was among the greater nobility, several of whom had married Jewish money in the past. As Sancho Panza was to say, 'being an Old Christian I was better than being the greatest nobleman alive'. The Inquisition was also a means whereby Philip kept tight control over the church. It was not coincidence that the Spanish bishops in Trent in 1563 attempted to revive the conciliar theory, and argued for the effective autonomy of national churches. The test case was that of Bartolomé Carranza, the archbishop of Toledo. Carranza had been in England with Philip, and had become closely associated with Cardinal Reginald Pole. At that time he had been highly in favour with Philip, but after they had both returned to Spain, Carranza's enemies used his association with Pole (who had been unsuccessfully accused of heresy) to discredit him with the king. He was arrested by the Inquisition, a process to which the pope objected on the grounds that an archbishop could only be tried in Rome. The Council of Trent declared his views to be orthodox, but in Spain as Cardinal Allesandrino reported 'The most ardent defenders of Justice ... hold that it is better to condemn an innocent man than to let the Inquisition suffer any diminution of its powers.' After seven years of deadlock the case was transferred to Rome, and Carranza was eventually acquitted, but died shortly afterwards. If any other bishop in Spain needed a dire warning of the consequences of offending the king, that was it. Every foreign influence, spiritual or intellectual, was considered to be suspect, and any indigenous religious movement which was slightly different. Ignatius Loyola, Theresa of Avila and St. John of the Cross all spent time in the prisons of the Inquisition, and it is not surprising that Spain has been described as a 'closed society' during this period. The cosmopolitan influence of Erasmus, which had been extensive in the early part of the century, was completely banished after the issue of the first Index in 1551, and the discovery of the *alumbrados* in 1558 provoked new and severe measures of repression. The second index of 1559 was draconian, and virtually all foreign books and intellectual influences were prohibited. Spanish students were prohibited from studying abroad, even in orthodox countries such as Italy and Bavaria. Nevertheless, the closure was never complete. The attitude of the Inquisition fluctuated somewhat with the personality of the Chief Inquisitor, and Spain remained a part of the Europe of the Counter-Reformation. That could hardly have been otherwise when Spain ruled Naples, Milan and a large part of the Low Countries. Successive viceroys of Milan quarrelled violently with the saintly archbishop, Carlo Borromeo, but that was over jurisdiction and not over doctrine. Culturally, Spain exported far more than it imported after 1550. Painters such as Valesquez; writers like Cervantes and Lope de Vega, and theologians such as Melchor Cano, made an impact commensurate with Spain's political and military status as a great power - but neither Philip nor his subjects were willing to learn anything from the outside world.

To some extent the image of enormous strength which Spain succeeded in projecting during the reigns of Philip II and Philip III was always fraudulent, owing more to the weakness of France and the distance of the Ottomans than to her own efficiency or resources. In spite of his early (and vain) hopes of military glory, Philip II was a civilian and a bureaucrat to his fingertips. After settling at Madrid in 1561, and even more after moving to the Escorial in 1584, he travelled little, even within Spain, and spent most of his waking hours in his study, surrounded by vast piles of state papers. In spite of the network of councils which he inherited or established for each of his dominions, he delegated little except the most routine work. His councils advised him by means of written *consultas,* which he read with great care, and annotated assiduously. The result was great consistency of policy, but endless and crippling delays, except in the most urgent of matters. 'If death came from Madrid', said one provincial governor, 'we should all be immortal'. Philip was also congenitally suspicious, which was one of the reasons why he delegated so little. Not only would he not trust the Council of State in the distant Netherlands, he would not trust the nobility of Catalonia (which provoked a crisis in 1568), or even his own viceroys and agents. The Duke of Alba was undermined by factional enemies at court, and the other Castilian grandees who (for the most part) ruled Naples, Sicily, Milan, Aragon, Catalonia, Valencia, and Navarre seldom had their commissions renewed, in case they should become too powerful. Always desiring checks and balances, the king used lawyers and clergy wherever possible to circumscribe the authority of his military commanders. Because he never attended Council meetings himself, his personal knowledge, even of his own most important servants, was very limited. Consequently those who did have access to him - the presidents of the councils, and his own secretaries - tended to exercise disproportionate influence. Both the system of government and the way in which Philip used it, meant that his own character and priorities dictated policy at every stage. Money, to him was only a means to achieve his ends. So he was never interested in how wealth was created, but only in how it could be taxed or otherwise diverted for his purposes. It is not true to say that he had no financial sense; it was, for example, acute awareness of the mounting cost which made him insist upon launching the Armada in 1588 instead of delaying until the following year, as Medina Sidonia would have preferred. However, he had no economic sense, and on several occasions confiscated the private bullion which was being imported from the New World, thus disrupting the operations of his own merchants and bankers, and driving some of them into bankruptcy. Always operating at the full extent of his resources, Philip regarded any temporary easing of financial constraints as an opportunity to discharge some further part of his religious or patriotic duty, rather than an opportunity for retrenchment. And in spite of the enormous quantities of money which he received from the royal control of the silver mines, he died more deeply in debt than he had succeeded.

Philip's style of government created numerous problems. Important decisions were delayed beyond endurance, and the non-Castilian provinces and populations of the Empire were frequently aggrieved. The great Morisco revolt of 1568-70 resulted in the dispersal of the defeated rebels all over Spain, and the large-scale resettlement of Granada, but the problem was not resolved, and between 1604 and 1612 the entire Morisco population was expelled. As we have already seen, discontent in the Netherlands in 1566, repressed in 1567, had turned into open revolt by 1572, resulting in the permanent loss of the seven northern provinces. Faction at court in the late 1570s between the Eboli and the supporters of Philip's bastard brother, Don John, resulted in the murder (with the king's connivance) of the latter's secretary, Escovedo in March 1578. Philip then turned against the Ebolis, and against his own secretary, Antonio

Perez, who had instigated the murder.Both Perez and the Princess of Eboli were arrested and the faction destroyed. After ten years in prison, Perez escaped to Aragon in 1590, and claimed the protection of the liberties of that kingdom - accusing the king directly of Escovedo's murder. Unable or unwilling to over-ride the privileges of Aragon, Philip then fabricated charges of heresy against Perez, and sought to have him arrested by the Inquisition. The Aragonese, outraged by these attempts to circumvent their liberties, rose in revolt in 1591. The revolt was suppressed, and many of the leaders were executed, but the Aragonese were not reconciled to Castilian domination. The last ten years of Philip's life was a decade of failure, starting with the failure of the hugely expensive *empressa* against England, in which the king had invested so much of his prestige and personal commitment. Defeat and then stalemate followed the victories of the 1580s in the Netherlands, and in 1596 the Spanish Crown again went bankrupt. After the failures of 1558 and 1575 there had been a substantial measure of recovery, but the third time was too much. The great fairs, such as that of Medina del Campo, collapsed, taking several of the surviving banking houses with them. After the failure of the Aragonese revolt, Perez escaped to France, and there continued his personal propaganda campaign. After Henry IV's conversion in 1593 the Spanish-backed catholic league in France also collapsed, and Philip's relations with the papacy reached a new low.

It would, of course, be unfair to measure Philip's reign by the last ten years. Not only had he maintained his authority over his Spanish and Italian lands, but he had successfully held back the Ottoman threat in the Mediterranean until it effectively ran out of steam, relieving Malta in 1565, and winning the great sea battle at Lepanto in 1571. The Spanish Empire in the New World developed both politically and economically, and extended greatly in area. The great silver mines of Peru not only fuelled (to some extent) the Spanish war machine, but also helped to transform the whole economic situation of Europe - although that was little to Spain's benefit. most dramatically, however, Philip succeeded in 1580 in establishing his hereditary claim to the throne of Portugal, and by a judicious use of law and force, took over the whole Portuguese Empire, and united the peninsula for the first time under a single ruler. In 1583 his great admiral, the Marquis of Santa Cruz, defeated an English/French/Portuguese fleet at Terciera in the Azores and confirmed the success of his coup.

After his death in 1598, and under a ruler with less charisma, the damaging effects of years of overtaxed resources began to become clear. Disadvantageous treaties of peace were concluded with England in 1604 and the United Provinces in 1609. Natural disasters were added to the effects of mismanagement. In 1598 and 1599 the harvest failed. Dearth was followed by famine, and famine by plague; about 15% of the population was wiped out, and the steady demographic growth of the sixteenth century was halted, and probably reversed. In some parts of Castile, as we have seen, the effects were much worse, coming on top of decades of heavy military recruitment. Pride and confidence were followed by depression, fatalism and cynicism. 'Queremos comer sin trabajar', we want to eat without working, became a popular motto. The society which had aspired to rule the world and conquer the infidel, turned in on itself in an agony of self-analysis. Don Quixote ruled. Philip III was a pallid and supine young man, whose government was quickly taken over by favourites; the currency was heavily debased, and the economy sank further into disaster. In 1621 Philip III died, and war was renewed in The Netherlands. The new king was a minor, and the new favourite was the Count-Duke of Olivares, a distinct improvement on his predecessors. Olivares, much blamed for corruption and self-interest, nevertheless kept the tottering Empire going for over twenty years, until his fall in 1643. Spanish armies still achieved occasional victories, and provided the backbone of the Imperial war effort in the early days of the thirty years war. But in 1640 Olivares, government, constantly weakened by a declining silver supply and no longer able to rely upon the resources of Castile, was faced with two major rebellions. That in Catalonia was eventually suppressed, but Portugal regained her independence, taking what was left of her Empire with her. Finally, in 1643 at the battle or Rocroi, the main army of Spain was routed by the French and the great age of Spanish military power finally came to an end. The shadow of Spanish Imperial power continued to haunt Europe until the Peace of the Pyrenees in 1659 (Oliver Cromwell still believed in it, for instance) but the substance had long since gone. Philip II like Louis XIV of France, ruined his country in pursuit of a great ideal, and both got good posthumous ratings from their own subjects, even when they were living with the consequences.

31. The Empire and the background to the Thirty Years War

The Thirty Years War was not so much the escalation of a domestic crisis within the Empire as a merging and intermingling of conflicts which already existed in various parts of Europe. To Spain, it was essential that the Austrian Habsburgs should retain their grip upon the Holy Roman Empire, because without that alliance her overland communications with The Netherlands - the so-called 'Spanish Road' would be critically threatened. After the re-emergence of France in the reign of Henry IV, peace between France and Spain was only precariously preserved during the minority of Louis XIII by the ascendancy of the ultra-catholic party (the *dévots*) at the French court. The Emperor Rudolf II had attempted to take advantage of the decline in Ottoman aggressiveness and efficiency to free Christian Hungary from the burden of tribute, and had declared war in 1593. However, he not only found the Turks still to be formidable opponents, but compounded his own difficulties by attempting to persecute the protestants among the Hungarian nobility at the same time. By the Treaty of Sitvatorok in 1606 he succeeded in escaping from the Ottoman tribute, but was compelled to placate the protestants with whose assistance this success had been secured. Bohemia was similar to Hungary in that the catholics formed only a minority of the population, and following his concessions in the latter kingdom, Rudolf found himself in 1609 compelled to issue Letters of Majesty, granting religious freedom to the largely Hussite nobility, and to the largely German and Lutheran townsmen. Such concessions were not only damaging to the Counter-Reformation, but also to any hopes which Rudolf may have entertained for the centralisation and strengthening of Imperial power. From The Netherlands to the Turkish border, religious dissent was everywhere associated with provincial autonomy and aristocratic liberties - catholicism with strong central government. This is the main reason why it is impossible to separate politics from religion in discussing the affairs of this period. The revival of catholicism in Germany after 1560 had made the protestant princes jumpy and suspicious, and none more so than the Calvinist Electorate of the Rhine, which was not covered, even by the somewhat fragile safeguards of the Peace of Augsburg. In 1606 their suspicions were raised to fever pitch when Rudolf intervened in a domestic dispute in the strategic town of Donauworth on the Upper Danube. The protestant town council was overthrown, and the town placed under the control of Rudolf's staunchly catholic ally, Maximilian of Bavaria. In response Christian of Anhalt, the chancellor of the Elector Frederick IV of the Palatinate, persuaded a number of protestant princes and cities to form an Evangelical Union for mutual protection, under Frederick's leadership and the patronage of Henry IV of France. This Union was mostly Calvinist, as the Lutheran princes were deeply suspicious of Frederick, and not anxious to promote a political polarisation within the Empire. Nevertheless, that is what happened. Spain was sharply alarmed by the threat to her Rhineland communications, and persuaded Maximilian of Bavaria to set up a Catholic League, to consist of himself and the Electoral archbishoprics, with Spanish subsidies. As an additional safeguard Philip III also endeavoured to negotiate an alternative route for the 'Road', not passing through Savoy, but further east through the Valtelline and the Grisons into the Tyrol. This route would cross the Rhine at Breisach, and avoid Frederick's territories by passing directly into friendly Lorraine.

When we also remember that the twelve year truce between Spain and the Netherlands was due to expire in 1621, and that Spain had every intention of resuming hostilities, it is easy to appreciate what a hair-trigger situation existed in the critical year of 1618. Indeed, hostilities would probably have broken out sooner if the assassination of King Henry IV in 1610 had not disorientated French policy, and the death of Rudolf two years later led to the election of his brother Matthias, who was already an old man, and never saw himself as much more than a caretaker. Matthias, however, was determined that his successor, both as Emperor and as king of Bohemia, should be his nephew Ferdinand, Archduke of Styria. Ferdinand had been educated in Spain, and was a ruthless and energetic exponent of Catholic and Imperial hegemony. His election to either office would have been certain to provoke the open conflict which everyone was by then expecting. He had already suppressed the protestants of Styria, whom his father had tolerated, and driven 10,000 of them into exile. When the Bohemian Diet met to pre-elect Matthias's successor, the old man was himself present. That fact, combined with the skill of his chancellor, Lobkowicz, guaranteed Ferdinand's success, and no sooner was the result declared than a new Council of State was created with a catholic majority. However, given the overall balance of power in the country, this was a highly artificial result, and when zealous Imperial officials tempted providence by making several early moves against protestant churches, the true feelings of the majority of the nobles were quickly revealed.

On 22 May 1618 a large crowd, led by a number of Czech nobles invaded the Hradcany Palace in Prague, the seat of government, and hurled the two most detested officials, Martinitz and Slavata, from a first floor window. A Hussite governing council was elected, and an army mobilised. When the news of this revolt reached him, Matthias was too sick to respond, and as long as he was alive Ferdinand had no authority. The only effective response came from the Spanish ambassador, Oñate, who, without authority and on his own initiative and credit, raised an army of 12,000 men to defend the Catholic cause. Philip III, understanding the crucial strategic importance of Bohemia in a finely balanced Electoral college, endorsed Ofiate's actions. Nevertheless for a few months it looked as though the Habsburg cause was lost. Supported by the Evangelical Union, the Estates of Bohemia, Moravia, Lusatia and Silesia formed a new constitutional league, in which all offices were to be reserved for Hussites and protestants, while Hungary and Upper Austria joined in the revolt, and a military strike against Ferdinand in Vienna was only frustrated by the Spanish troops. Matthias had died in March 1619, and by the summer Ferdinand (who refused to accept the constitutional league) appeared to be fighting for political survival. Given the situation in Bohemia, the three protestant Electors had only to stick together to break the Habsburg succession to the Empire, but John George of Saxony detested the Evangelical Union and voted with the Catholics, so that Ferdinand was elected Holy Roman Emperor on 28 August, just two days after the Bohemian Estates had formally repudiated his earlier election as King. In his place, the Bohemians offered their crown to the leader of the Evangelical Union, the Elector Frederick V of the Palatinate. Both the other princes of the Union and his father-in-law James I of England urged him to refuse, not least because as king under the new constitution, he would have virtually no power. However, Frederick was as zealous for his faith as was Ferdinand. He described the offer as '...a divine calling which 1 must not disobey and duly arrived in Prague in October 1619.

The situation was delicately balanced. On the one hand both Upper and Lower Austria had decided to join the Bohemian Confederation, and the Hungarian prince Bethlen Gabor was prepared to support them. On the other hand, there was a sizeable Spanish army undefeated on Bohemian soil, and the Dutch, who were among Frederick's most enthusiastic supporters, were in the middle of a domestic crisis which made it impossible for them to intervene. It soon transpired that Frederick, for all his enthusiasm, was not the right men to handle such a situation. He filled his court with Germans, and offended both the Hussites and the Lutherans with his extreme Calvinist views. Within a few months his position had begun to crumble. The lack of English and Dutch support dismayed the Bohemians, and when Bethlen Gabor had to withdraw to deal with a Cossack threat in January 1620, they began to look distinctly isolated. Meanwhile the Spanish army in Austria had doubled to 24,000, and Maximilian of Bavaria had mobilised the Catholic League in Ferdinand's support. His price (undeclared at the time) was the secession of the Upper Palatinate and Frederick's Electoral title. Neither the Lutherans, nor the other members of the Evangelical Union were prepared to support Frederick, and the latter declared their neutrality in July 1620. Confronted by two powerful armies, one under Maximilian and the other under Spinola, and without any outside support, the Bohemians were completely defeated in a single campaign, ending with the battle of the White Mountain on 8 November. Frederick made no attempt to redeem the situation; while Maximilian occupied the Upper Palatinate, he fled to the Netherlands, and the Bohemians began to quarrel fiercely among themselves. In the summer of 1621 the Evangelical Union disbanded and by the summer of 1622 the whole of the Palatinate had been overrun by the army of the Catholic League, now commanded by Maximilian's general Tilly. The only good news, if it can be called that, was that the truce between Spain and the United Provinces came to an end in the autumn of 1621, and Spinola withdrew his Spanish army to face the Dutch, whose prevarication was thus abruptly brought to an end - but too late to be any use to Frederick. By 1627 Bohemian protestantism had been completely crushed, most of the rebel leaders executed, the powers of the Estates curtailed, and the Letter of Majesty annulled.

However, such overwhelming success carried its own nemesis. The war in Germany was over by 1622, but in the process the seeds of a new conflict had been sown. The Imperial Diet at Regensburg in 1623 objected to Ferdinand's action in transferring Frederick's Electoral title to Maximilian, an action which was contrary to Imperial law, and which caused many Catholic princes (as well as the protestants) to feel seriously menaced by the revival of Habsburg power. More seriously, in 1621 the Spaniards had invaded the Valtelline and established their own garrisons there. The reasons for this lay in the importance of the 'Road', with The Netherlands war about to restart, and in the unstable politics of the region, where religious factions contended for power. The Spanish action immediately offended France, whose benevolent neutrality had placed a significant part in the catholic triumph in the Rhineland, and in 1623 France, Venice and Savoy signed a treaty aimed at freeing the Valtelline from Spanish control. War was briefly averted when Philip ceded control over the area to the Pope, with whom Louis XIII had no desire to be in conflict. But tougher councils prevailed in France with the rise to power of Cardinal Richelieu in 1624, and by the end of that year a French army had also moved into the region. Neither side wanted an all out struggle, and by 1626 a compromise had been agreed, by which both sides were to withdraw and all the Spanish forts were to be demolished. This was a set-back to Spain, but did not eventually prevent them from using the route for the remainder of the northern war. It was that war, and the ancillary conflicts connected with it (like that in the Valtelline) which led to extended and protracted strife in Germany, rather than the Bohemian revolt, which had merely precipitated matters by bringing catholic armies into being sooner than would otherwise have been the case. Having failed Frederick, and indirectly caused both the collapse of the Evangelical Union and I of England was a non-starter. By 1622 the main focus of his policy was a forlorn attempt to persuade Spain to return a part of Frederick's territories, and to damp down the fires of religious conflict by a marriage alliance between Prince Charles and the Spanish Infanta. The other possibilities were Gustavus Adolphus of Sweden and Christian IV of Denmark. Both had legitimate interests in north Germany (Christian already held Holstein, Verden and Halberstadt), and were willing to promote those interests on the pretext of assisting Frederick and the beleaguered protestant cause in the Empire. The Dutch could afford to be generous with subsidies, and from their point of view any attack upon the Habsburgs would relieve the pressure on them, even if it did not involve the direct engagement of Spinola's forces. Since most of the Habsburg money still came from Spain, the more overstretched those resources were, the better.

In the summer of 1625 Christian was elected Director of the Lower Saxon circle of the Empire, and moved his army with the intention of engaging that of the Catholic League.

However the campaign was aborted by an accident to the king, and it was not until the following year that there was any effective action in the north. Meanwhile an extraordinary new phenomenon had appeared upon the scene, which was also to play a large part in the excessive protraction of the wars. This was the mercenary army of Albrecht von Waldstein (usually known as Wallenstein). Wallenstein had made a dubious fortune out of being military governor of Prague after the suppression of the revolt, speculated in confiscated land, and purchased a huge estate in Friedland, near the Sudeten mountains. This estate he then turned into a military base aiming to produce enough food and equipment to supply a full size army. That army he then planned to hire out to the highest bidder, making his profit by exacting protection money from the towns and countryside among which he was operating. He calculated (rightly) that an army which was regularly paid and efficiently served would be much more amenable to discipline, and would consequently be a more efficient fighting machine. Wallenstein was probably not quite as cynical as this outline suggests. Although he was willing to hire any competent mercenary soldiers, whatever their faith or nationality, he himself was a catholic, and seems to have hoped from the start that it would be the Emperor who would take up his services. And so it proved. By 1525 Ferdinand was acutely aware that he had no usable army of his own. Spinola was engaged in the Low Countries, and the army of the League under Tilly could not be relied upon in all circumstances,   given the growing suspicion of Habsburg ambitions. So when Wallenstein approached him, he found the terms irresistible. In the summer of 1625, before the Danish invasion, he agreed to hire 21,000 men. After Christian's abortive operation, realising that he might now be facing a serious war in the north, he increased the number to 40,000. This was still short of Wallenstein's estimate of his own capacity, but it was the first test for the military entrepreneur, and in the winter of 1525/6 he moved his army into Saxony to collaborate with Tilly against the expected invasion.

32. The Scandinavian intervention

1626 was a year of grand strategy, significantly orchestrated by the United Provinces on one side and Spain on the other. By the treaty of the Hague, Christian of Denmark was to engage the forces of the Catholic League, thus enabling Christian of Brunswick to invade the Rhineland and restore Frederick to the Palatinate. Meanwhile Count von Mansfeld was to evade the forces of Wallenstein, with the objective of reaching Bohemia and resurrecting the protestant and Hussite revolt. The money for this ambitious plan was to be provided by The Netherlands. On the other side, Philip IV's chief minister, Olivares, aimed to strike at the vulnerable and important link between Holland and the Baltic ports. To achieve this he intended to use both the stick and the carrot. The carrot was to be a monopoly of northern trade with Spain and the stick was to be Wallenstein's army. Wallenstein was to advance to the Baltic coast, and link up with a Spanish fleet which was intended to reassure the Hanseatic ports that they could safely break their links with the Netherlands. Since Wallenstein had his own ambitious plans to carve out another principality in north Germany, he was quite happy to co-operate in this scheme. In the campaigns which followed, both sides were disappointed. Christian of Brunswick's campaign was aborted by his death in June, and Mansfeld was out-manoeuvred by Wallenstein. He reached Moravia, but was unable to break back into Bohemia, and was gradually edged out towards the Hungarian border, where he died in November. Christian of Demnark advanced into Saxony as planned, but was completely defeated by Tilly at the battle of Lutter, lost over half his army, and spent the rest of the year trying to extricate himself from the mess. On the other hand, neither Wallenstein nor the Spaniards made any progress towards disrupting Dutch trade in the Baltic. Mainland Denmark was invaded and over-run in 1628, but Tilly was badly injured in the process, and Wallenstein, following his own priorities, seized the Duchy of Mecklenburg. By the beginning of 1628 he had 128,000 men under arms, and turned back to the original strategy of two years before by laying siege to the port of Straslund.

However, in spite of promises, he was still without sea power. Straslund was supplied by sea from Denmark and Sweden, and after a few weeks he abandoned the siege. Meanwhile the southern end of the Spanish road was again causing problems. The important strategic fortress of Casale, between Milan and Savoy, was controlled by the Duchy of Mantua. In 1628 the Duke died and his lands was passed by inheritance to the French Duke of Nevers. The Spanish military governor of Milan decided upon a pre-emptive strike against Casale before the French could occupy it, but failed, and the French quickly installed a strong garrison. So in spite of the great battle of Lutter and the defeat of Denmark, the Habsburg cause made little further progress between 1626 and 1629. Christian made an easy peace at Lubeck in the same year, surrendering all claims to north German territory and resigning as Director of the Lower Saxon circle. In return, all his Danish lands were restored.

With friends like Wallenstein, Ferdinand hardly needed enemies. Not only was the general stirring up widespread discontent in north Germany by his exactions, both the Electors as a group and the Catholic League had protested in 1627 against his unbridled operations. They feared him as a possible agent of Habsburg absolutism, but Ferdinand now had grave doubts about whether he controlled him at all, especially as he was heavily in his debt. This being so, the Emperor seems to have concluded that he might as well be hung for a sheep as a lamb, and determined to enforce a literal interpretation of the Peace of Augsburg. In March 1629 he issued the Edict of Restitution, which had three major implications. In the first place, it outlawed Calvinism, which had not been included in the Peace of Augsburg, thus not only destroying any possibility of Frederick's restoration, but also placing a number of minor principalities under the ban of the Empire. Secondly, it required the return of all ecclesiastical territories secularised since 1555 (the dubious ecclesiastical reservation), which would have meant an extensive redrawing of the map of Germany, and the enforced conversion of populations which had been protestant for two or three generations. Thirdly, the Edict was issued without reference to the Diet, and in terms which clearly indicated a bid for Imperial absolutism. The archbishoprics of Magdeburg and Bremen, a dozen dioceses and many monastic estates were to be handed over to Imperial commissioners simply by the force of the Emperor's writ. The Princes of the Catholic League were almost as alarmed as their protestant counterparts, seeing the enormous army of Wallenstein behind this unprecedented boldness. In fact it seems that Wallenstein did not approve of Ferdinand's actions, but he carried out his orders on this occasion in the manner of an exemplary official. Magdeburg and Bremen were occupied, and Augsburg was forced to submit to a catholic bishop. To rub in the lesson, the Emperor then bestowed Magdeburg upon Leopold William, his youngest son.

In the circumstances, it is not surprising that the Imperial Diet, summoned to Regensburg in 1630, should have spelled trouble. Ferdinand wanted to secure the election of his son as King of the Romans, he wanted support in Mantua, and he wanted to repay his debt to Spain by supporting her armies against the Dutch in Brabant. In an attempt to bargain, he took the risk of dismissing Wallenstein, on the pretext that he had refused to serve in Mantua, but he got nowhere with any of his projects - the League princes led by Maximilian setting an example of opposition. Without the support of the Diet, the Emperor eventually lost the contest for Mantua; once Richelieu had defeated the ultra catholic party in France in November 1630, he was able to prosecute the war there with vigour, and by the treaty of Cherasco in June 1631 the Duke of Nevers was firmly installed in the contentious city. Meanwhile, Gustavus Adolphus of Sweden had landed in Pomerania in July 1630, and the whole military situation in the north was transformed. Gustavus was, almost literally, the nemesis of Ferdinand's success. He had been deeply concerned by Wallenstein's advance to the Baltic in 1628, and by his seizure of Mecklenburg - that was why he had come to the assistance of Straslund. He was also as genuinely protestant as Ferdinand was catholic, and was horrified by the implications of the Edict of Restitution. Finally, and less altruistically, he wanted his own base in northern Germany, from which to operate (as need might required) against his traditional enemies, the Danes and the Poles. He cleared the decks by signing a truce with Poland in September 1629, and had no sooner landed than he found himself the object of French diplomatic attentions. By the treaty of Barwälde in January 1631 he accepted a hefty French subsidy in return for agreeing to fight against the Emperor, which he intended to do in any case. There is no sign that Gustavus's priorities were at all influenced by this treaty, because although the subsidy was useful, it was not in any sense necessary to, maintain his war effort. Richelieu had struck a bad bargain in one sense, because Gustavus was no more amenable to French control than he had been before. On the other hand, the French were again relieved of the necessity for direct military intervention.

As a result of Richelieu's intervention, both the pace and the confusion of events then increased. The Lutheran princes were just as suspicious of Gustavus and his motives as they were of Ferdinand, and John George of Saxony (who was busily recruiting an army for his own protection) offered to ally with the Emperor if the latter would withdraw the Edict of Restitution. His offer was refused, and most of the Lutheran states remained in uneasy neutrality. At the same time Maximilian of Bavaria signed an agreement with France, undertaking not to assist the Emperor provided that France guaranteed his Electorate and Rhineland possessions. Since Richelieu's other ally, Gustavus Adolphus, was committed to restoring both to Frederick, the French were going to have some difficulty in honouring their pledges. Maximilian's neutrality had meanwhile transferred Tilly and his army to the Emperor's service, and the dismissal of Wallenstein placed most of the latter's troops also under Tilly's command. Unfortunately Tilly did not have Wallenstein's resources, and the Emperor did not have enough money to keep him supplied. As a result, in May 1631, Tilly moved against Magdeburg, one of the few cities to declare for Gustavus and reputedly well stocked with provisions. The city was taken, the army got out of control, and the resultant sack caused some 25,000 casualties and the destruction of the desperately needed provisions. Without either money or supplies, Tilly's army had become little better than a huge band of marauders. Shock and fear drove both Saxony and Brandenburg into the Swedish camp, and by the end of the year Gustavus had both full control of Mecklenburg and Pomerania (his chief military target), and the alliance of all the main north German princes. He marched south and decisively defeated Tilly at the battle of Breitenfeld in Saxony - the first pitched battle of his campaign. The sequel then demonstrated the fragility of his French alliance, because instead of attacking the Habsburg lands, as Richelieu would have wished, he marched into the Rhineland, at the same time forcing the reluctant Saxons to invade Bohemia and 'liberate' Prague. In November 1631 he captured Frankfort, and established his winter quarters there. Thoroughly alarmed by this extremely independent ally, the French then also moved troops into Alsace and Lorraine, and between them the French and the Swedes completely blocked the 'Spanish Road'. From this position of enormous strength, Gustavus then brought forward his own plan for the solution of Germany's problems, which required no less than the secession of the protestant Princes from the Holy Roman Empire, and their union with Sweden.

The reaction was predictably unenthusiastic. Gustavus may have seen himself as the saviour of German protestantism, but he was also a very obvious imperialist. The Lutherans could hardly reject the proposal outright, as they feared the alternative subjection to Ferdinand even more, so they stalled and played for time. By the beginning of 1632 Gustavus had restored Frederick to the Palatinate, and overrun most of Bavaria. His spring campaign would clearly be an advance down the Danube towards Vienna. In this desperate emergency, Ferdinand recalled Wallenstein, apparently giving him a free hand to conduct the war as he saw fit. As the only man who could afford to pay and supply an army on the catholic side, he could in any case hardly have been tied to conditions. Wallenstein swept the Saxons out of Bohemia, and then moved north, apparently to threaten Pomerania. This effectively diverted Gustavus from his earlier intention, and he pursued Wallenstein, catching him at Lutzen in November 1632. There the Swedes gained a second decisive victory, but Gustavus was killed in the battle, leaving the political victory to the Imperialists. However, the king's death was not without its advantages from the protestant point of view. The extremely able Swedish Chancellor, Axel Oxenstierna, immediately took over the command, and with Gustavus's threatening personality removed, found the Lutheran princes much more amenable. Within weeks he had put together a new alliance, the League of Heilbronn, embracing all the protestant states except Saxony (which was striving to return to a position of neutrality), and once again subsidised by France. Nor was the disappearance of Gustavus good news for Wallenstein, because much of the aggressiveness had now gone out of the Swedish army, and the League of Heilbronn was more concerned with defence than attack. He was therefore no longer indispensable, and faced the bitter hostility of Maximilian for having done nothing to recover Bavaria. Scarcely disguising his own ambitions, Wallenstein began to negotiate with all sides like the independent power which he in fact was, and the Emperor dismissed him for a second time in January 1634. The general then made a serious mistake, by failing to take into account that some of his officers took their allegiance to the Emperor and the catholic church seriously. When it was rumoured that he was proposed to take his army over to the League of Heilbronn, these officers mutinied and killed him. Wallenstein's death, following that of Gustavus, cleared the ground for a new phase of the struggle. Most important, Ferdinand regained the initiative. His son and namesake took over the command of the army (and its supply base, which was now available), recovered Bavaria, and defeated an attempt by the League to recover Bohemia. In the summer of 1634 the situation was further improved by a renewed Spanish effort against the Netherlands. A fresh Spanish army set out from Genoa, and joined forces with Ferdinand in the Tyrol. In September the combined force met the army of the League of Heilbronn at Nordlingen completely defeated it, and recovered control of the Rhineland. Both militarily and politically, it was as though the Swedish victories had never taken place, and Richelieu was brought face to face with the failure of his vicarious policies.

33. The France of Henry IV and Richelieu

The conversion of Henry IV to catholicism in 1593 guaranteed him (as it was designed to do) the support of the great majority of Frenchmen, who were loyal to the crown and not over-demanding in their religious standards. But it naturally alarmed and distressed the Huguenots. How should they react? Some were totally disillusioned and wanted to renew the civil war. They tightened their political and military organisation, and were still capable of putting 25,000 men into the field. On the other hand many still had a close rapport with their former leader, and were inclined to trust his promises of generous terms. What became immediately clear was that the Huguenots were still a force to be reckoned with, and that a negotiated settlement was therefore imperative. The negotiations were tough and prolonged, but the Edict of Nantes which eventually emerged in April/May 1598 contained nothing that was new or original. The protestants were granted freedom of conscience, and the right to worship where they had worshipped before, except in and around Paris. All public offices were to be open to them (a major concession which did much to reconcile the Huguenot aristocracy), and a special chamber was added to the Paris *parlement,* in which a mixed panel of catholic and protestant judges would hear disputes between parties of different confessions. To guarantee the observance of the edict, the Huguenots were allowed to garrison about one hunfred towns at the king's expense; on the other hand, catholic worship was now to be allowed in those areas where the protestants had hitherto been strong enough to prevent it. As with all realistic compromises, no one was entirely satisfied with the Edict, but the strength of the king's position and the urgent desire for peace eventually overcame the consciences of the scrupulous. The ultra-catholic *parlements* were the toughest nut to crack, particularly that of Paris, which refused ratification. A mixture of cajolery, and the threat of a *lit de justice* eventually prevailed, in what was to be held as a classic demonstration of Henry's political skill, but active co-operation was more than could be hoped for, and the administration of the Edict creaked from the start. Pope Clement VIII was naturally offended, regarding any settlement with heretics as *ipso facto* void. But papal censures did not have much effect, except upon those who wished to use them for their own purposes, and fortunately for Henry Clement also needed his support to secure control of Ferrara, so he accepted the Edict, although with (face saving) bad grace. The Edict of Nantes had little to do with toleration, in which neither side believed. It was a *modus vivendi,* creating two religious communities, very different in size and resources, within the same state. For the time being it fulfilled its purpose, reuniting the country behind the king, but in the long term it was a failure. The Huguenots had dwindled from 2000 congregations to about 800, and the unsatisfactory enforcement of the Edict after Henry's death made them increasingly vulnerable - a vulnerability which they did nothing to alleviate by periodic rebellions.

Having settled the religious issue, and finally defeated the remnants of the Spanish-backed League, Henry was faced with two main tasks - to restore the commercial and agricultural prosperity which alone could fill his coffers with taxation, and to recover as far as possible royal control over the administration. A series of edicts freed the trade in grain, forbade the felling of mature trees without licence, and prohibited the nobility from hunting across the peasants' fields in the three months before harvest. These, and many other similar measures, were partly the result of the king's own awareness of what needed to be done, and partly of the enlightened advice of his chief adviser, the Huguenot Due de Sully. Sully was an old comrade in arms, and was much trusted by Henry, becoming *surintendant, de sfinances* in 1599, but his was not the only influential voice, and the king's own initiative counted for much. Canals were built, roads and bridges repaired, and internal markets assiduously fostered. A navy was also built for the purpose of protecting the reviving merchant marine and fishing fleet; but so strong was the Dutch grip upon the carrying trade by this time that French merchant shipping was a negligible factor during this period, and although deep sea cod fishing continued to flourish, attempts to revive North Sea fishing failed in the face of Dutch and English competition. At the same time, neither Henry nor Sully, nor Sully's great rival, the chancellor Belliévre, ever lost sight of the fact that commercial prosperity was not an end in itself. Between 1599 and 1610 the king's revenue increased from 27 million livres a year to 60 million, and the debt fell from 300 million to 196. The price of this success was high, and taxes remained heavy, in spite of the fact that the country was at peace, but the most spectacular improvement was achieved by tough accountancy, and by cutting out the middlemen in the tax-farming chain, rather than by actually increasing the burden on those who paid. On the other hand, nothing was done to make the chief personal tax, the *taille,* any more equitable. Indeed it became less so. Noble exemption spread from the *pays d'états* to all regions, and bourgeoise exemptions became more numerous as patents of office or nobility were purchased. Consequently, although the peasantry could support the burden in good years, there was little margin, and no capital to plough back into improvements. Henry's celebrated concern for the peasants' standard of living was more a publicity coup, and a reflection of his general popularity as an effective king than of any specific measures which he took to improve their lot.

Politically, the main problem continued to be with the aristocracy. The gentry or *seigneurs* were again out of employment with the ending of the wars, and lacking both income, and an outlet for their energies. Most of them were not sufficiently educated to be much use as genuine administrators, and Henry therefore spent very large sums annually out of his household budget on fees, annuities and insubstantial court offices. These not only purchased their loyalty to some extent, but also improved their attachment to the regime by bringing them within the confines of the court - which expanded greatly in consequence. They remained a turbulent element within society, but were permitted to turn their violence upon each other in the form of duels which sometimes assumed the scale of gang warfare, and resulted in hundreds of casualties every year. Both the League and the Huguenots had been to some extent constitutionalist in their political thinking, and the ultimate victory of a kind of politique catholicism had therefore also been a victory for absolutist principles. This success had also been emphasised by the failure of the Estates General to make any independent stand. The meeting of 1593 had been dominated by the extreme wing of the League, a party which had collapsed in discredit within a year, leaving a sour taste of Spanish domination behind, and the king in sole possession of the patriotic credentials. On the other hand the wars had seen a drastic reduction of crown rights, particularly to lands, reversions, escheats and revenues, either through a process of usurpation which would take time, energy and application to reverse, or through grants necessitated by the need for military support. Some towns had become virtually autonomous franchises, and provincial governors had assumed the right to appoint royal officials, particularly Henry's two main allies, Montmorency-Damville in Languedoc and Lesdiguières in Dauphin. The king's main remedy for this situation was a process of attrition. The higher nobility were excluded from his Council, the chief instrument of central government, which was filled mainly with the *noblesse de robe* (like Sully), and this exclusion gradually reduced their power in the regions by cutting them off from the source of royal patronage. No dramatic action was taken, and it was consequently difficult for the disgruntled to find a point upon which to stand, but their disillusionment was nevertheless real, and at least two of Henry's former noble supporters conspired against him. However, as long as royal absolutism was seen to be succeeding, in terms of more efficient government, peace and national recovery, conspirators had little leverage. During the troubles many appointments had been simply usurped from the Crown, particularly by Leaguer nobles, and after 1593 the holders of such offices, fearing dispossession, had been among the first to make their peace with the king, thus contributing substantially to the rapid increase of his power. Many of these offices had in any case been purchased, and the anxiety of the holders to protect their investment also contributed to their compliance. In 1604 Sully decided to add another dimension to this well-established practice by introducing the *paulette*. This was an annual tax of about 4d in the pound on the return from purchased offices, in exchange for which the office became hereditary. This added to the value of the purchase, both for the king and the purchaser, and also had the incidental effect of reducing the patronage of the nobility - many of whom had usurped the king's right to sell the offices in the first place. It did nothing to improve the quality of administration, but that had never been a consideration in the sale of offices. The real work was always done by genuine officials, over whose appointment the king was at great pains to recover control.

Much of Henry's success in retrenchment depended upon the preservation of peace. From 1595 to 1598 Henry needed a war with Spain to pull the country together, but with the Edict of Nantes and the Treaty of Vervins in the same year he could turn his attention to the process of recovery. And yet, ironically, that peace would also certainly have been broken had he lived. A dispute in 1609 between the Emperor and the protestant princes over the succession to the duchies of Jüllich, Berg and Cleves threatened to lead to an increase of Habsburg power on the lower Rhine, and Henry decided to intervene. It was hardly essential to French interests that he did so, and with both England and the United Provinces indifferent, he would have had to sustain the war unaided. In the event he was assassinated on 14 May 1610, and with his death the threat of war evaporated. It is interesting to speculate whether his reputation as the rebuilder of France would have survived if he had lived.

Louis XIII succeeded at the age of thirteen and the regency was placed in the hands of the Queen Mother, Marie de Médici; the Edict of Nantes was confirmed, and most of Henry's advisers were retained. However, continuity was a hopeless prospect. The great nobility flocked back to Paris with their retinues, and Sully was forced out of office within a year. Marie abandoned her husband's intended war, and signed a new treaty with Spain, but combined pressure from the towns and the nobility compelled her to summon the Estates General - a sure sign that the government was in difficulties. However, having launched a joint attack upon the management of the country's finances, the two groups fell out over the proposed abolition of the *paulette*, and the Estates were dissolved in 1615, with only a vague promise to investigate the grievances which had been complained of. Marie preserved herself in power with the aid of her favourite, Concini, and by exploiting the chronic disputes among her many noble enemies.

She also alienated her son, largely by neglect, and in April 1617, when he was 20, and consequently of age, Louis had Concini murdered, and his mother imprisoned. For the next two years the government was conducted by his own favourite, de Luynes, who was no improvement upon Concini. In 1619 Marie escaped, and endeavoured to put together a coalition of her former enemies against the king. The result was a fiasco, partly because of the mutual distrust of all those involved, and partly because it was one thing to complain about incompetent favourites, and intrigue for the recovery of power, and quite another to fight an open war against the king. The rebellion collapsed, and Luynes continued to govern, albeit with the increasingly important participation of Louis himself. Luynes only notable act of policy before he died in 1622 was to provoke a major Huguenot rebellion by enforcing catholicism upon the Pyreneen state of Béarn. After his death this rebellion was not so much defeated as bought off, and the great protestant fortress of La Rochelle became virtually a separate state, under English protection. Louis then tried a succession of short lived ministers, none of whom could square the circle between an anti-Habsburg foreign policy (made increasingly necessary by events in Germany) and the suppression of religious dissent at home. Paradoxically, it was through reconciliation with his mother that he found the answer. Richelieu was originally her favourite, and it was she who secured the Cardinal's hat for him in 1622. After the reconciliation, it took him two years to win the king's confidence, but he was admitted to the council in April 1624, on the 'orthodox catholic' ticket, and became its head in August.

From 1624 to 1630 Richelieu was the king's chief minister, but his power was limited by the influence of other councillors, to whose pressure he occasionally had to bow, as over the affair of the Valtelline. His commitment to the king and to the royal power was total, and was rewarded with increasing friendship and trust. In the process he fell out with his former patron, the Queen Mother, and she made numerous attempts to have him dismissed. However, after the 'Day of Dupes' in November 1630 (a confrontation between herself, the king and Richelieu) it was she who was dismissed, and fled into exile. Thereafter, until his death in 1642 his hold upon the king's confidence was complete and unchallenged. Richelieu was not, in fact, an unadulterated absolutist. He realised that a stable system of government had to take some account of aristocratic power, and therefore strove to restructure the king's council in such a way that the nobility would be guaranteed a certain amount of effective participation. He also realised that it would be more efficient to govern the provinces with the co-operation of the nobility, rather than against them, and endeavoured to take some account of local vested interests in re-structuring the system of *intendants,* who were already the main agents of the central govermnent. In 1629 he introduced a series of financial reforms, including the abolition of the *paulette,* although some of these were subsequently abandoned in the face of political opposition which he was always wise enough to recognise and take notice of. At the same time the king's authority was significantly extended in one important direction. In 1627 La Rochelle revolted, with English support (this was the occasion of the Duke of Buckingham's expedition to Isle de Rhé). The English were beaten off, and the town forced to surrender in November 1628. In June 1629 the Edict of Nantes was reaffirmed, but with one major exception, the garrison towns were withdrawn, and the separate Huguenot political and military organisation brought to an end. Thereafter the king's writ ran uniformly in both catholic and protestant France. One result of this was a steady increase in the power of the *intendants,* who were given enhanced supervisory powers, particularly over local financial officers, with a mandate to stamp out corruption and partiality in the collection of taxes. Another was a clipping of the wings of the provincial *parlements,* whom the king accused of excessive and obstructive legalism. Richelieu used both political surveillance and successful foreign war to increase the unity and morale of France, and appeared to have succeeded better than any of his predecessors, even Sully. But appearances were to some extent deceptive. In spite of the care with which he had handled aristocractic aspirations, and to some extent built them into the system, there could be no disguising the fact that he had made Louis XIII more absolute than his father, not less, and the stability which he sought depended too much upon his own ability to maintain it. There was still another major round of aristocratic rebellion to be coped with before Louis XIV finally capitalised upon his efforts.

34. France and the Thirty Years War

The battle of Nordlingen re-established Habsburg supremacy in the Rhineland. Frederick fled for a second time and the princes of the League of Heilbronn submitted to the Emperor.This process was greatly eased by Ferdinand's belated willingness to abandon the Edict of Restitution, and John George of Saxony was the first to sign the terms of the Treaty of Prague in May 1635. He was confirmed in all his ecclesiastical possessions, and in his recent acquisition of Lusatia, but was required in return to make no alliance with the Emperor's enemies. Since the Swedes remained in Germany, and the French were about to declare themselves, this was a rather more substantial undertaking that he had bargained for. As the other princes followed Saxony's lead, the position of the Swedes became increasingly difficult. There was no longer any civil war in Germany to exploit, and neither money nor supplies were to be had. The French were willing to renew their subsidies, but only on the unacceptable condition that the Swedes abandoned their positions in the Rhineland. In 1635 also the truce of Altmark between Sweden and Poland expired, threatening a renewal of war on that front. Oxenstierna decided to buy off the Poles rather than yield to the French, and the treaty of Stuhmsdorf released 10,000 fresh men to join the Swedish commander, Baner, in Germany. Nevertheless by the following year he had retreated into Pomerania, that being Sweden's main territorial interest. Meanwhile, Richelieu tried to rebuild his shattered anti-Habsburg alliance, and remarkably, succeeded within four months. The Swedes were willing partners, in spite of their unwillingness to accept conditions, and the Dutch were equally looking for allies against Spain. Less obvious, however, was Bernard of Saxe-Weimar, who was subsidised to renew hostilities in the Rhineland, and the minor but strategic north Italian states of Mantua, Modena and Parma. Unfortunately, this alliance turned out to be as insubstantial as it was instant. The Swedes and the Dutch were preoccupied with their own concerns, and neither Bernard nor the Italians were sufficiently substantial. In 1636 the Spanish and Imperial armies won a series of victories, and towards the end of the summer they joined forces to overrun Picardy. Richelieu had been a shade too clever for the good of France, and Paris was in imminent danger of attack.

In the midst of this victorious campaign, the Emperor Ferdinand II died. He had not accomplished the establishment of Habsburg absolutism, which had seemed imminent in 1623, but he had certainly brought about a major revival of Imperial power, which made it unrecognisable from the office held by Maximilian II or Matthias. In fact the summer campaign of 1636 must have seemed like a return to the great days of the victory of Pavia, over 100 years before. However then, as before, it was one thing to invade France, and another to make any substantial conquest. In spite of their inexperience and lack of pay, the French were a tough proposition when they were defending their own soil. Louis XIII personally rallied his northern army and retook Corbie, while the southern Imperial army was turned back in Burgundy. By the end of the year both Imperial armies had retreated from France. As some compensation for what had otherwise been a bad year for the alliance, in October 1636 the Swedes won a substantial victory at Wittstock, and overran Brandenburg. By this time the native Swedish troops whom Gustavus had led into Germany six years before formed only a minority of the army, and were mostly deployed in garrison duties. The bulk of the field army consisted of German mercenaries, paid partly out of Swedish taxes and partly out of French subsidies. It was a relatively stable system, which seemed likely to survive as long as hostilities continued, not being dependent either upon windfalls or upon particular personalities. Stability, however, guaranteed survival rather than success, and the main action of 1637 saw the Swedes again pushed out of Brandenburg by a low key Imperial offensive. By the end of that year they were again confined to Pomerania. Oxenstierna was prepared to negotiate peace with the new Emperor, but only in return for the secession of Pomerania, and that Ferdinand III was determined not to concede.

More flexible than his father on religious issues, he was no more willing to surrender a square foot of Imperial territory. Consequently, Sweden renewed its French alliance on 15 March 163 8, by the treaty of Hamburg. The price for continued French support over Pomerania, and a renewed subsidy was the withdrawal of all Swedish claims to the Rhineland. The Rhine was now the key element in Richelieu's strategy, and Bernard of Saxe-Weimar, who had so conspicuously failed to make an impact in 1636, was again pressed into service. This time he did notably better, defeating an Imperial army at Rheinfelden in March 1638, and joining forces with the French Marshall Turenne to capture the key strategic fortress of Breisach (one of the main crossing points of the Rhine) at the end of the year. Success, however, made Bernard independent, and he attempted to establish his own claim to Alsace. This disrupted the alliance, and he was of no farther use to Richelieu before he died in the summer of 1639. It soon transpired that the campaign of 163 8 was the turning of the tide. The fall of Breisach had once again severed the Spanish Road, and the Spanish forces in The Netherlands, now struggling to contain the Dutch under Frederick Henry of Nassau, were in no position to rescue the defeated Imperialists. On 10 October 1639 Breda fell to the Dutch, and in the same month Spanish sea communications were also cut by the victory of admiral Tromp at the battle of the Downs, a shattering defeat which destroyed Spanish sea power for many years. In 1640, the year of the great Catalan and Portuguese revolts, it seemed as if the whole Spanish state was going to break up. It survived, thanks to the final great effort of Olivares, but was barely able to maintain the war in the Netherlands, and had neither men nor money to spare for Ferdinand. Indeed the boot was now on the other foot, and Philip IV called in vain for assistance from the Austrian Habsburgs, who owed so much to his father's servants - and his own. The Swedes on the northern front won a couple of minor victories in Saxony, and advanced as far as Prague, but it was now far too late to stir any flicker of the religious and national passions of twenty years earlier. They were unable to take the city, and withdrew before the end of the year. In 1640 a messy campaign resulted in stalemate, which in the circumstances should probably be counted as an Imperial success, and Ferdinand hastened to summon an imperial Diet before the situation should get any worse, and while there was still some prospect of rallying support. The Diet met at Ratisbon in September 1640, and was sympathetic to the Emperor, until an unfortunate turn of events deprived him of the initiative. This was the death in December of George William, the peaceable and incompetent Elector of Brandenburg, and his replacement with his ruthless and energetic son, Frederick William. Frederick William seized the initiative in the Diet by renouncing the Peace of Prague, which formed the basis of the existing relationship between the Emperor and the Lutheran princes and signing his own truce wtih Sweden in July 1641. His priority was to withdraw his battered country from hostilities, and to clear his lands of all foreign troops. The diet responded, as all enthusiasm for war had long since evaporated (and in many cases had never existed), and when it ended its sessions in October 1641, the prevailing call was for peace. The Emperor had failed to obtain the support he had looked for, and his leadership had been severely undermined.

However, the war had long since developed a terrible momentum of its own. Armies divided, coalesced and devoured each other like amoebas, continually acquiring larger and larger trains of ancilliaries and camp followers. Disbanding and paying off these ever-growing hoards was a more expensive proposition than keeping them in being. In some parts of Germany the only protection from these marauders was to join them, and while this solved the recruiting problem, it devastated the normal civilian life of town and country alike. The Papacy had made intermittent attempts to bring the war to an end since 1635, and the death of Ferdinand II, which reduced the religious temperature, led to a renewal of those efforts in 1638.

By this time the wars had obviously become another round in the long running saga of the Habsburgs versus the rest, and the genuine catholic and protestant zeal which had inspired both the older Ferdinand and Gustavus Vasa in their different ways had almost entirely disappeared. From 1638 to 1641 talks about talks went forward sporadically, and in December 1641 the French, the Emperor and the Swedes at last agreed to set up two simultaneous peace conferences. One was to be held at Munster, where France would negotiate with Ferdinand, under the mediation of the Pope and Venice; the other would convene at Osnabruck, and there the Emperor would deal with the Swedes under the mediation of Demnark. All parties had accepted this arrangement by the summer of 1642, but with an urgency which makes 20th century disarmament conferences appear positively frenetic, it was 1643 before any serious discussions began. There was no provision for a temporary cessation of arms, and each side stalled repeatedly, waiting for better news from the battle front.

Richelieu renewed the Swedish alliance in 1641, and between then and his death in December 1642 France was steadily rather than spectacularly successful. Artois in the southern Netherlands and Rousillon in the Pyrenees were occupied as Spanish strength steadily ebbed away. Louis XIII followed his great minister to the grave in May 1643, and was succeeded by his infant son, Louis XIV The minority government was theoretically led by the Queen Mother, Anne of Austria, but in practice by Richelieu's hand picked successor, Cardinal Mazarin. Mazarin continued his mentor's policies with the same success, and within a few days of the old king's death the last great Spanish army was defeated at Rocroi on the borders of the Netherlands. This victory not only set the seal on Spain's military decline, and made her war in the Netherlands, a hopeless quest, it also established the rising reputation of the young Due d'Enghein, who, as the Duke of Condé, was later to be one of Louis XIV's greatest commanders. On other fronts, the struggle was more evenly balanced. The Emperor had no commanders to compare with Enghein or Turenne, but he did have the support of some able Bavarians, notably Werth and Mercy, and the old veteran Piccolonomi, although the latter was long past his best. Baner, the best Swedish general, died in 1641, but he was succeeded by the competent Tortensson, and after 1646, by Wrangel. The main problem which afflicted them all was the increasing difficulty of obtaining supplies from a country repeatedly devastated, and afflicted by disease and harvest failure. Time after time victories would prove fruitless because they could not be followed up, and there was no longer any urban wealth to draw upon. Money to pay the troops could be brought in from France, or Sweden, or from the Emperor's lands further to the east and south, but money could not purchase food or horses which did not exist, and each campaign was slower and more frustrating than the last in consequence.

In 1646 the Imperial army captured Freiburg, and fought, a bloody but indecisive battle with the French nearby, but the French, who were better supplied, were able to hold the field, and occupied the left bank of the Rhine as far as Mainz. In August 1645 the French were victorious in a second battle at Nordlingen, but this time they were unable to hold the ground they had won, and retreated to Alsace, where it was still possible to obtain food. Tortensson similarly won a victory in Bohemia in March 1645, and advanced to within a few miles of Vienna, but was forced to retreat when the supplies ran out. However, in September 1645 a Swedish invasion of Saxony finally forced the Elector out of the war, and the Imperial position began to crumble away. In July 1646 Turenne and Wrangel combined to invade Bavaria, and by March of the following year the country was so devastated that Maximilian also agreed to a truce. The war was now moving to its final phase. Official peace negotiations had been going on at Munster and Osnabruck since December 1644, and by the summer of 1648 were reaching their conclusions. Maximilian was unwise enough to break his truce in September 1647, and in May of the following year was again defeated by the combined Franco-Swedish forces, and saw his country overrun a second time. On 20 August 1648 Enghein defeated the Archduke Leopold, Ferdinand's brother, at the battle of Lens, and further reduce the Imperial and Spanish presence in the Low

Countries. That was just about the last engagement of the war, as the two treaties which are together known as the Peace of Westphalia were signed on 24 October. Ironically, at that very moment a Swedish army was besieging Prague. It had been investing the city for some three months, but had been unable to overcome the stubborn resistance of the strongly catholic population, who had refused to abandon their Imperial allegiance. After 1648 only Spain and France fought on, a struggle which was to last for another eleven years before being finally concluded at the Peace of the Pyrenees. On every other front, 1648 was the great year of the pacification, and the battered and exhausted powers of central and northern Europe were left to count the cost, and to make what provision they could for economic and political recovery. By the time that they had done so the climate of international affairs had markedly changed. The era of religious wars was not only over, but seen to be over

35. The treaties of Westphalia

As befitted the immensely complicated struggle that the Thirty Years War had become, the negotiations which finally brought it to an end were extremely protracted. The first approaches had been made in 1638, and in 1641 a preliminary treaty had been signed providing for the setting up of two peace conferences; one at Munster (where the Emperor would negotiate with France, Spain and the catholic princes) and the other at Osnabruck (where the Emperor would meet the Swedes and the protestant princes). This strange arrangement was necessitated, not so much by the sensitivities of the belligerents themselves, as by those of the papal nuncio, who would not sit in the same room with heretics. It had originally been intended that the Danes should act as mediators at Osnabruck, but war between Denmark and Sweden between 1643 and 1645 made their participation in such a role impossible. At the same time, when the French delegation arrived at Munster in the autumn of 1643, they were furious to find the Spaniards present, because Mazarin was determined to exclude the Franco-Spanish conflict from any general settlement. For these and a number of other reasons, for which protocol was the usual excuse, the two conferences did not open until December 1644. Meanwhile, as we have seen, the war continued, and both sets of negotiations were subjected to frequent delays and filibusters as each party strove to take advantage of the temporary swings of the military situation. For example the French at Munster refused to deal with the Emperor's representative, Isaac Volmar, because they deemed him to be of inadequate social status, and only when count Trautmansdorff arrived to take his place in November 1645 could any progress be made. Thereafter it took some time to clarify the issues which had to be resolved, but they were eventually set out under four headings: First, the complaints of the Imperial Estates, going back to the cases of Donauworth and Cleves Jillich, including the Edict of Restitution and the withdrawal of the Letter of Majesty - in other words the originally acknowledged causes of the war. Second the position of those dispossessed in the first round of the fighting, particularly Frederick of the Palatinate - and consequently the future of the Palatine Electorate. Thirdly, the satisfaction of those outside powers who had entered the war ostensibly as allies of one or other of the German parties - in other words, should Sweden have Pomerania, or France Alsace? And fourthly, what compensation should arise from the resolution of (3) - most particularly, what should Brandenburg receive if it was forced to give up Pomerania? At the same time two important conflicts were not on the agenda - that between France and Spain, and that between Spain and the Netherlands. Since both of these had been important in determining the pattern of fighting, it was by no means certain that even success at Munster and Osnabruck would finally bring the war to an end.

The satisfaction of the outside parties made the most rapid progress, which was hardly surprising, given the ability of each to disrupt any alternative approach. Agreement in principle was reached over Alsace as early as September 1646, whereby France was to receive the whole territory with the exception of the Breisgau. However, given the complex jurisdictional structure of Alsace, it was by no means clear exactly what this secession actually meant. Even the final treaty was full of contradictions, giving the King of France full sovereignty over both Upper and Lower Alsace, and then reserving certain liberties which would inevitably detract from that sovereignty. However, because it was in no one's interest to delay the treaty over such an issue, they were left for time and practice to resolve. In fact France had gained most of her objectives in that direction, including a seat in the Imperial Diet. The resolution of this issue had been made easier from the French point of view by the support of Maximilian of Bavaria, a support which had its price in the furtherance of his own interests, as we shall see. Sweden was less easily satisfies not because the Swedes were greedier than the French, but because Duke Bogislav of Pomerania had died in 1637 leaving the Elector of Brandenburg as his undoubted heir, and

Frederick William was fiercely opposed to any transfer. The Emperor was anxious to get the Swedes off his back, and supported their claim, while the French, with an eye to the future, supported Frederick William. The inevitable result was the partition of Pomerania, which was agreed in September 1647. Sweden received western Pomerania, together with several Baltic islands which gave her the coastal control which she had sought, and the secularised bishopries of Bremen and Verden. Frederick William received eastern Pomerania, together with the secularised bishoprics of Halberstadt and Minden, and the reversion of the secularised archbishopric of Magdeburg. In fact, Frederick William did very well out of this deal, which not only gave him the largest territory in the Empire after the Habsburgs, but also lands worth approximately three times as much as those was surrendering. It is no exaggeration to say that the future power of Brandenburg Prussia rested upon this treaty.

The constitutional settlement of the Empire took rather longer, because these were issues which could not be resolved by trading territories. The French wanted to break the Habsburg hold on the Imperial title. They failed to achieved that, but in alliance with several of the princes, succeeded in making it little more than an empty dignity. Such power as had been left to the Emperor by the Golden Bull of 1356 was virtually eliminated by clauses which gave the princes the right to conclude treaties, either among themselves or with outside powers, and to exercise 'territorial superiority in all matters ecclesiastical as well as political'. The liberties of the princes thus became effective sovereignty; the Empire became an honorary federation (rather like the British commonwealth); and the last bid for effective Habsburg power was completely snuffed out. At the same time the Diet was divided into catholic and protestant sessions, and hedged about with such conditions that the United Nations General Assembly looks effective by comparison. These treaties brought the Holy Roman Empire to an end in all but name, and caused the Habsburgs to concentrate their full attention on Austria-Hungary, which was to remain their power base down to 1918. The greatly reduced importance of the Electoral College, which was one of the consequences of these developments, made the solution of another hitherto difficult problem straightforward. Maximilian could keep his Electoral title, together with the Upper Palatinate two thirds of his original price for supporting Ferdinand. At the same time an eighth Electorate could be created for Charles Lewis, Frederick's heir, who was restored to the Lower Palatinate.

The solution found for the religious problem was likewise based upon compromise - made possible by the fact that so much of the heat had gone out of the issue since the deaths of Ferdinand II and Gustavus Adolphus. In the first place the Peace of Augsburg was widened to include Calvinism. This did not mean a general toleration, which would still have been unacceptable (from habit as much as conviction), but it did mean that all the substantial churches were now included, and a new level of stability achieved. The Ecclesiastical Reservation had been abandoned at the Peace of Prague in 1635, but a further concession was now made to the holders of secularised church property, in that the date of recognition was moved back from 1627 to 1624, thus surrendering those lands which had been retaken after the defeat of Christian of Denmark. In addition, the lay administrators of such lands were given seats in the Diet - an empty concession by this time in political terms. At the same time the Augsburg principle of *cuius regio...* was modified in a manner which would have been unacceptable even twenty years earlier. A prince who changed his religion was now no longer able to enforce his conversion upon his subjects - an acknowledgement of the declining importance of religious uniformity. Dissidents were in theory to be given five years in which to settle their affairs and move their property to a new home, but in practice many were to enjoy toleration *in situ,* except in some parts of the hereditary Habsburg lands. A general amnesty was declared backdated to 1618, except in the cases of Bohemia and Austria, where it went back only to 1630 - thus leaving

Bohemia as a major Habsburg and Catholic gain, and no doubt sweetening the pill of so many humiliating failures.

In January 1648 Spain and the United Provinces signed a separate peace, in which the independence of the Provinces was finally acknowledged. This did not please everyone, however, as it meant surrendering any chance of reconquering the southern provinces, a prospect which some thought to be imminent. It also upset the French to some extent, since they now faced the prospect of continuing their war with Spain on their own. In an attempt to mitigate the effects of this, they insisted that the Emperor must agree to remain neutral, a condition which delayed the final settlement at Munster for several months, but was eventually conceded. The only remaining obstacle was then Sweden's demand for a massive twenty million Imperial dollars to pay off her armies and serve as an indemnity. Probably such a sum was intended as a bargaining counter, because after a prolonged negotiation, she eventually settled for five million, and the treaties were signed simultaneously on 24 October The European state system as it was settled in Westphalia survived down to the French revolution, and religion ceased to be a principle motivating force for international strife. This was not the end of the Ancien Regime; most states were not yet nations, and dynastic warfare continued as it had existed for centuries. But with trade and colonial expansion taking the place of confessional strife, a new era of international relations had been entered.

The war which continued had never been religious in its inspiration, and it seemed at first as though Mazarin had made a disastrous miscalculation in insisting that it continue. Even before the treaties of Westphalia were concluded, in the summer of 1648, discontent against the Cardinal's regime had led to open defiance by the Paris *parlement,* and before the end of the year the civil wars, known as the Frondes had broken out. For several years central government virtually ceased to exist, and the armies of Spain found themselves fighting only against a faction, often with the support of its enemies. Thus in 1650 Turenne was leading his army against the royal army of France, and in 1653 Condé besieged Rocroi in alliance with Spain. For almost the whole of 1651 the Spanish forces were virtually unopposed and they had overrun Picardy, advancing to within a few miles of Paris before French national feeling, and Turenne's return to his allegiance finally drove them out. It is a measure of Spain's relative weakness by this time that she was not able to make more effective use of the paralysis of France. By the end of 1653 the opportunity for a decisive strike was past, and Mazarin was back in control of the situation. The war ground on inconclusively. In 1655 Mazarin came to terms with the republican government of England, and in 1656 the Spaniards suffered a decisive defeat at the hands of the rebel Portuguese, which marked the effective end of Spanish rule in Portugal. In 1657 English and French troops began to campaign together against Dunkirque, and in the following year a combined Anglo-French army under Turenne won another decisive victory at the battle of the Dunes. By that time Spain was anxious for peace, and Mazarin held out the prospect of a marriage between Louis XIV and the Infanta. The negotiations, which had been going on in a desultory fashion since 1656, became real and earnest in the summer of 1659, and by November the peace of the Pyrenees had been concluded.

Apart from the marriage, the terms were essentially a postscript to Westphalia. The renegade Condé was pardoned, but France,acquired almost the whole of Artois, the Flemish towns of Gravelines and Landrècies, and some other border fortresses, such as Thionville. The Catalans and the Portuguese were abandoned, while Rousillon was finally acquired in full possession and a stranglehold upon the supposedly independent Duchy of Lorraine. In many ways, therefore, it was the peace of the Pyrenees rather than the Treaties of Westphalia which marked the end of the Thirty Year war. But it was also the first stage in the hegemony of France. When the marriage of Louis and Maria Theresa took place in June 1660, the Infanta renounced her claim to the Spanish succession, on condition that her dowry of 500,000 crowns was paid within eighteen months. However, thanks to the impoverishment of the Spanish crown, it never was paid. Instead, Philip IV's second wife bore him a son, the future Charles II, known also as Charles the Sufferer from his defective constitution. Charles lived until 1700, but when he died, as a consequence of the Peace of the Pyrenees, the crown of Spain passed to Louis' grandson, the Duke of Anjou, and a fresh round of European wars was generated.

Suggested Reading

This list is by no means comprehensive but most of the books listed below   have excellent bibliographies and since many are new those bibliographies are comprehensive and up-to date. For reference purposes Cambridge Medieval History and The Cambridge Econmic History volumes are invaluable.

Arblaster, P., *The Dutch Revolt witnesses at 's-Hertogenbosch* (Source Doc.) (2001

Baker, A.R.H, *Historical Geography* (2002)

Beneke, G. *Society and politics in Germany, 1500-1750* (1974)

Bergin, J. (Ed.) *The Seventeenth Century, Europe 1598-1715* (2000)

Bonney, R. *The European Dynastic States 1494-1660* (1991

Brecht, , M. Trans, J.L. Schaaf, *Martin Luther: His road to Reformation, 1483-1521* (1985)

Breisach, E. , *Renaissance Europe , 1300-1517* (1973)

Brotton, J. *The Renaissance Bazaar: from the silk road to Michelangelo* (2002)

Brown, A., *The Valois Dukes of Burgundy* (2002)

Cameron, E. *The European Reformation* (1991)

Cameron, E. *Early Modern Europe* (2001)

Chadwick, O. *The Early Reformation on the Continent* (2001)

Coles, P. *The Ottoman Impact on Europe* (1968)

Duke, A. *Reformation and Revolt in the Low Countries* (1990)

Elliot, J.H., *Imperial Spain 1469-1716* (1963)

Evans, R.J.W., *The Making of the Habsburg Monarchy* (1979)

Evennett, H.O. *The Cardinal of Lorraine and the Council of Trent* (1930)

Forster, M. *Catholic Revival in the Age of Baroque* (2001)

Fragnito G. (Trans Belton,A.) *Church Censorship and Culture in Early Modern Italy* (2001)

Gauci, P. *The Politics of Trade: the overseas merchant in state & society 1660-1720* (2001)

Goffman, D., *The Ottoman Empire and Early Modern Europe* (2002)

Greengrass, M.., *France in the Age of Henry IV* (1984)

Hagen, W.W., *Ordinary Prussians: Brandenburg Junkers and Villagers 1500-1840* (2002)

Holt, M., *Renaissance and Reformation France* (2002)

Holt, M *The French Wars of Religion 1562-1629* (1995)

Hook, J., *The Sack of Rome* (2003)

Knecht, R.J., *Catherine de' Medici* (1988)

Knecht, R.J. *Francis I* (1982)

Königsberger, H.G. *Monarchies, States Generals and Parliaments: The Netherlands in the Fifteenth and Sixteenth Centuries* (2001)

Law, John, *Lord of Renaissance Italy* (2002)

Loades, D.M.,*Charles V and the Ottomans* (2002)

Loades, D.M.*Essays in European History 1450-1648* (2003)

Loades, D.M. *The English Crown and the Papacy in the Sixteenth & Seventeenth Centuries* (2002)

Lynch, J. *Spain under the Habsburgs* (1981)

McGrath, A.E. *Intellectual Origins of the European Reformation* (1987)

McNeilll, W.H. *Venice: the hinge of Europe 1081-1797* (1974)

Marino, J., *Early Modern Italy 1550-1796* (2002)

Miskimin, H.A. *The Economy of later Renaissance Europe 1460-1600* (1977)

Mattingly, G., *Renaissance Diplomacy* (1955)

Mentzer, R. & Spicer, A., *Society and Culture in the Hugenot World, 1559-1685* (2002)

Osborne, T. *Dynasty and Diplomacy in the Court of Savoy: political Culture and the Thirty Years War* (2002)

Parker, D., *The Making of French Absolutism* (1983)

Parker, G., *Empire War and Faith in Early Modern Europe* (2002)

Parker, G. *The Dutch Revolt* (1977)

Parker, G. *Spain and The Netherlands* (1979)

Parker, G. *Philip II* (1979)

Parker, G., *The Thirty Years War* (1985)

Parrott, D. Richelieu's Army: war, government and society in France 1624-1642 (2002)

Parry, J. *The Spanish Seaborne Empire* (1966)

Rodrigues Salgado, *The Changing Face of Empire, Charles V, Philip II and Habsburg Authority* (1988)

Rowlands, G., *The Dynastic State and the Army under Louis XIV* (2002)

Ruff, J., *Violence in Early Modern Europe, 1500-1800* (2001)

Schmidt, B. *Innocence Abroad: The Dutch Imagination and the New World, 1570-1670* (2002)

Signorotto, G. & Visceglia M.A.(Eds.) *Court and Politics in Papal Rome 1492-1700* (2002)

Tracy, J.*Emperor Charles V, Impressario of War* (2002)

Scammell, G., *The First Imperial Age: European expansion 1500-1715* (1987)

Scarisbbrick, J.J. *The Jesuits and the Catholic Reformation (1988)*

Vaughan, Richard, *Charles the Bold*. (new edn. (2002)

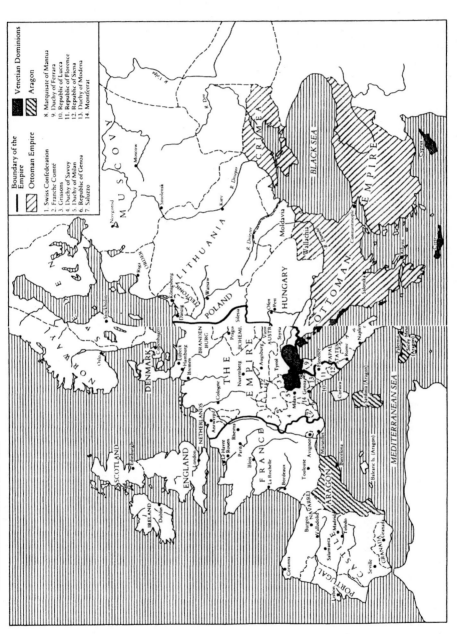

Boundary of the Empire
Ottoman Empire
Swiss Confederation
Venetian Dominions
Aragon

1. Swiss Confederation
2. Franche Comté
3. Grisons
4. Duchy of Savoy
5. Duchy of Milan
6. Republic of Genoa
7. Saluzzo
8. Marquisate of Mantua
9. Duchy of Ferrara
10. Republic of Lucca
11. Republic of Florence
12. Republic of Siena
13. Duchy of Modena
14. Montferrat

Map 1   Europe: frontiers about 1500

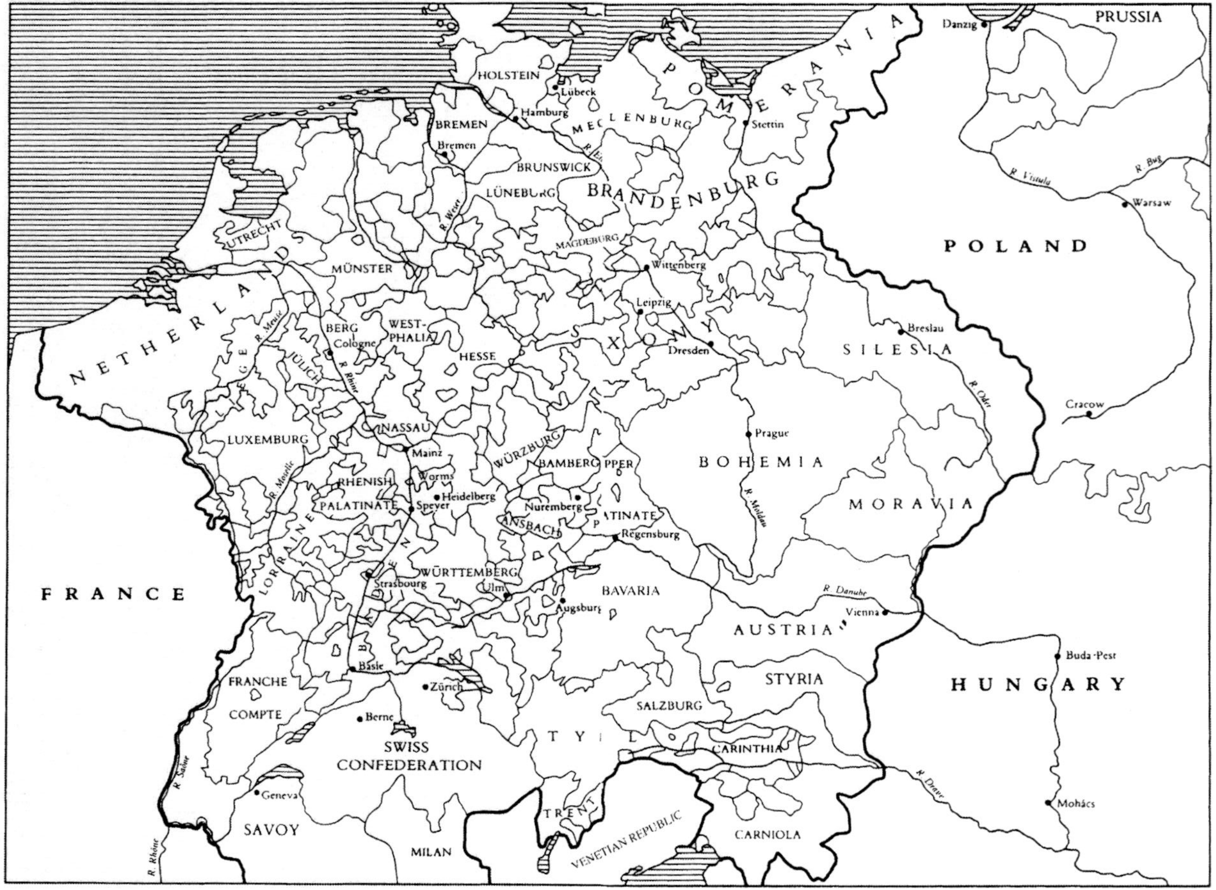

Map 2 The Empire (Germany) at the time of the Reformation

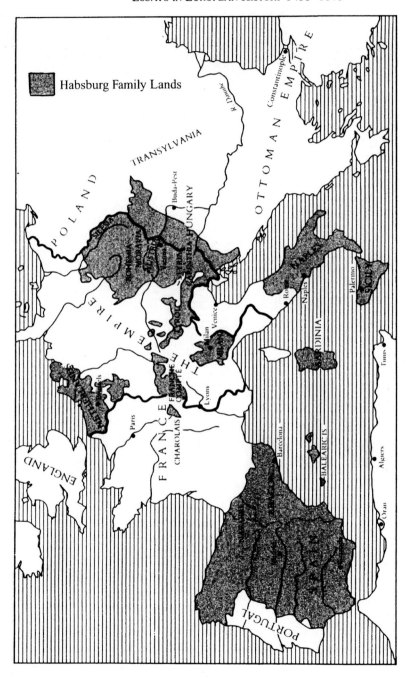

Map 3 The Empire of Charles V

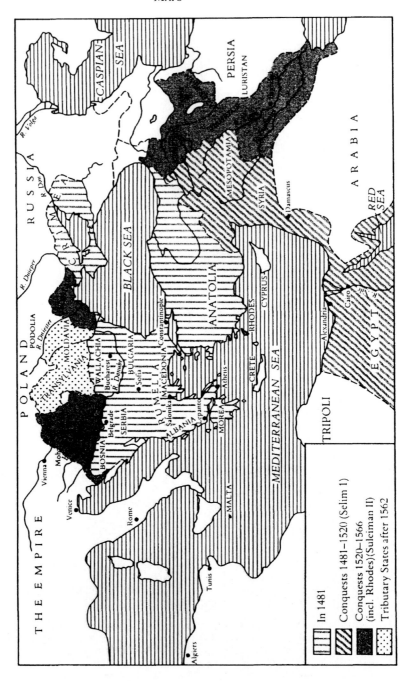

Map 4 The Ottoman Empire

Map 5 The Portugese and Spanish Overseas Empires

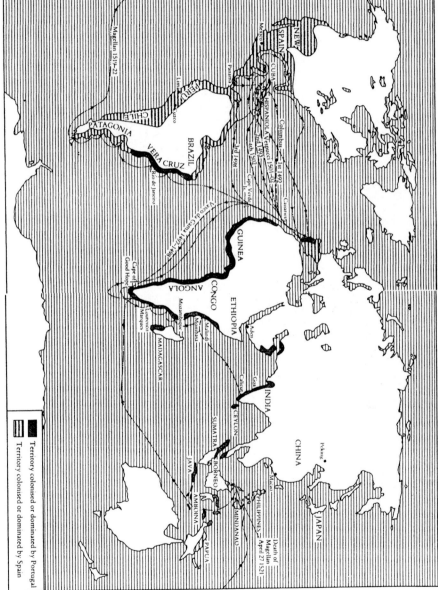

MAPS

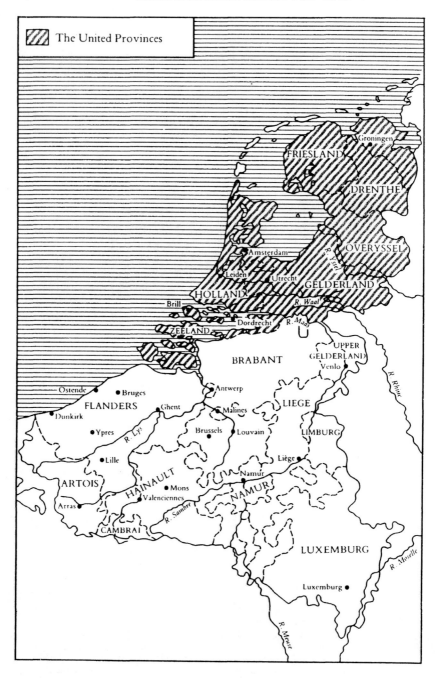

Map 6   The Netherlands in 1609

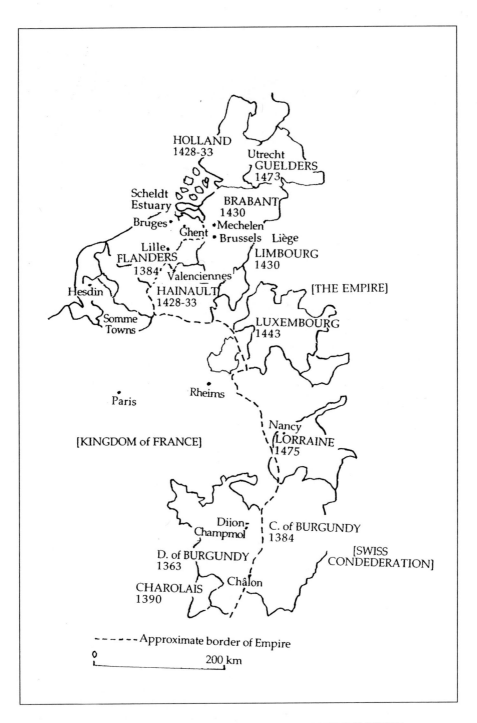

HOLLAND
1428-33

Utrecht
GUELDERS
1473

Scheldt
Estuary

BRABANT
1430

Bruges

Ghent

Mechelen
Brussels Liège

Lille
FLANDERS
1384

Valenciennes

LIMBOURG
1430

Hesdin

HAINAULT
1428-33

[THE EMPIRE]

Somme
Towns

LUXEMBOURG
1443

Paris

Rheims

[KINGDOM of FRANCE]

Nancy
LORRAINE
1475

Dijon
Champmol

C. of BURGUNDY
1384

[SWISS
CONDEDERATION]

D. of BURGUNDY
1363

Châlon

CHAROLAIS
1390

- - - - - Approximate border of Empire

0   200 km

TERRITORIES OF THE VALOIS DUKES OF BURGUNDY
(with dates of their acquisition)

Map 7